Victorian Connections

Victorian Connections

EDITED BY

Jerome J. McGann

University Press of Virginia

Charlottesville

This is a title in the series

VIRGINIA
VICTORIAN
STUDIES

THE UNIVERSITY PRESS OF VIRGINIA
Copyright © 1989 by the Rector and Visitors
of the University of Virginia

"*Praeterita* and the Pathetic Fallacy" copyright © 1989 by J. Hillis Miller

First published 1989

Printed in the United States of America

Contents

Victorian Connections

Jerome J. McGann

Introduction:
The Privilege of
Historical Backwardness—
American Scholarship
after World War II
and the Career of
Cecil Y. Lang

§

*I*n 1985 Cecil Lang had behind him a long and distinguished career as an editor of Victorian materials. The edition of Tennyson's letters, produced with Edgar Shannon, was entering its final phases, and Lang was turning to take up the task of editing the letters of Matthew Arnold. In the brief period between those two editorial ventures, however, Lang wrote and published an article of great importance—"Narcissus Jilted: Byron, *Don Juan,* and the Biographical Imperative."[1]

This essay quickly became a point of reference in Byron studies for two reasons. First, it connected with the longest and most important tradition of Byron criticism—biographical criticism; and second, it made that connection through a retrospective assault upon those modes of criticism which had marginalized Byron, on one hand, and anathematized biographical and historical methodologies on the other. That is to say, Lang set his essay as an attack upon formalist critical procedures in general, and upon the New Criticism in particular.

We confront here one of those small moments in history—the history of criticism and scholarship, in this case—that brings into focus, as with a flash, an invisible world. It is a world from the past which overlaps the work of this book, and which lives on here as a series of transformed lives.

To understand the importance of Lang's essay we have to fill in a few small but crucial details. In 1985 Lang was sixty-five years old. After studying at Duke University before the war with the distinguished scholar and editor Paull F. Baum, Lang took his degree from Harvard in 1949. That same year he began teaching at Yale. He would travel across the country to teach at three other institutions—Claremont Graduate School, Syracuse University, and University of Chicago—before finally arriving, in 1966, at the University of Virginia, where he has remained ever since.

Lang's student years at Duke and at Harvard overlapped the most vigorous period of the New Criticism. But his own work did not move with that new current. Besides Baum at Duke, Hyder Rollins at Harvard had the greatest influence on Lang's interests. When Lang arrived at Yale, therefore, he came as a well-trained philologist and historical scholar. He was, in other words, already moving out of fashion in 1949.

Lang's scholastic and pedagogical skills were of so high an order, however, that his hermeneutical backwardness (so to speak) would never count against him in his literary career. Lang in fact produced highly significant work in "literary criticism": the introductions to his great edition of Swinburne's *Letters* and to his important *Pre-Raphaelites and Their Circle*[2] are both remarkable pieces of criticism, but neither attracted much general attention at the time. In the first place, both dealt with subjects which seemed strange and peripheral to an academy still dominated by a commitment to the idea of *a* Great Tradition; second, Lang's critical approach followed (and recalled) the procedures of scholars who were philologically and historically trained—critics like Baum, Rollins, Henri Peyre, and Douglas Bush. Lang thus became a distinguished presence in "the profession," though a presence categorized in those pigeonholes of "editing" and "scholarship." While he and a small band of scholastic angels like him went on with their pedagogical work, skirting the Scylla of theory and the Carybdis of thematized and formal hermeneutics, American literary studies passed into the final years of the New Criticism and its amazing aftermath.

These are the years in which we may follow as well the career of another important academic figure, Paul De Man. The comparison is most instructive. After serving in the navy in the Pacific theater during the war, Lang came to Harvard to resume his studies and to take his Ph.D. De Man came to study at Harvard after the war as well; but while he came there—also like Lang—already well-schooled in philology, his background—in both its sociopolitical and its scholastic aspects—was very different. There is no need here to stress the sociopolitical differences. As for the scholastic differentials, Lang's work came out of a highly pragmatic and empirical tradition, whereas De Man's had been shaped by German philosophy and hermeneutics, and especially by Heidegger. Lang came to Harvard to study with certain scholars, like Hyder Rollins, whereas De Man came in order to place himself in the orbit of New Critical hermeneutics, with its strongly thematic, text-centered, and ahistorical interests. De Man would eventually preside over the deconstructions of both the New Criticism and structuralism, and his name—perhaps more than any other—would inscribe itself deeply into those processes of deconstruction. Along with names like Bloom, Derrida, and to a lesser extent Geoffrey Hartman and J. Hillis Miller, De Man forged a global authority in English literary studies. In De Man's case, as we now know, it was an authority advanced under the Nietzschean sign of forgetting.

Lang's name, of course, has had a far more localized authority. In this respect his work epitomizes what became of "scholarship" and historical criticism in the period of late– and post–New Criticism: they were seen to be, in Wellek's words, "extrinsic" to the central ("intrinsic") interpretive concerns of literature and criticism.[3] Because interpretive work could not proceed without editors and historical scholars, however, the latter were maintained in the institution as marginalized presences and local heroes, untheorized at the core of literary studies. Lang's great distinction as a "Victorian editor and scholar" is an index, perhaps an emblem, of at least two generations of people like him, and hence of at least two generations of a largely forgotten history.[4]

The importance of Lang's essay on Byron lies precisely in the way it calls attention, obliquely, to this larger pattern of literary history. Crucial here is the remarkable belatedness of Lang's piece. Anyone whose schooling developed "After the New Criticism"[5] will instantly recognize the older dialect in which his commentary is framed. Lang's repudiation of the New Criticism was matched by his subsequent refusal of its theoretical aftermath; he has scorned those languages of criticism all his life, and his own style constantly reflects that resistance movement to which he has so fiercely adhered.

That style, in other words, calls attention to the post–New Critical context in which Lang's essay made its appearance. As part of a collection of *Historical Studies and Literary Criticism* published in 1985—that is to say, in a context where the now well-known "return to history" in English and American literary studies, both practical and theoretical, was being programmatically brought to the fore—Lang's "antiqued" essay constituted in itself a statement of immense critical significance. This was an older voice, near the end of its career, executing an important interpretive maneuver "out of the past," as it were.

Lang could have written his Byron essay years before, as anyone who knows him might attest. He had never published anything on Byron, but he had (and has) been, all his life, an assiduous scholar, teacher, and student of Byron. The essay only *appears* to come from nowhere. In fact it is deeply funded, and the meaning of its appearance has far less to do with Byron studies than with general hermeneutics and the history of American literary studies since World War II. The essay is in itself a comment on both, and a comment that had been held in reserve for a time when what it had to say would once again find a sympathetic audience.

In this sense Lang clearly gauged the situation correctly. But the piece has a historical significance (and meaning) which transcends its most apparent interpretive aims (the critique of the New Critical program and the elucidation of certain biographically located meanings in *Don Juan*). This other dimension of the essay stems from its belatedness: from its attack upon New Criticism at a point in time when the struggle against that movement had long been over; and from its deployment of a sociohistorical hermeneutic which was innocent of all those many important contemporary methodologies which gave such theoretical impetus to the development of the "return to history" in criticism.

The really trenchant character of Lang's piece emerges from its own historicity. In the first place, that historicity sets clear bounding lines—clear limits—to the arguments Lang makes. The attack upon the New Criticism and the commentary on *Don Juan* are localized, set out from a point of view which is always clear to us. In the second place, the historical marginality which that point of view endured is suddenly thrust to the fore. As a consequence Lang's essay, appearing in 1985, lays out a brief biography (as it were) of a certain literary way of life which had all but disappeared from *critical* consciousness after the Korean War.

In a sense, then, Lang's critical work in 1985 seemed to have found a larger environment within which it might flourish once again. And while this is partly (and plainly) true, it is a view which obscures the larger and more important truth. For Lang's piece did not emerge ex nihilo. We have to search the scholarly journals to find, after the war, work of this kind: not because it was not being written, or because it is not in fact to *be* found, but because it was not being *read* by the dominant lines of critical activity. It was not being read because hermeneutic theory in those years was grounded in various kinds of immemorial and thematic interests, and sociohistorical work seemed at the time deeply resistant to such interpretive programs. Peripherally situated with respect to the ordinary public media of institutionalized literary discourse, Lang was imagined by that discourse to have "become an editor."

In taking on that public role, however, his most influential interpretive life went, so to speak, underground. He was able to pursue this route, as have many others, because the academy has two principal spheres of institutional activity: on one hand the writing of scholarship and criticism, and on the other the praxis of pedagogy. For some thirty years Lang presided as the dominant critical presence in his classrooms. While his external or public life was being carried on in scholarship and editing, his secret life retreated to the local and day-to-day scenes of teaching. There he lived a kind of fifth-column existence, a confessed atheist before the gods whose comings and goings he had observed for more than forty years.

His students and many of his colleagues, on the other hand, were all believers of one kind or another, at one time or another: in New Criticism, in structuralism, in theory and deconstruction, in Marxism, intertextuality, postmodernism. Lang has always held these several beliefs in scorn, as he has their originary religious types. What he never scorned were those who believed, and particularly his fideist students who were seeking to find ways of practicing literature in a world which seemed without either divine or human commitments.

Jerome J. McGann

As a consequence, Lang's classrooms, and the pedagogical arenas which he extended beyond those classrooms, became the locus of some of his most far-reaching work. If we see his editorial work as a series of important "scholarly resources," which they most certainly are, others of us have seen them as exemplars of an astonishing critical practice—a kind of vision of spring kept in the winter of shifting beliefs. But that practice was most actively pursued in the pedagogical arena. There the philological and historicist protocols in which he was trained, and to which he remained committed, preserved a diminished but insistent life. Lang did not "preach" historicism between 1950 and 1980. He let that god die as well, but he preserved carefully the materials and tools which were the human source of its existence: first of all, a materialist orientation toward the texts, their producers, and their reproducers; second, an uncompromising insistence upon accuracy and procedural rigor at every level, from the most abstract areas of critical method to the local details of prose style; and third, a clear understanding that memory—not forgetting—is the mother of the muses, and one of the essential bases of all culture as well. Equally central has been the peculiar way he has of removing himself from the center of one's intellectual attention, as if the subject (and object) of inquiry had to be preserved as the predominant, and differential, presence.

No one who has worked or studied with Lang has left his presence unmarked by these protocols. Important as they are in themselves, it is their pedagogical context which is finally crucial. Because the classroom and its extensions became the *figura* of criticism as Lang understood it, critical enquiry in his orbit has always been an applied science. In such an environment one comes to understand that criticism is a social activity, and that individual authority, including (perhaps primarily) the authority of the teacher, discovers its full realization through its disappearance, through its subsequent transformations in the dialectic of various critical encounters. One may well recall that contradictory proverb from *Song of Myself:* "He most honors my style who learns under it to destroy the teacher."

§

These considerations have dictated the apparently "loose" organization of this book. The essays here all deal with "Victorian" matters, of course, and while the book is largely (but not exclusively) "historical" in orientation, one will look in vain for a shared theoretical or methodological outlook.

Each of the authors was set free to write about anything in the Victorian period, and only one proviso was made: that the essay seek to draw connections with other disciplines, fields, periods, methodologies, or authors. This freedom was sought partly to secure work which represented the real current interests of the writers, and partly to reflect back upon the work of the person who stands behind this book.

The diversity of the collection is a gloss on Lang's work, and on the imperatives he set for those who learned from him. Outside the field, or to a specialized eye, he is known as the most distinguished living editor of Victorian epistolary materials. He set a standard for such work which has not been surpassed, and has seldom been equaled, even to this day of the large, well-funded, and cooperative editorial institution. That standard is measured in two ways: first, by the accuracy and rigor of his editorial work; and second, by the extraordinary range of his historical understanding.

These virtues are evident enough in Lang's published work. A secondary text like this one may or may not witness his personal achievements. What it does witness is the endurance, in multiple transformed styles, of the critical attitudes he sought to perpetuate. In this sense his work as a teacher and colleague is set forth here in order to be seen and understood; and in this sense these essays are *historically* framed in a way that none of them, by or in themselves, could have managed.

Also important is the historical field covered by the essays. A great deal could be said on this subject, not least in the present context. The development of the critical ideologies of the New Criticism and its aftermath inclined to swerve away from the Victorian period and preferred to search for resources in other, more ideologically integral, fields of the English literary inheritance. (The work of J. Hillis Miller, represented here, is a notable—and a significant—exception.) Study of the Victorian period in literature offers problems which are not at all like those encountered in, for example, the study of neo-classicism, modernism, or romanticism in England. If the latter have their extended historical aftermaths, they are relatively coherent cultural and ideological phenomena, and localize themselves

Jerome J. McGann

in convenient ways. But what we designate as Victorian stretches over a much longer period of time and encompasses a vastly larger and more diverse range of materials.

Lang recognized this situation very clearly, and set his work in two complementary directions. First, his personal scholarly work concentrated on making available the necessary primary materials for studying Victorian culture. Second, he directed the work of a large number of students who were to take up various problems in Victorian culture, and he did this by pointing them toward that diversity of issues, and then by letting each of them go. That encouragement of diversity is witnessed in this book, where a number of his students and colleagues have written on different subjects from different points of view.

Very little has been alien to Lang, and this is not simply a characterological trait; it is in the end a critical principle (one of the very few principles—of any kind—that he would care to profess). Representing that principle in this book is, however, not simply an act of deference to Lang. Once defended, if not theorized, as "critical pluralism," and once held more as a position than a principle, it has reacquired some of its critical salience in recent years.

The principle assumes that not only are the phenomena to be studied complex and heterogeneous, so too are the critical tools and approaches which we have inherited or made up for ourselves. In such a situation one does not proceed either from (or perhaps even toward) a "unified field theory." The material will not submit to such an ordering, it is too wealthy and unstable. Rather, the goal is (to borrow a Blakean insight) to "open the doors of perception," to proceed in such a way that one's investigations are constantly forced to encounter those differentials and limiting cases which release the energies of knowledge through procedures of destabilization. In this way the method of investigation is married to the subject(s) of the investigation.

Drawing "connections" of various kinds is one way of encouraging such procedures. This may be done along any of those traditional avenues of comparative criticism—for example, by drawing poems and paintings into critical relationships. Or it may be done in other ways—interrogating fictions and poetry in sociological, historical, or political frames of reference; mapping the forms of literary discourse along intertextual lines; investigating ideological formations and deformations, either within or between periods; and so forth. Any or all of these procedures may themselves be joined with another connective method: the method of antithetical or negative hermeneutics. This may involve the exposure of antitheses in the material being studied (the exposure of its inherently unstable connections) or it may appear as a critical move against the materials themselves (the deployment or definition of antitheses between the material to be studied and the investigating subject).

All of these procedures are illustrated in this volume. In addition, each stands in an incipiently antithetical relation to the others, so that the collection is itself unstable. We do not have uniformity here (a series of Marxist essays, or feminist, or formalist, or New Historicist), neither do we have a dialectic of points of view. Rather, the essays diverge, and in this they do not so much contradict each other as they expose their various limitations. The compliment they pay to each other—the way they complement each other—lies exactly in their dispersion.

Such has seemed to me, at any rate, and to a number of others, the pedagogical—dare I say the theoretical?—meaning of the work of Cecil Lang. This book has taken the form that it has partly because his life as a scholar has taken the form that *it* has. Lang's comparatist and historicist leanings, along with his decision to keep pedagogy at the center of his work, developed in him a special kind of "resistance to theory."[7] In Lang the resistance to theory has been at all times the reciprocal of his commitment to history and to memory. In this respect, the historical and pedagogical orientation of Lang's work would find a new life on the far side of the deconstructive movement, where the importance of theory (including the importance of contemporary theory) is being rediscovered through the definition of its concrete sociohistorical goals and frames of reference. Current "theory" is a certain set of historically determinate practices.

Those contributing to this book have been influenced—some far more than others—by the very different approach to "theory" which Lang transmitted (even if he did not invent that approach, and even if he would spurn the very idea of calling it a theory). Though some of us have sometimes sought to expose *its* limitations or to pursue other paths, we have remained connected to it—more or less, for better and worse. It has seemed important, therefore, to pay it, and a person who stood for it, the homage it is due. No mere act of

Jerome J. McGann

genuflection, this payment is a practical effort to demonstrate what Trotsky called "the privilege of historical backwardness." In these essays that privilege is remembered and recovered through what may be its most salient form: its dispersal across a set of unprivileged and self-limiting texts. Critique of autonomy and totalization is a type of deconstruction, of course. Carried out under the sign of "historical backwardness," however, it is an activity which simultaneously undermines its own inertias toward a final privilege.

Authority is something assumed, something historically imagined. We are at present imagining the authority of gender studies, as well as certain other critical and pedagogical modes; and this is as it must and should be. One may set a quietist, retrograde face toward these events, of course, and imagine them as simply (con)temporary and fashionable. That is, as one might say, "the privilege" of a certain kind of historical backwardness, but it is not the privilege imagined by Trotsky's idea, which is in fact a kind of historical progressivism. Alienation is a privilege only so far as it develops, through its own conditions, objective and nonpersonal forms of resistance.

Lang's career in literary studies can and perhaps should be seen in terms of that larger, historically grounded form of critical resistance.

Notes

1. Cecil Lang, "Narcissus Jilted: Byron, *Don Juan,* and the Biographical Imperative," in *Historical Studies and Literary Criticism,* ed. with an introduction by Jerome J. McGann (Madison, Wis.: University of Wisconsin Press, 1985), pp. 143–79.

2. See "Introduction," *The Swinburne Letters,* ed. Cecil Y. Lang (New Haven: Yale University Press, 1959), pp. xiii–l; "Introduction," Lang, *The Pre-Raphaelites and Their Circle* (Boston: Houghton Mifflin, 1968), pp. xi–xxix.

3. The terms in text are those established in René Wellek and Austin Warren's *Theory of Literature* (New York: Harcourt, Brace, 1942).

4. But see Gerald Graff's two attempts to bring some historical light to the development of the American academy in the area of literary criticism: *Criticism in the University,* ed. Gerald Graff and Reginald Gibbons (Evanston, Ill.: Northwestern University Press, 1985); and Graff's *Professing Literature: An Institutional History* (Chicago: University of Chicago Press, 1987).

5. The phrase "After the New Criticism" is, of course, the title of Frank Lentricchia's excellent critical survey (Chicago: University of Chicago Press, 1980).

6. See Paul De Man, *The Resistance to Theory* (Minneapolis: University of Minnesota Press, 1986).

Karen Chase

" 'Bad,' was my commentary"—
Propriety, Madness,
Independence in Feminist
Literary History

§

*T*he present essay has a triple purpose. It means to make tribute to Cecil Lang by following a problem in historical development which he has taught us to take seriously. At the same time it means to consolidate diverse strains in the study of women in the nineteenth-century novel; and finally it hopes to suggest some emerging continuities in feminist theory and feminist literary history.

One might begin cultivating these three areas of inquiry by recalling an institutional puzzle which most of my readers will quickly recognize. I have in mind the deep intimacy between nineteenth-century fiction and the feminist critic, and more particularly the tie between the study of nineteenth-century women writers and the elaboration of a feminist critical theory. One sometimes hears—when one's presence behind the door has not been detected—that women go in for the nineteenth century because they have never outgrown novels that end in marriage. A better explanation is needed—or at least a less sloppy one. As a way of approaching such an explanation, let me invoke the titles of three significant histories not chosen at random: first, *The Proper Lady and the Woman Writer* by Mary Poovey; second Sandra Gilbert and Susan Gubar's *The Madwoman in the Attic: The Woman Writer and the Nineteenth Century Literary Imagination;* and third Martha Vicinus's *Independent Women.*[1]

These three works by these four women make scant reference to each other; they define their own problems and pursue their own ambitions. But on a deep stratum of the critical imagination they interpenetrate and interanimate, and in so doing they offer a way to reformulate our puzzle. Mary Poovey on the ideology of the proper lady in late'eighteenth and early nineteenth century, Gilbert and Gubar on the topos of the madwoman in the Victorian period, Vicinus on female independence in the late Victorian and early modern period—the historical domain of these three studies overlaps in such a fashion that the works, for all their differences in tone and tenor, inadvertently stand as companion pieces charting distinct phases in the history of women during the last two centuries. And it is a mark of the developing coherence of feminist literary history that the force of each of the books becomes greater when set alongside the others and three signal individual accomplishments combine to suggest an ongoing collective project.

Propriety, Madness, Independence—these distinct and distinctly powerful concerns of the three studies raise the question of how such concerns can be brought into theoretical configuration and historical coherence. For those of us who study the history of women in the nineteenth century, one large task must be to interrogate the subterranean connections that link propriety, madness, and independence and to ask just how the eighteenth-century Proper Lady became the Victorian Madwoman, and how the Madwoman engendered modern Independence?

We need to be wary of supposing that these problems are behind us or that they are a difficulty for the women we study and not the women we are. And here may be the beginnings of an explanation as to why feminist criticism has been so intimately bound to the literary history of the nineteenth century. For it seems clear that in significant and illuminating respects, the vicissitudes of women's position in the nineteenth century have been recapitulated in the institutional problems confronting the feminist critic. We who interpret our nineteenth century predecessors find that we have been predicted by them. And seen from our present standpoint, propriety, madness, and independence not only describe the historical condition of the woman writer but also the terms of our relation to the norms of an academic discipline. This is what gives the persistent double focus to the feminist critical project: the historical urgency that seeks to recover lost accomplishment and the institutional urgency that seeks to secure a position for an ongoing academic task.

We all have felt, men and women have felt, the weight of institutional norms—but women who have written on women have particularly felt that to challenge intellectual propriety, to depart from the norms of the discipline, is to invite madness, where madness in a disciplinary context signifies research that is anomalous, asystematic, indecorous, unpublishable, unpromotable.

And yet one of the perceptions suggested by a conjunction of the three works here invoked is that madness forms a middle term between propriety and independence, that a broad cultural historical arc extends from propriety *through* madness to independence. The readiness of a first generation of feminist critics to be seen as mad, their willingness to divest the portfolio of propriety, is surely what allows us in a second generation to feel that we are independent scholars at last. But are we? As long as there remains such intellectual uneasiness between the tasks of feminist literary critics and the discipline that institutionalizes them, the suspicion will linger that we are madwomen after all—or worse still, only proper ladies.

This institutional question will remain in the background of the argument to come, but everything that follows presupposes the view that feminist criticism has a theory only insofar as it has a history, and that its history lies less in a critical tradition than in an imaginative tradition where women have made a place and found a way to preserve it.

§

In beginning, and only just beginning, to spin out the historical thread which connects those moments described separately by Poovey, Gilbert, Gubar, and Vicinus, we might confront two nineteenth-century novels whose apparent dissimilarity will provide the impetus we want, two works which pose the difficulty of literary transition in imposing form. The novels are *Mansfield Park* and *Wuthering Heights*. Each gives rise to a textual crux which opens to wide historical and theoretical concerns and which might be referred to as the Fanny Price problem and the Nelly Dean problem.

Fanny Price was a problem before the emergence of feminist literary history, but she is more of a problem now. In order to see just why this is so, we may distinguish two separate traditions in the recent construction of a woman's literary history. First, and most obvious, is a tradition of women writers, a tradition that has, notoriously, put in question the problem of the literary canon. Second, and less prominent, is a tradition, not of women writers, but of female characters—a lineage of heroines as exemplary precedents from the cultural past.

What makes *Mansfield Park* such a difficult work for the feminist critics, and what makes for a detectable uneasiness in those who address the novel, is that it marks a place where the two traditions conspicuously collide. Jane Austen—always Jane Austen, above all Jane Austen—stands as anchor to any tradition of women writers, and *Mansfield Park* gives weight and bite to that anchor. But at the same time the portrait of Fanny Price stands as a deep embarrassment for that second tradition, the tradition of fictive precursors through whom we hope to devise a moral identity. Here, then, is what gives us the Fanny Price problem: that Austen's imaginative activity should realize itself in the passivity of her heroine, that an ironist should celebrate a prig, and more particularly, that our great novelistic matriarch should enshrine the loyal daughter of patriarchy.

Marilyn Butler has offered a reading of *Mansfield Park* that may serve as a useful standard for all attempts at refinement. Butler characterizes the novel as an ideological work, an anti-Jacobin novel principally concerned with defending the conservative cause against a set of radical social tendencies. In her view the first part of the novel succeeds as a withering critique of a failed modernity. Modern skepticism, hedonism, egotism, the fall from Christian faith and Christian humility, the neglect of domestic authority, the encouragement of lawless desires—these are the novel's targets. The conservative critique exposes a festering decay which can only be remedied by the recovery of lost ideals of moral integrity.

The difficulty in the book, according to Butler, is that Austen is not satisfied with the conservative critique; she is intent to portray the *conservative ideal;* and she means to do so through the portrait of Fanny. This is how Butler accounts for the most telling feature in the form of the novel, the shift in narrative perspective between the first and second books. The impersonal standpoint of the opening, which is well suited to Austen's satiric critical purposes, gives way to an increasingly personalized point of view, Fanny's point of view, which is designed to reveal the ideal workings of the conservative temper.

"'Bad,' was my commentary"

Butler argues that the fatal weakness in the novel, the source of its unpleasantness and our unease, lies in the discrepancy between the impersonal social critique and the subjective moral idealizing—the movement, as Butler puts it, "from the plane of what could happen to the plane of what should happen, from the actual observable world to the ideal." The essential problem is that the attempt to render the moral consciousness of the individual—the attempt, that is, to render Fanny's subjectivity—cannot be reconciled with the novel's conservative ideology, which is anti-individual, antipersonal, antisubjective. The ultimate failure of *Mansfield Park* for Butler is that the conservative case is weakened by "the attempt to use the inward life of a heroine as [its] vehicle."[2]

Butler makes a compelling argument for the ideological failure of *Mansfield Park*, but what she persuasively describes as the novel's weakness as a conservative social tract is precisely what opens it to a feminist rereading. What Butler takes to be the fatal fissure in the work, the break between impersonal social comedy and the inwardness of subjectivity, might instead be taken as its most arresting and most radical feature. This is because it points to an essential disjunction between values and experience. Put another way, it points to a rupture between ideology and subjectivity—that is, the rupture between dominant social beliefs and lived individual experience. Instead of seeing this as a flaw, we might take it as the novel's subject.

For fictive men as well as fictive women, there always looms the possibility of a subjectivity that cannot be assimilated, that remains fugitive, unofficial, marginal. But for men the paths from the margins back to the center were well charted, and it is surely no accident that the nineteenth century history of the bildungsroman is an overwhelmingly male history, that *bildung* is habitually conceived as male *bildung*. Where men get educated and cultivated, women get married; marriage is the female counterpart to *bildung:* in place of growth there is a wedding. And where the bildungsroman typically offers continuity and development, the marriage plot most often depends on a magical transformation, a sudden change of state, without transition, without development: "Reader, I married him." No matter how gratifying the resolution, it cannot remove the strain between the experience of women and the values they are asked to bear. Our persistent contemporary urge to undo the marriages of our heroines need not be interpreted as a desire to send them off to public life—to have them run for office, to have them found a colony—but more fundamentally and more simply as a desire to display female subjectivity, unencumbered, unadorned, unassimilated.

Female subjectivity may be considered one great and abiding provocation to the Victorian imagination; the overcoming of that provocation, the restoration of propriety, the taming of madness, the marrying of solitaries, is a dominant fictive task, and a chief instrument of that task is commentary. Within the theory of fiction, commentary continues to be a neglected subject, yielding first place to narrative, second place to description, and narrowing generally to those passages of overt evaluation whose effect, we are told, is to control readerly judgments—as Forster controls our judgment of Dolly Wilcox in *Howards End:* "She was a rubbishy little creature and she knew it."

But if this is the effect of commentary, then we must surely grant that it is not confined to those instances of overt intrusion, but that it is ubiquitous. The attempt of a text to tell the reader how to take it, the attempt to persuade, to cajole, to plead, to convert, occurs at every level of the work—from the choice of descriptive terms to the sequence of narrative incident. And once this evident fact is acknowledged, then it becomes impossible to see commentary as a special minor function which appears only when the machinery of narration and description stops working for a moment and an authoritative voice whispers in the reader's ear.[3] In fact, the whisper never ceases. Commentary must be recognized in all those acts which bring a fugitive and unformed experience into a regulative moral order. Commentary, in short, is the text's ideology.

So conceived, commentary is no static body of gnomic utterances; it is, rather, an activity that a work must ceaselessly perform upon itself. Fiction, especially nineteenth century fiction, obeys a rhythm of invention and self-regulation. A female body is imagined. It is promptly dressed, its hair is coiffed, its eye tamed, its walk steadied. But every new invention tests the old regulation, raises the possibility that the body will tear its dress, loose its hair, free its eye, and run in mad flight from the restraints of commentary. A way, then, to formulate the problem here is to cast it in terms of a struggle between female subjectivity and the fictive commentary that encloses it.

In *Mansfield Park* the struggle, almost always submerged, breaks the surface at rare moments, one of them being a short passage at the beginning of the novel's last chapter, where the narrator speaks in tones of unmistakable intimacy: "My Fanny indeed at this very time, I have the satisfaction of knowing, must have been happy in spite of every thing. She must have been a happy creature in spite of all that she felt or thought she felt, for the distress of those around her. She had sources of delight that must force their way."[4] On the one hand, this is an act of romantic appropriation which makes Edmund's fondness for Fanny seem all thin milk and water; here at the novel's denouement it is the narrator, not Edmund, who breathes "My Fanny" through finely pursed lips. On the other hand, there are subtle signs of tension in this ideal romance between narrator and character. The narrator, we learn, enjoys not only the power of affection but the added and incomparable "satisfaction of knowing." It is the narrator, not the husband, who can recognize the difference between what Fanny feels and what she thinks she feels, a superfine distinction upon which the complexity of the novel hangs suspended.

Indeed, the striking formal turn in *Mansfield Park* can be understood in terms of this distinction. As the novel substitutes narrative summary for dramatic scene, as it virtually eliminates dialogue, as it disregards social comedy, as it settles its point of view on Fanny, it finds a way to render its heroine's feelings in all their ineliminable immediacy; but at the same time it finds a standpoint from which to criticize the illusions of feeling. Out of the energetic comedy of the novel's opening phase two perspectives ascend to dominance: the heroine's and her commentator's. Surely Butler is right to emphasize that *Mansfield Park* veers sharply in the direction of Fanny's subjectivity, but we need to add that, simultaneously, it veers towards the perch of the authoritative commentator who encloses Fanny's agony within the broader vista of moral stability. The movement from dramatic tableau to narrative exposition at once consolidates subjectivity and seeks to correct it.

§

Here, perhaps surprisingly, we have a point of access to the novel's other great crux, the outrage created by the home theatricals rehearsed at Mansfield. The moral fuss has seemed so disproportionate to the fault (an "advanced" drama rehearsed in the billiard room) that it has reasonably been felt that we need deeper sources of explanation. But leaving aside all the explanatory niceties—anthropological, psychological, political, cultural historical—we can content ourselves with a dull and direct thought: namely, that the suspicion toward the drama expresses a novelist's wariness before a rival genre. A worker in prose fiction fastidiously separates herself from dramatic expression: what makes the issue so pointed is that Austen herself inclines instinctively towards the methods of drama, the first movement of *Mansfield Park* representing an unquestioned triumph of theatricality.

The condemnation of domestic theater stands, then, as the thematic counterpart to the work's great structural ambition, the attempt to develop a novelistic form which would be consistent with the book's moral aims and which would accordingly discard and even discredit the reliance on dramatic devices. Within the terms offered by *Mansfield Park,* drama is associated with flirtation (as opposed to marriage), with erotic chafing (as opposed to love), with wit (as opposed to eloquence). At the same time the multivoicedness of drama is incompatible with Austen's pursuit of a secure moral and formal center, and the great change in the method of her novel can be seen as enacting a movement away from the dramatic model to another model which the fiction conveniently invokes.

In the last confrontation between the upright but disinterested Edmund Bertram and wittily impertinent Mary Crawford, Mary endures his moral criticism and then responds, "A pretty good lecture upon my word. Was it part of your last sermon?" (p. 418). Earlier, Mary's brother Henry had put a similar point in more respectful terms. "A thoroughly good sermon," he tells Edmund,

> "is a capital gratification. . . . There is something in the eloquence of the pulpit, when it is really eloquence, which is entitled to the highest praise and honour. The preacher who can touch and affect such an heterogeneous mass of hearers, on subjects limited, and long worn thread-bare in all common hands; who can say any thing new or striking, any thing that rouses the attention, without offending the taste, or wearing out the feelings of his hearers, is a man whom one could not (in his public capacity) honour enough. I should like to be such a man." (pp. 309–10)

Jane Austen, we might say, wants (at least intermittently) to be such a woman, and the sermon, as Crawford describes it, becomes an alternative to social comedy as a paradigm for the novel. Eloquence, decorum, novelty without offense, tradition without repetition, a broad appeal to a heterogeneous audience—plainly these are not only signs of the successful sermon but marks of the novelistic success which Austen envisioned for *Mansfield Park.*

But if the sermon is a model for the novel's author and its narrator, the confession is a generic lure for its heroine. Throughout the second half of the book the unrelenting concentration on the immediacies of Fanny's experience raises the possibility that she will at last break her unearthly silence; speak in her own voice what has been spoken for her; confess her passion, her suffering, the horror, the love. Indeed, in the final chapter a future is projected in which Fanny will "tell [Edmund] the whole delightful and astonishing truth" (p. 430).

Confession and sermon stand cautiously side by side, parallel but distinct modes of moral speech. *Mansfield Park,* in effect, gives us two exemplars of propriety, in the person of its heroine and in its narrator, and far from coinciding, they disclose a division within the canons of propriety—a division, roughly speaking, between moral anguish and robust moral conviction. Fanny Price desperately feels her way to thought, while the narrator dispassionately separates what she feels from what she only thinks she feels. In this division, all the paradoxes of self-transparency unfailingly come into play. What we think we feel cannot be thought away: it feels like a feeling.

Part of the great strength of *Mansfield Park* is that it is no more concerned with moral precept than it is concerned with moral sensation. And in asking so probingly how it *feels* to be a moral woman—whether or not one only thinks one feels it—the book opens up a space between ideology and subjectivity. That Fanny is a prig, that she bows low before the Father, that she prefers propriety to freedom, that she drinks deep of the ideology of conservatism—these facts are not in doubt. But what is striking is that this defender of established community is herself so isolated, that this champion of home comfort is herself so agitated, that *in spite of herself* this moral conservative makes a domestic revolution. Fanny's unrelenting Propriety is what makes her an exile through the long course of the novel—the Proper Lady as the Marginal Woman.

At a moment of crisis during her emotional trial, Fanny comes to the wearying recognition that she must expect still more agony, that "the vicissitudes of the human mind had not yet been exhausted by her" (p. 340). It is an unsettling remark, especially when set against the view of Fanny as the prig's own prig, the one who longs for moral stasis before all. Moral stasis is indeed what Fanny seeks, but the vicissitudes of the human mind are what she endures. If we are beguiled by the moral categories that organize the novel, we may find Fanny merely a prig and merely repellent. In so doing, we then obscure the novel's deepest layer of excavation, the layer of experience that *underlies* moral categories, Fanny's terror, her solitude, her self-doubt and self-estrangement, her horror of certain smells, her fear of dirt and pollution—all those immediate sensations, perceptions, and emotions that *precede* and *exceed* ideology.[5] Suppose, then, that instead of seeing the "inward life of a heroine" as a retreat from Austen's ideological purposes—suppose that we see it as an attempt to locate a region deeper than ideology, where even one's own values seem external to the self, where even Fanny Price is not good.[6]

It is likely to be objected, especially from the standpoint of a certain Marxism, that there is no place for the body to flee, and no place for subjectivity where it will be immune from the system of values that dominate an epoch. But this is a theoretical and methodological assumption that feminist history is well positioned to contest. For just to the extent that women have been, not the agents who fashion ideology, but the objects of ideological refashioning, and just to the extent that ideology has located women on its margins, we may expect to uncover a stratum of female experience which cannot be resolved into the values of the epoch. Deprivation has had this benefit: in keeping women on the margins of public life, it has left us room to develop private lives radically distinct from public aims, and it is then no surprise that in the emergence of a literary form, the novel, which sought to excavate the inwardness of experience, it would so often fall to the *heroine* to be the bearer of subjectivity.

In this respect feminist literary history has a double aim, a double aim that can be cast in terms of two slogans that have served as homemade signposts for critical reflection. One slogan tells us that "the personal is political" and the other speaks of "the authority of experience"—two simple formulations which have crystallized much feminist thought but which stand in perceptible tension.

To assert that the personal is political is to insist on the interpenetration of private and public lives, on the presence of power in domestic life, on the continuity between personal and social struggle. But to acknowledge the authority of experience is to refuse that continuity: it is to grant a privilege to subjectivity and to deny that our lived experience must be assimilable to the categories of social life. Tension though this be, it is a productive one for feminist literary history, setting complex tasks for the historian of women. On the one hand, our aim must be to take seriously the insight in the phrase "the personal is political" and to pursue the reach of politics into the furthest recesses of personal life. On the other hand, the goal is to respect the authority of experience even when—indeed, especially when—experience challenges moral norms and political values. At the limits of ideology there is Woman.

§

At this point, we might usefully distinguish two sources for fictive commentary, two species of extraliterary discourse that inform the way fiction makes judgments, invokes values, applies standards, embeds ideology. The first is Scripture—preeminently Scripture in the biblical sense but also in the derived sense of any canonical text that claims, and is granted, an authoritative privilege. The characteristic and paradigmatic locution in all Scripture is the phrase "It is written"—a phrase which obliterates all traces of the living speaker and which names a text as the source of authority. "It is written" acknowledges no tie to the sound of the speaking voice and its limitations, claiming for itself an impersonality, an asexuality, even an inhumanity, that exempts it from the finite circumstances of human speech.

The claim to authority in novelistic commentary—this is the initial point—is a claim for the novel as a form of Scripture; and a marked tendency in prose fiction, especially marked in fiction of the nineteenth century, is a tendency to aspire beyond the constraints of individual speech, to expunge the marks of personality, history, and gender, and to present the judgments within the text as sanctioned merely by the *writing* of the text. The biblical "It is written" incites a dream of mastery in fictive commentary, a dream of uncontested scriptural authority which owes nothing to the community it governs, which does not emanate from the community but descends upon it.

The paradigm of the sermon in *Mansfield Park* is the derived oral form of this scriptural authority. The novel in the view offered here goes in tireless search of an appropriate mode of spoken discourse, a nondramatic form of speech, but this ambition itself rests upon another, the desire to establish a written text as a basis for all other rhetoric. In short, if the sermon is a model for characters' speech, scripture is the paradigm for the text itself, and as with preacherly eloquence, the successful verbal performances of fictive characters emanates from, and resolves back into, the authoritative writing which underlies it.

In general, one of the persistent aspirations of the novel has been to efface its origins in merely human gifts and to present itself as the word, the fictive Logos—but that is only one persistent aspiration. I have suggested that there are at least two extraliterary sources for commentary, two paradigms for novelistic judgment. The second, standing at the greatest distance from scripture, is gossip. If on one side, that is, the novel has aped the tones and privileges of biblical authority, on the other side it has assumed the casual informality of the gossipy tongue which carries on its moral valuations, not in the spirit of impersonal conviction and disembodied impartiality, but with a frank acknowledgment of its own homely origins.

The implacable "It is written" of scripture has its counterpart in the jaunty "And *I* say" of the gossip. And in these two phrases—"It is written" and "And *I* say"—we have not only two paradigms of moral judgment but two conventions for the narrative act. The history of the Victorian novel plays out an uneasy negotiation between these paradigms, and within individual works we can detect a nervous alteration from the novel as self-validating text which asks for no human sanction and the novel as the intimate utterance of a neighbor.

Patricia Spacks's study of gossip has not yet found its due place in feminist theory, but by situating her work on the concept in opposition to the antithetical term that I am naming scripture, it should be possible to reconceive a prevailing theoretical orthodoxy as a way of reconceiving dominant historical assumptions.[7] Perhaps the most prominent strain in the Derridean program has been the effort to rehabilitate an allegedly degraded writing and to contest the exorbitant privileges of speech. This critique of phonocentrism needs to be more directly met in feminist theory: until now, the upward revaluation of writing and the downward revaluation of speech have largely been either ignored or casually presupposed. But what Spacks's work encourages us to see—though this is admittedly not part of her goal, and she is to be exempted from my own polemical intentions—is that from the standpoint of women, the relations of speech and writing look quite different.

Where women are concerned, *speech* rather than *writing* has been the degraded term. The conversations of women have been made to appear a spectacle of thoughtless chatter: prattling, gabbling, clucking. Indeed, as Gilbert and Gubar have definitively shown, when conceived in the terms of gender, writing has had an abiding prestige, a prestige traditionally associated with male genius, male power, and the male anatomy—and even as the written text and the male sex are mystically married, the abuses of speech, the inability to keep silent, the promiscuity of the tongue have been generously reserved for women.

To cast the issue in terms of gossip and scripture is to suggest how one might reverse the Derridean reversal—how one might recognize that for women the difficulty has not been the tyranny of sacred speech but the indignity of profane conversation. And it is a special merit of Spacks's account of gossip that she implicitly opens the way for a second revaluation of the speech/writing distinction, a revaluation that should have consequences for the relationship between feminism and poststructuralism.

Gossip, as Spacks points out, generates "interpretations out of shared belief in the comprehensibility of motive and action," and its "collaborative oral narratives" represent a form of "communal authorship."[8] To see gossip in these terms—not as essentially frivolous or demeaning, but as a form of moral solidarity—is to refuse the current theoretical gambit; it is to make a counter-Derridean move towards a recovery of value in speech rather than writing, the value of our wagging female tongues. Furthermore, to recognize the proposed distinction between gossip and scripture is not only to give the specificity of gender to the prevailing concern with speech and writing but also to suggest a way of understanding the literary historical problem that is broached here under the heading of the Fanny Price problem, the question of the inward life of the heroine within the close confines of novelistic ideology.

Within the terms of fiction, the succession of historical phases which I have derived from my feminist precursors—propriety, madness, independence—may be seen as moments in the emancipation of female subjectivity from the constraints of commentary. Poovey's proper lady is one who has been made to yield to the coercions of narrative comment: propriety is achieved when the heroine coincides not so much with the hero as with the narrative norm. The madwoman of Gilbert and Gubar eludes the moral vocabulary brought forth to define her; she is named mad because the commentator has no other terms in which to cast her. And Vicinus's independent woman—only glimpsed in Victorian fiction—is one who comes bearing a new moral vocabulary which sits obstinately and indigestibly within the old.

This historical progression—a halting uneven *bildung* that we can recover for our heroines, not as individuals, but as members of the species—may be associated with the two phases of commentary which this essay is at pains to distinguish. As the heroine passes from being the object of scriptural abjuration to the subject of neighborhood gossip, she begins to make the long march from propriety through Madness to independence. And it is just here that the Fanny Price problem gives way to the Nelly Dean problem.

§

Early in *Wuthering Heights,* a curious Lockwood hopes that Nelly will "prove a regular gossip," and indeed as Nelly begins to spin her tale, she promises to follow it through "in true gossip's fashion."[9] That Nelly identifies herself as a gossip and that a gossip's curiosity governs the rhythm of the plot is no incidental feature but an essential, even determining, aspect of the book. It is perhaps most clearly displayed in the passage from *Wuthering Heights* which suggested my title, a passage which occurs in the ninth chapter, where Nelly quizzes Cathy about her love for Edgar Linton.

> "Why do you love him, Miss Cathy?"
> "Nonsense, I do—that's sufficient."
> "By no means; you must say why."
> "Well, because he is handsome, and pleasant to be with."
> "Bad," was my commentary.
> "And because he is young and cheerful."
> "Bad, still." (p. 97)

"Bad" is her commentary, and no act of moral evaluation could be less ambiguous. But that the act of commentary is named as such, that Nelly avows it as "my commentary," that it no longer circumscribes the plot, but falls within it—this is the change that must concern us. For it means that now commentary must enter into a dialogue with the heroine.

We may put the point just the other way, since it is also true that now the heroine may enter dialogue with commentary. When Cathy makes her memorable utterance "I *am* Heathcliff" (p. 52), she is, in effect, presenting the problem of subjectivity in its most uncompromising form—she is a subjectivity refusing to be herself. Standing alone, the statement offers an unsurpassable epitome of the third paradigm for fictive commentary, the paradigm of confession, commentary as self-appraisal and self-projection. But for heroines (as for critics) this remains only a partially realized mode of speech; the act of confession becomes quickly entangled within the ideological web; it is highly notable, for instance, that in Cathy's celebrated avowal, the complete form of the sentence is not "I *am* Heathcliff," but "Nelly, I *am* Heathcliff," a detail which makes plain that passion in the novel is, not a two-term, but a three-term relation. Joseph's invocation of God as "Him as allus makes a third" might equally be an invocation of the voice of commentary, the third who intrudes on the narrative of intimacy, opening the insides of passions for outsiders to see.

Indeed, Joseph, with his constant recourse to biblical precedent and his remorseless application of biblical rule, might be seen as a relic of what I am calling scriptural commentary—now no longer poised on an invisible pinnacle, but reduced to carping from dark corners, laying claim to a moral authority which others refuse to grant. It is not Joseph with his scripture but Nelly with her gossip who works her way to the center of events and who is chiefly responsible for one of the most startling aspects of *Wuthering Heights:* its reliance on the methods and the motives of voyeurism.

Observing, overhearing, snooping, skulking, eavesdropping—these are not incidental lapses, they are central activities in a book where being is never clearly distinguished from seeing. Cathy and Heathcliff glimpsing the Lintons through a window; Heathcliff overhearing Cathy's reasons for marrying Edgar; Nelly a bystander at the most passionate kiss in English literature; these are only the most vivid instances of a motif that is uncannily persistent. On the one hand, we may see this in terms of an urge to bring commentary close to its object, to allow the evaluating eye to peer closely at its specimen. For after all the celebrated passion of *Wuthering Heights,* it is worth noting that it is the *critique* of passion which most occupies the novel's principals—the endless, restless scrutiny of the emotions of others.

On the other hand, the risk in any voyeurism is that those who watch will be seen seeing. Cathy and Heathcliff come to observe the Lintons only to find themselves fatefully observed. When Heathcliff comes to retrieve his son, the terrified Linton, in a phrase that we may take as another epitome, lifts his eyes in order "to inspect the inspector" (p. 254). The reversal of gaze contained in this act—the act of inspecting the inspector—may be the novel's most radical gesture: it is also the first act of any feminism. Moreover, it represents a decisive stage in the struggle sketched here, the struggle between commentary and subjectivity. *Wuthering Heights* repeatedly allows the hierarchy to be inverted—it initiates oppressive acts of moral vision and then turns to examine the examining eye.

Commentary, we need always to remember, is never an isolated act of moral reflection; it is always part of a network of competing statements struggling to establish dominance over the interpretation of the text. For an utterance to function as commentary, it is not enough for it to express an evaluation; it must achieve a rhetorical force which will coincide with the governing forces of the text and which will thus appear to the reader, not as an isolated judgment from a single perspective, but as a truth about the world. When the narrator of *Mansfield Park* serenely expresses the "satisfaction of knowing" that Fanny "must have been happy in spite of every thing," we are in the presence of textual power in its clearest form. The narrator may well be complacently knowing because we have been reminded that the act of narrative constitutes the truths to be known.

Wuthering Heights continually subverts the aspiration to the power of commentary. Throughout the novel individual characters will position themselves as controlling voices, only to discover that in this world such power can always be disarmed. Laughter is chief among the disarming instruments, a fact keenly sensed by those who seek to consolidate authority. Mr. Earnshaw, we are told, "did not understand jokes from his children" (p. 52), and Heathcliff, when he has achieved power of his own, rebukes Catherine by saying, "I thought I had cured you of laughing!" (p. 387). Laughter is the enemy of authoritative commentary; the sniggering lips, the braying voice, the convulsed body offer rudely direct ways of inspecting the inspector.

In the novel's most directly staged encounter between the moral eye and the rebellious voice, the dying Mr. Earnshaw asks Cathy "Why canst thou not always be a good lass?" to which she laughingly, unabashedly, parodically responds, "Why cannot you always be a good man, father?" (p. 53). The reprobate scolds the judge—the heroine parodies the commentator's decree. The tones of parody are never far from the tones of passion in *Wuthering Heights,* and that is because parody becomes a form of revenge upon those moral magistrates, a way of neutralizing the edicts of authority: parody creates a space that allows the passions to enjoy themselves. And so the Bible-quoting Joseph, my figure for scriptural commentary, finds that his perpetual "reproofs" meet Cathy's perpetual "bold, saucy look" (p. 102).

When through the offices of Nelly Dean, Edgar Linton learns that Cathy and Heathcliff are meeting in his kitchen and learns too what they have said, he surprises them and addresses his wife from the high ground of moral outrage: "what notion of propriety must you have to remain here, after the language which has been held to you by that blackguard? I suppose, because it is his ordinary talk, you think nothing of it—you are habituated to his baseness, and, perhaps, imagine I can get used to it too!" Whereupon Cathy retorts, "Have you been listening at the door, Edgar?" and Heathcliff gives a "sneering laugh" (p. 140).

This is a telling instance of that reversal of gaze which the novel persistently enacts, and during the space of this moment our three governing terms—propriety, madness, independence—jostle uneasily. For Edgar to sustain the canons of propriety is to consign Cathy and Heathcliff to moral madness, and the activity of commentary in *Wuthering Heights* is largely in pursuit of this end. But contained in Edgar's remark is the frightened acknowledgment that madness has its own proprieties, that even the unspeakable has its habits, its norms, its table manners. And from this it is only a short step to the unnerving suspicion that what we have named madness might be called independence.

Such a daunting reversal depends on the ambiguity that inheres in gossip—gossip, not as idle chatter, but as a form of moral relatedness. In every act of gossip there lives a tacit acknowledgment of a rival subjectivity, there lives the recognition that I who speak may soon be spoken of. Nelly Dean has been our emblem of this ambiguity. She is the figure of the commentator as gossip and the gossip as failed voyeur. She is repeatedly caught in the act, repeatedly seen seeing; and yet just this failure of concealment ensures her importance—because to be seen seeing is to become at once subject and object, a constituting eye and a constituted body, a critic and a thing criticized. This is the deepest implication of that reversal of gaze which informs *Wuthering Heights* at every level and which allows it to become an exemplary text for heroines and also for historians.

§

For there is a continuity, after all, between the commentary that a fiction devises for itself and the commentaries that we, the critics, devise for fiction. And if I have been suggesting that we can see in gossip and in scripture two paradigms for fictive commentary, so we might also recognize them as competing paradigms for our own activity. Spacks remarks acutely that "It is a paradox essential to gossip that those who engage in it must in the process combine the roles of insider and outsider,"[10] and this is what makes gossip rather than confession the attractive institutional alternative. The gossip is an insider because the object of her speech is a member of the community to which she too belongs, and she is an outsider because in turning a critical edge on the community, she cannot coincide with it.

But is not that ambiguity of insider and outsider essential to our own position?—as literary historians in general, but more particularly as feminist literary historians, who feel so often that the community we seek was already found by the writers and heroines we study. Our own acts of critical commentary seem to place us outside the tradition, but when in the spirit of our self-reflective enterprise we submit ourselves to scrutiny, we find that the tradition folds back to contain us.

This is a difficult position, the literary historian as latter-day gossip, but the prevailing alternative is another form of scripture— the pretense that we can occupy a position detached from the tradition we encounter and that we can deliver authoritative judgments unaffected by the community from which they emerge. My improbable suggestion is that we critics should take the gossip as the mother of us all—because if we see criticism as ascending from gossip rather than descending from scripture, then we may be encouraged to understand the project of feminist literary history, not as the pursuit of individually authoritative utterances, but as the chatter of a community reflecting on its own history as a way of reflecting on itself, a chatter that has its own rigor, which is the rigor of individual beliefs seeking to mold the consensus of the group. Indeed, it is among the brighter ironies of our institutional lives that within the larger field of literary studies so unsure of its disciplinary coherence, feminist criticism—with its shared program of research, its mutually respectful individual coworkers pursuing common problems, its stable and increasing audience, its widely read journals, its well-attended conferences—has the emerging coherence of a discipline, a discipline born of gossip.

If propriety and madness will at last yield independence, that will only be because communities of women have made independence possible. Then we will gossip freely without fear of being overheard, and when we ourselves are the target of gossip, we will turn to inspect the inspector. When the male critic wearily asks, "Why canst thou not always be a good lass," we can saucily respond, "Why cannot you always be a good man, father?"

Notes

1. Mary Poovey, *The Proper Lady and the Woman Writer: Ideology as Style in the Works of Mary Wollstonecraft, Mary Shelley, and Jane Austen* (Chicago: The University of Chicago Press, 1984); Sandra M. Gilbert and Susan Gubar, *The Madwoman in the Attic: The Woman Writer and the Nineteenth-Century Literary Imagination* (New Haven: Yale University Press, 1979); Martha Vicinus, *Independent Women: Work and Community for Single Women, 1850–1920* (London: Virago Press, 1985).

2. Marilyn Butler, *Jane Austen and the War of Ideas* (London: Oxford University Press, 1975), pp. 245, 249.

3. See Wayne Booth for a rare subtle understanding of the ambiguities and impalpabilities of commentary: *The Rhetoric of Fiction* (Chicago: The University of Chicago Press, 1961).

4. Jane Austen, *Mansfield Park* (Oxford: Oxford University Press, 1986), p. 420. Hereafter, references to the novel will be to this edition and will be cited parenthetically in the text.

5. Ruth Yeazell has made several astute observations on the motif of physical taint in the novel, remarking that "the sense of pollution . . . is characteristic of the design of Austen's most troublesome novel." Ruth Bernard Yeazell, "The Boundaries of *Mansfield Park,*" *Representations* 7 (Summer 1984): 134.

Karen Chase

6. Compare D. A. Miller's judgment that "Fanny's curious disbelief and excessive disgust are inadequately served by the moral terms in which they are accounted for." *Narrative and Its Discontents: Problems of Closure in the Traditional Novel* (Princeton; Princeton University Press, 1981), p. 58.

7. Patricia Meyer Spacks, *Gossip* (New York: Alfred A. Knopf, 1985).

8. Ibid., pp. 230, 257.

9. Emily Brontë, *Wuthering Heights* (Oxford: The Clarendon Press, 1976), pp. 40, 78. Hereafter references to the novel will be to this edition and will be cited parenthetically in the text.

10. Spacks, *Gossip*, p. 212.

Ross C Murfin

Novel Representations
Politics and Victorian Fiction

*An ancient English Cathedral Tower? How can the
ancient English cathedral tower be here? . . . Ten
thousand scimitars flash in the sun-light, and thrice
ten-thousand dancing girls strew flowers.*
　　CHARLES DICKENS, *The Mystery of Edwin Drood*

*With a single drop of ink, the Egyptian sorcerer
undertakes to reveal . . . far-reaching visions of the
past. . . . With this drop of ink at the end of my pen, I
will show . . . the roomy workshop of Mr. Jonathan
Burge . . . as it appeared on the eighteenth of June,
in the year of our Lord 1799.*
　　GEORGE ELIOT, *Adam Bede*

§

*O*pium visions. Inky revelations.
But also the Negro, women, Ireland, America, liars, the Jew. Reflections in warped, spotted, and broken mirrors: poignantly distorted,
painfully sharp. Lines and scratches swirling a polished pewter pier
glass. Symbols appearing, reappearing, changing, evolving in
nineteenth-century British fiction. Symbols both of reality and of its
representation, for if the world is confused or bizarre, then so may be
its reflecting portrait; if it is not, then the surface that images it may
be as clear, airy, sharp, and bright as was the roomy workshop of Mr.
Jonathan Burge. If the world yet to be represented is dark, female,
poor, and non-Christian, then perhaps she who reflects and represents it should someday be the same. Perhaps. But the thought

frightened the world of nineteenth-century England, even as it frightens many living in the world today.

Truly novel representatives, after all, are people who seem to be liars—at least until their shattering stories and themes are finally perceived to be truths, often of a new and subtler order. In Charles Dickens's *Oliver Twist,* Doctor Losberne proves one of several novel representatives—one of several representatives of the novel, too— for he serves the truth through what seems to be falsehood. He tells a tall tale to save Oliver Twist, a true innocent if ever there was one, from policemen who are technically correct in thinking the boy an accomplice of thieves. Losberne is, at the same time, of course, a symbol not just of novel and radical representation but also of the world to be represented, the world whose motives and relationships are but dimly understood. So is Father Holt, the creation of William Makepeace Thackeray. This devious, revolutionary, Jacobite priest saves another bastard child, Henry Esmond, and thus allows *The History of Henry Esmond* to be told. With his ciphers, codes, and countless disguises, Holt represents both radical representation and the complex social and political reality that militiamen, magistrates, and members of Parliament often fail to see, let alone understand.

Other such figures—some human, some inhuman—abound. There is George Meredith's Diana of the Crossways, the Irish woman with English and Spanish blood who writes anonymous political commentary, as well as novels, under an assumed name. Examples would also include the diamond referred to by the title of Wilkie Collins's *The Moonstone,* as well as the Eustace Diamonds in Anthony Trollope's novel by the same name. All these are multi-faceted gems that can shatter a single, simple-seeming light source into myriad, multi-colored reflections. Equally powerful symbols, both of the world's complexity and of novel but powerful represen-tation, are mesmerism and the "new" drugs—potable opiates such as laudanum or chlorodyne—that are proffered and prescribed by characters in Victorian novels. In *The Moonstone* laudanum is the exotic, unsuspected ingredient in a diamond heist; later, however, in the hands of Doctor Ezra Jennings, it becomes a means of re-presenting the night of the crime, of discovering the long-obscured truth about what really happened. (Mesmerism, too, comes into play; associated with inscrutable Indians seeking to recover the Moonstone, it is the medium through which they see the lost gem's whereabouts.) In Eliot's hands, medicinal opium is associated with a different kind of obscured reality and a different form of representation. In a chapter which begins by associating Doctor Tertius Lydgate's struggles for "Medical Reform" with the "Natural struggle for another kind of reform," Lydgate counters "the . . . political writer," Will Ladislaw, by warning him that "There is nothing more thoroughly rotten than making people believe that society can be cured" by an extension of the suffrage, which Lydgate calls "political hocus pocus." Will reasserts his view that "cure must begin somewhere" and declares that the Reform Bill of 1832 is "something to begin with." Lydgate reasserts his opposition to the act: "When I say I go in for the dose that cures," he says, "it doesn't follow that I go in for opium in a given case of gout."[1]

Opium, obviously, was considered a dangerous prescription by some—almost as dangerous as mesmerism was thought to be.[2] So, clearly, was the 1832 reform bill. Almost equally inimical, in the eyes of many, were works of fiction, especially those that represented a low, unsavory, hitherto unseen side of life. Lady Carlisle found *Oliver Twist* repulsive because she didn't like hearing what the criminal class had to "say to one another," and Prime Minister Melbourne read no more than two chapters of the same novel, commenting that "It is all among workhouses and pickpockets and coffinmakers. . . . I do not like them in reality and therefore do not like to see them represented."[3] Still other "representative" men and women refused to believe that a criminal class of the type represented by Dickens even existed in reality. When the radical Sir Francis Burdett read *Oliver Twist*, Steven Marcus tells us, "he couldn't believe the conditions it described really existed, and determined to inquire into them."[4]

Thus, even some radicals preferred to think that new, realistic-seeming works of fiction in fact misrepresented reality. In the view of countless, more "respectable," Victorians, novelists were illusion-mongers, unsavory characters hawking lies that masqueraded as truths. As Janice Carlisle reminds us in her book entitled *The Sense of an Audience*, the novel was held in low esteem, throughout the first half of the nineteenth century, by both "Evangelical and utilitarian schools of thought," and "the fact that fiction is false was the principal source of its disfavor." Even Thomas Carlyle, whose *Sartor Resartus* bears more than a little resemblance to a novel, stood on his

Presbyterian principles and declared that "Fiction . . . partakes . . . in the nature of *lying*"; then he went on to ask his reader to "bethink him how impressive the smallest historical *fact* may become, as contrasted with the grandest *fictitious* event."[5]

And yet the times were already changing. One young, evangelistic student of theology named Mary Ann Evans became the agnostic novelist who called herself George Eliot. Whig historians sympathetic with utilitarianism were nonetheless skeptically reviewing the accepted "facts" about the past. Forty thousand Chapman and Hall subscribers laughed sympathetically as Dickens's one-legged derelict, Silas Wegg, referred to *The Decline and Fall of the Rooshan Empire* and then atoned for his blunder by making a sobering point: histories of Rome and Russia are not really so different, since all tell the stories of Caesars, czars, what Wegg calls "scarers."[6] As for one-legged quasi-literates, Dickens suggests, they were and are unrepresented in Rome, Russia, and the history books written by proper historians.

But they and their illiterate friends existed—in Rome, in Russia, and in Victorian England. Their living conditions were deplorable, even more deplorable than was the preeminent historian Macaulay's claim that the life led in nineteenth-century workhouses was vastly preferable to the life led by university scholars in the sixteenth century.[7] In Victorian England, in spite of the fact that the vote had been extended, in 1832, to £10 householders, the still-unrepresented were demanding recognition, reform, representation. A second reform bill that would further extend the suffrage was in riotous demand by the mid-1830s—and still in demand when Dickens published *Our Mutual Friend*, in 1865. (Benjamin Disraeli wrote a powerful account of the earlier Chartist fever in his fine historical romance entitled *Sybil.*) Only slightly less frenzied was the hunger for other reformed, representational mirrors, mirrors *like* that afforded by Disraeli's historical romance, mirrors in which whole groups could for the first time see themselves reproduced and, consequently, could feel real.

Novel representatives were, of course, as much in demand as were novel representations. Dickens was begged to stand for Reading. Thackeray, who agreed to be a candidate in Oxford, failed to win a seat, as did Trollope, who lost a hotly contested election in Beverley, Yorkshire. But Disraeli's successes have become legendary.

A Jew born in a nation in which Jews could not stand for election—a politician who cut his representational teeth, not on legal writing, but on novel writing—Disraeli serves as yet another symbol. He symbolizes the strange, mixed, confusing new world without, a world whose story cannot be told by one old, old one. (A reform-minded Tory, a Jew baptized into Christianity, a pragmatic dandy, and a novelist-become-politician, Disraeli was himself a bundle of contradictions and conversions, some of them perpetually in process.) At the same time, Disraeli symbolizes the novel representative, the figure needed to mirror change and the contradictions that inevitably accompany it. Disraeli brought to British history exactly that touch of illegitimacy and romance that the fiction of the age brought to the world of "facts" as they were conventionally seen. The novel—precisely because it offered a romance of history—was able to show new sides, often shocking sides, of British reality that had long been overlooked by those who might instead have overseen their restoration and representation.

§

From the "conservative Liberal"[8] Trollope, to the liberal Tory Disraeli, to Dickens—who in the view of one critic was by the time of his death in 1870 "all but a Marxian communist"[9]—all of the representative Victorian novelists that I have so far alluded to saw clearly that the inevitable challenge of the century would be to avoid revolution by reforming representational structures in such a way as to get the unrepresented represented.[10] As a brief survey of even a few selected letters and papers will show, however, the degree of commitment to representational reform—and the reasons for supporting the various reform acts—varied greatly from novelist to novelist.

Dickens, who was arguably the most radical of the great mid-century novelists, was an "ardent reformer"[11] from the time when, as a reporter for *The Mirror of Parliament*, he watched the final battles over the 1832 reform bill from the gallery of the House of Commons. Although he refused to stand for election to the House when asked to in 1841 by a group of citizens from Reading, he refused because he felt he could better represent the unrepresented and their needs in fiction. He followed parliamentary politics closely throughout his career as a novelist and always supported radical programs for reform. "How radical I am getting," Dickens wrote to John Forster in the same year he was asked to declare from Reading.[12] In fact, Edgar Johnson tells us, Dickens had been, throughout the 1830s, "sympathetic to the Chartist program of manhood suffrage, vote by ballot, annual Parliaments, abolition of property qualifications for election from Parliament, payment of members, and division of the country into equal electoral districts."[13]

Whereas other writers lent uneasy support to the second, 1867, reform act, Dickens felt calmly confident that it would improve the nation: "the greater part of the new voters," he wrote in a letter, "will in the main be wiser as to their electoral responsibilities and more seriously desirous to discharge them for the common good than the bumptious singers of 'Rule Britannia'."[14] As early as 1858 he had coauthored, with Collins, an essay entitled "A Clause for the New Reform Bill," in which he and his longtime collaborator had half humorously suggested an amendment preventing lavish, expensive preparations for visits by the queen to the nation's cities and towns. One thing, though, that Dickens and Collins make clear in the essay is that they are entirely serious in their support for a new, second reform bill, one significantly altering the reflection of the nation produced by that still-distorting mirror of Parliament.

Their most serious doubts concern whether what is ultimately passed will be strong enough. "Whether it is destined to show that Tories are Radicals, and Radicals Tories, and Whigs nothing in particular," Dickens and Collins write, "whether it be an artful Bill of the old sort, which at first delights us with magnificent professions, and then astonishes us with minute performances; or whether it is to be a Bill of original character, and of unparalleled resources in giving practical advantage to the people at large—seems to be more than the wisest of our political sages can tell us." Once again, a connection is made between representational reform and a "dose" of something, in this case healing medicine for a sick nation: "All that we really know . . . is that a new Reform Bill is being compounded somewhere. What the strength of the political mixture may be, which of the State Doctors will send it out, and what it will taste like when the British patient gets it, are mysteries."[15] No doubt Dickens thought the bill that eventually passed in 1867 was a dose of insufficient strength. In a speech he gave in 1869 he reconfirmed his faith in the advantages of extended suffrage (while showing little in the ability of politicians to represent their constituents): "My faith in the people governing is, on the whole, infinitesimal; my faith in the People governed is, on the whole, illimitable."[16]

If there was a novelist as radical as Dickens writing during Victoria's reign, it was Meredith, whose "interests and attitudes . . . throughout the [1850s and 1860s] were," in Jack Lindsay's words, "closely linked with those of the advanced sections of the working class." Meredith shows his radical colors in "The Old Chartist"; indeed, by subscribing to the principles set forth in People's Charter of 1848, he identifies himself as "a left-wing Radical."[17]

Thackeray, who stood for Oxford as an Independent in 1857, never expressed radical views like those Meredith penned in "The Old Chartist." Indeed, in a speech he wrote to be given to the Administrative Reform Association of Parliament on July 11, 1855, Thackeray is far more cautious in urging reform than Dickens had been when addressing the same group on June 27. Nonetheless, Thackeray says many things in the speech he wrote—but never delivered—that both Dickens and Meredith would have approved of. Having written, "I take it A. R. [administrative reform] means P. R. [political reform] for you never will get one without the other," Thackeray goes on to needle his prospective audience, as if to suggest that its members are halfhearted in their liberalism:

> I take it that you mean an ameliorated representation in Parliament, and an amended franchise without. You mean that men shall be eligible to sit in the House of Commons without these enormous expenses which befall candidates nowadays. . . . I fancy some of you may possibly mean that in lieu of the present system . . . [allowing voter] intimidation, stupid coaxing wheedling treating back-door persuading, . . . popping off five pound notes into drunken voters' hands—you will prefer a system that shall do away with all this wickedness & humbug and if you say for instance that you will adopt the [secret] Ballot I for one will give my most hearty concurrence. . . . If you don't—then this Society is mere Bosh.[18]

Thackeray then proceeds, though, as if the society is *not* "Bosh," writing words surely meant to stiffen the resolve of reformers. "The governing classes," he warns, will be "against you. They always are." Expect trouble from the House of Lords, Thackeray advises, the body "we are bidden in venerable print nowadays to thank God we have . . . , which can restrain any immature and indecent popular ardor for reform," which "can interpose its august big-wigs between the mob and the desires which they have in view." But "by those big-wigs," Thackeray reminds his audience, "people were kept for years out of rights which are acquired and historical now:—the Catholics were kept out of their citizenship . . .—that modicum of justice called the Reform Bill was kept back: and, at this very minute . . . it is by that assembly of Lords that our Jewish fellow-citizens are kept out of . . . the house of commons."[19]

Two years later, in his address to the electors of Oxford, Thackeray is less specific in identifying injustices (and somewhat cloyingly kind to those he once labeled "big-wigs"), but he shows a continuing commitment, both to extended suffrage and to the secret ballot: "With no feeling but that of good-will towards these leading aristocratic families who are now administering the chief offices of the State, I believe it could be benefitted by the skill and talents of persons less aristocratic, and that the country thinks so likewise. I think that to secure due freedom of representation, and to defend the poor voter from intimidation, the ballot is the best safeguard . . . , and would vote . . . for that measure. I would have the suffrage amended in nature and number."[20]

For George Eliot, to amend the suffrage in "nature" meant something different than what it meant to Thackeray. For her it meant what it meant to John Stuart Mill, who tried to amend Gladstone's 1867 reform bill in such a way as to give women the vote, and to John Morley. Through the *Fortnightly Review,* which he edited, Morley supported Mill's amendment vociferously. To him Eliot wrote: "Your attitude in relation to Female enfranchisement seems to be very nearly mine. I would certainly not oppose any plan which held out any reasonable promise of tending to establish as far as possible an equivalence of advantages for the two sexes, as to education and the possibilities of free development." Eliot continues in this, a personal letter to Morley, by revealing her reason for writing it: she felt that Morley had misunderstood an offhand remark she had made at a dinner party. He had thought she had said something antifeminist, something critical of the women's suffrage proposal, whereas what she had meant was something very much the opposite: "I fear you may have misunderstood something I said the other evening about nature. I meant to urge the 'intention of Nature' argument, which is to me a pitiable fallacy. I mean that as a fact of mere zoological evolution, woman seems to me to have the worst share in existence. But for that very reason I would the more contend that in the moral evolution we have 'an art which does mend nature.' "[21]

It is not difficult to see how Morley "may have misunderstood" Eliot, thinking she was opposing him when she was in fact in agreement. Even in this letter, in which she tries to set the record straight, there is something curiously halfhearted about her support for women's suffrage; it is as if she feels an ambivalence she cannot mask. "Your attitude . . . seems to be very nearly mine" could be read two ways, and what Eliot goes on to say does little to make us think that her own views are more liberal than Morley's: "I would certainly not oppose any plan which held out any reasonable promise of tending to establish as far as possible an equivalence of advantages. . . ." Is Eliot talking, in this wildly equivocating statement, about the vote? If so, *does* she think it holds out reasonable promise of *tending* to establish more equivalent advantages? It almost sounds as if Eliot, were she able to vote on the matter, might just vote against the vote for women. It almost seems she is "urging" the "intention of Nature" argument in what has become the more usual sense of the word *urging*.

Certainly, Eliot's support for the second reform bill seemed qualified by second thoughts. She wrote her "Address to the Working Man" just before the 1867 legislation went into effect, in response to the John Blackwood's fear that "When the new Reform Bill comes into operation the working man will be on his trial and if he misconducts himself it will go hard with the country, but in all events his class would be the greatest sufferers."[22] Although Eliot had supported the passage of the bill, she had been adamantly opposed to the secret ballot, which promised to allow a poor tenant or operator to vote his conscience, whether or not his landlord or employer had bought him a beer or given him a sovereign for his vote: "I am moved to congratulate you on writing against the Ballot," Eliot wrote to Charles Bray in 1868; "It has been a source of amazement to me that men . . . can believe in the suppression of Bribery by the Ballot. . . . They might as well say that our female vanity would disappear at an order that women should wear felt hats and cloth dresses."[23]

Eliot's self-undercutting rhetoric is embarrassing, but it is not so embarrassing as it would be if it were not mirrored, to greater and lesser degrees, in the statements of so many other Victorian novelists "urging" representational reform. Even Meredith, who, like Dickens, was for the most part unsusceptible to retrogressive outbursts, is occasionally curmudgeonly in his novels. And a touch of conservatism shows in his letters, too—usually when the subject of America comes up. In a letter written in 1861, he expresses nothing less than ruling-class indignation over the seizure of Confederate envoys from an English ship by the American North. Later, his post–Civil War expressions of aversion to the (re)United States do not smack nearly so loudly as Trollope's do of a suppressed distaste for democracy, but Meredith's lyrical letter to Morley, in which he characterizes Americans collectively ("Themselves they know not, save that strong / For good and evil they grow"), makes the young democracy sound like an unself-conscious, adolescent Frankenstein.[24]

It is Trollope, though, who most deeply and disturbingly counterpoints arguments made in favor of reform with rhetorical slips, reactionary misfires. In his *Autobiography,* in the chapter entitled "My Political Theory," he writes of the "injustice" of "inequality" but then, after alluding to his belief that it "is the work of God," wonders that the "consciousness of wrong had induced in many enthusiastic and unbalanced minds a desire to set all things right by a proclaimed equality."[25] Perhaps fearing, like Eliot, that he may be misinterpreted, Trollope reassures his reader with a (guardedly) negative definition of conservatism. "The so-called Conservative, . . . being surely convinced that such inequalities are of divine origin, tells himself that it is his duty to preserve them. . . . But this man, though he sees something, . . . sees only a little. The divine inequality is apparent to him, but not the equally divine diminution of that inequality. . . . Such, I think are Conservatives;—and I speak of men who, with the fear of God before their eyes and the love of their neighbors warm in their hearts, endeavor to do their duty to the best of their ability." As for "the equally conscientious Liberal," Trollope goes on to say, that man is "equally averse to any sudden disruption of society" but "alive to the fact that these distances [between unequals] are day by day becoming less, and he . . . is even willing to help the many ascend the ladder. What is in his mind is,—I will not say equality, for the word is offensive, and presents . . . ideas of communism, of ruin, and insane democracy,—but a tendency towards equality." Having noted that the Liberal "knows he must be hemmed in by safeguards, lest he travel too quickly," and that, therefore, "he is glad to be accompanied on his way by the repressive action of a Conservative opponent," Trollope declares that "Holding such views, I . . . am an advanced conservative Liberal."[26] It may be worth noting that, being a conservative Liberal, Trollope, like Eliot, opposed the secret ballot. Indeed, he continued opposing "the Ballot" even after being defeated in Beverley by a Conservative candidate who, by all accounts, bought his votes. "Up to ten o'clock," the story in *Beverley Recorder* ran, "it seemed that the Liberal candidates were likely to be the victors," but "by the aid of bought votes the Conservatives gained . . . what may turn out to be a short-lived triumph."[27]

Thackeray, who supported the secret ballot, undercuts his own liberalism more subtly than does Trollope. Or, at least, he is less obviously self-contradictory in his nonfiction prose writings; his novels, on the other hand, fully justify George Henry Lewes's assertion that he was "a Janus bifrons," with a "pre-dominating tendency to antithesis."[28] Even in his nonfiction prose, though, we may occasionally catch a glimpse of Thackeray's two faces. There is that election speech in which he expresses "no feeling but that of goodwill" toward those very aristocratic families he mordantly calls "bigwigs" in another speech—that he never delivered. And in that same undelivered address to the Administrative Reform Association, there are passages that make it sound as if Thackeray wants all men represented, not because it is right, but, rather, because the country can survive it (and cannot survive without it): "The 1832 Reform Bill was got & no bones were broken—the Emancipation Act was passed & nobody's head was chopped off. . . . The Corn Laws were repealed. The nation did not go to the dogs."[29] Thackeray's critics, including Dickens, often maintained that there was a certain sham quality to his liberalism. In 1858 Edmund Yates published, in *Town Talk*, the following account of a series of lectures given by Thackeray: "The prices were extravagant, the Lecturer's adulation of birth and privilege was extravagant. No one succeeds better than Mr. Thackeray in cutting his coat according to his cloth: here he flattered the aristocracy, but when he crossed the Atlantic, George Washington became the idol of his worship, the 'Four Georges' the objects of his bitterest attacks."[30] Thackeray fired off a letter of protest, and Yates responded apologetically—but in a letter he never sent. "Unfortunately," Lewis Benjamin tells us, "Yates showed his letter to Dickens," who apparently thought Yates had nothing to regret and "drafted another."[31] Dickens' version of Yates's reply so offended Thackeray that he appealed to the Garrick Club to expel Yates, both for writing the inflammatory review in the first place and for later refusing to apologize for it properly.

What lies at the heart of the inconsistency Dickens must have noticed in Thackeray's positions—of the ambivalence I have tried to tease out of the writings of Trollope, Eliot, and, to a lesser extent, Meredith? Must we simply conclude that the "true" politics of Thackeray and Trollope were fairly conservative, but that, able as they were to "cut their coats according to the cloth," they put on an (imperfect) outward show of reform-mindedness?

Such an answer, though possibly true, is at the same time too simple. Trollope's evident ambivalence toward democratic principles is only one manifestation of a larger ambivalence—toward everything. Thackeray is a "Janus bifrons" when it comes to politics because, as Carlyle told Emerson, the man as well as his writings were "very uncertain and chaotic in all points." J. Y. T. Grieg agrees, saying that Thackeray's novels entirely lack "that integrity and coherence which we find in seemingly shapeless novels by Dickens and Hardy."[32] And how could they not, given Thackeray's views (they are also Trollope's views) both of "truth" and of writing? In *Vanity Fair,* where ink is associated with other novel elixirs, a famous passage implies that writing is, at best, false medicine—false because the "truths" it represents turn out to be falsehood. Thus, those "quacks . . . who advertise indelible india ink should be made to perish along with their discoveries. The best ink for Vanity Fair use would be one that faded utterly in a couple of days, and left the paper clear and blank."[33]

As Catherine Gallagher has recently suggested in *The Industrial Reformation of English Fiction,* politics cannot be separated from epistemology—or, ultimately, from aesthetics. Every writer I have mentioned in this essay "supported" reform, but to support representational reform unequivocally means to believe in "right" vs. wrong, to believe that there *is* a right way to represent the political reality of a nation. But what if one were to believe that both the "right" and the "real" are ephemeral and subjective? One would surely be prone to suspect, and suggest, that every political and aesthetic representation is only one of the many possible ones, based on assumptions that seem true—for the moment—from the perspective of the mirror holder. In the fiction of Thackeray and Trollope, that suspicion is nothing less than a singular conviction. In the novels of Eliot and Meredith, it is suggested more guardedly, in the form of what might best be described as cautiousness.

In her copy of Molesworth's *History of the Reform Bill of 1832*, Eliot marked a passage suggesting that, in some ways, that democratic instrument had backfired, "greatly impair[ing] the direct influence of working classes."[34] Eliot probably never wished that the 1832 act had been written in vanishing ink, but she did demonstrate, in her fiction, a carefulness born of the fear that well-intentioned representations, political and aesthetic, can wreak havoc if they are not carefully worked out.

§

In *Felix Holt, the Radical,* Eliot suggests that the passage of reform bills further extending the vote will have to wait on society's recognition that those to whom the suffrage has not yet been extended are ready for it. That recognition, in turn, will wait on a new national image of the as-yet-unenfranchised. Eliot is not ready, however, to devote her career as a novelist to refashioning the image of the lower classes. The new image will have to be a true one if it is to compete successfully with the images projected by other, more "legitimate," media. To be able to truly and attractively represent the novel potential of an electorate without property, novelists may *first* have to create an unprecedented groundswell of public interest in improving the lot of the poor. Felix Holt, the namesake of Eliot's novel about the 1832 reform bill furor (who is in some sense George Eliot as seen in the mirror of her own fiction), is painfully aware of the fact that the struggle to accurately represent the entire spectrum of political reality will be a long one—if it is to be successful. Replying publicly to claims made by another radical orator, one who would like to see the ballot extended to those poorer than the £10 householders benefitted by Lord Russell's 1832 proposal, Holt says:

> I think he expects voting to do more than I do. I want the working men to have power. . . . But there are two sorts of power. There's a power to do mischief—to undo what has been done with great ex-

pense and labor, to waste and destroy, . . . to talk poisonous non-
sense. That's the sort of power ignorant numbers have. . . . Ignorant
power . . . comes to the same thing as wicked power; it makes mis-
ery. . . . While public opinion is what it is—while men have not better
beliefs about public duty—while corruption is not felt to be a damn-
ing disgrace—. . . no fresh scheme of voting will much mend our
condition.[35]

For Eliot, the novelist and politician must proceed carefully, mod-
erately, if she is, herself, to wield power wisely. The age is simply too
fraught with change and perplexity to be represented by Dickensian
blacks and whites. In *Middlemarch*, published in 1872 but about the
years just preceeding the passage of the 1832 reform act, Eliot asks
the following question: "How could men see which were their own
thoughts in the confusion of a Tory ministry passing liberal measures, of Tory nobles and electors being anxious to return liberals
rather than friends of the recreant Ministers?" (ch. 37). The confu-
sions of a changing age may be decreased by the writer willing and
able to see novelties evolving: novelties such as a new and therefore
underrepresented town like Middlemarch, for instance, or such as
the "new" woman, as represented by Dorothea Brooke or Rosa-
mond Vincy. The representation of such novelties may even help to
advance social justice by hastening the day when they will be right-
fully represented in Parliament as well as in fiction. But novel representations will only banish confusion if they are fair and accurate,
the product of painstaking precision and patience. And social justice
will only be advanced by the extension of the ballot if those to whom
it is extended are ready for it.

George Meredith, more the radical, more than agrees with Eliot
that repressed truths, persons, classes, and communities must ultimately all be fully represented. Meredith is particularly concerned
about the need of women to achieve full representation. In *Diana of
the Crossways*, published in 1885 just after the ballot had been extended all the way to lower-class men dwelling in rural counties, but
set in the 1840s—well before male, urban laborers had been given
the vote—he comments that "Our temporary world, that Old Cre-
dulity and stone-hurling urchin in one," has "not yet been taught to
appreciate a quality certifying to sound citizenship as authoritatively
as acres of land in fee simple, or coffers or bonds, shares, and stocks,
and a more imperishable guarantee."[36] Women with that quality—

"brainstuff," Meredith later calls it—seem even less likely ever to be accorded a political voice than do men of the lower classes who have it, for the laws and traditions of patrimony, the workplace, and the marketplace handicap any woman trying to acquire the primary passing signs of "sound citizenship": acres, shares, bonds, and fees. Furthermore, the same laws, traditions, and men who make it difficult for a woman to make her own fortune, would—should she succeed in spite of their efforts—have it that the qualities normally "certifying to sound citizenship" do *not* so certify to the sound citizenship of a woman. (Meredith's *Diana of the Crossways* is, of course, a roman à clef based on the life of Lady Caroline Norton, a brilliant woman who influenced politics indirectly, through her close friendship with Prime Minister Melbourne. For her interest in Melbourne and in politics she was repaid with a scandal, her husband and other detractors insisting that she was Melbourne's mistress.)

Like other novelists of the period, Meredith measures fiction against other systems of signification and representation. His figuration of the legitimate, respectable, entirely male world as a "stone-hurling urchin" suggests the degree to which he wishes his fiction to seem a novel system of representation, one turning inside out the values inherent in more usual, acceptable media. In all of his major novels he suggests that the novelist will be no better or worse a representative of human truths than historians of the Victorian past and present have been if he or she cannot understand and represent fairly fully half of the human race.

Finally, though, Meredith, like Eliot, is a conservative radical when it comes to his views on novel representation. As did Disraeli, Meredith often seems to advocate slow political reform to stave off radical revolt. "They create by stoppage a volcano, and are amazed at its eruptiveness," the namesake of his novel comments at one point, speaking forebodingly of the volcanic way in which those who are denied education, land, shares, and citizenship may ultimately represent their desire for all, eruptively, at once (ch. 1). The future political representation of women, Diana and her author suggest, does not have to be so sudden or so explosive. Nor does the future representation of women in fiction have to be militant, sensational. But men in power will have to be reasonably generous and open-minded, ready like Eliot's Sir James Chettam (in *Middlemarch*) and Lord Augustus Debarry (in *Felix Holt*) to lay down their traditional stones of repression and to be open to the idea of novel representation. They will, conversely, need to be unlike Eliot's Casaubon and *very* unlike Meredith's Westlake and Rhodes, who become more than a little bit defensive upon hearing that Diana wishes ". . . to write a sketch of women of the future—don't be afraid!—The far future. And what a different earth you will see!"

"'And very different creatures!' the gentlemen unanimously surmised. Westlake described the fairer portion, no longer the weaker; frightful hosts. Diana promised a sweeter picture, if ever she brought her hand to paint it." In spite of such assurances, the young men feel threatened, and so they fearfully brandish their stones and sticks (and even larger weapons). If she were to write such a romance, according to "Arthur Rhodes, evidently firing a gun too big for him, [she] would be offered up to the English national hangman" (ch. 28).

Meredith, like Eliot, does not relish the arrival of the day when representations of the narrative, pictorial, or political variety will be shocking, volcanic, "frightful." "Matter that is not nourishing to brains can help to constitute nothing but the bodies which are pitched upon rubbish heaps," Meredith writes in the first chapter of *Diana of the Crossways*, thus sympathetically predisposing us toward his heroine's cerebral tendencies (as well as his own). "Brainstuff is not lean stuff; the brainstuff of fiction is internal history," he goes on to say. "Instead of objurgating the timid intrusions of philosophy, invoke her presence, I pray you," he says: "History without her is the skeleton-map of events: Fiction a picture of figures modelled on no skeleton anatomy. . . . There is a peep show and a Punch's at the corner of every street, one magnifying the face-work of life, another the ventral tumulus, and it is these for you, or dry bones, if you do not open to philosophy" (ch. 1). We are left to infer that the "peep show" artist is Dickens. (His sarcastic use of the word *philosophy* was well-known, and his works were avoided, when they were avoided, because of their shocking, sensational qualities.) Meredith leaves no doubt, though, as to the identity of the other writer. That operator of "Punch's" now "departed, . . . groaned over his puppetry" but "dared not animate" his creations "with the fires of positive brainstuff," Meredith's narrator continues by declaring, making it patently clear through allusions to puppetry as well as to *Punch* that it is William Makepeace Thackeray who showed only life's "face-work," or surface. "Had he dared he would (for he was Titan enough) have raised Art in dignity on a level with History, to an interest surpassing the narrative of public deeds as vividly as man's heart and brain in their union excel his plain lives of action" (ch. 1).

Meredith, then, would seem to see Dickens and Thackeray as writers offering extreme forms of representation: one radically sensational and obsessed only with life's underside, the other shallow and superficial and dedicated mainly to escapist entertainment. Like Eliot, Meredith would see novelists—and painters and members of Parliament—work steadily, philosophically, at painting a "sweeter picture" of the age: that is to say, a portrait at once thoughtful, moral, and balanced. Like Dickens, though, he insists on the novelist's responsibility to afford representation to those whose forerunners lived and died unrepresented by those "narrative[s] of public deeds" we too often learn our lessons from. "The historic muse," according to the philosophical narrator of *Diana of the Crossways*, has only "Learnt to esteem" what it calls "facts, . . . those brawny sturdy giants marching club on shoulder" (ch. 1). But what, Meredith asks implicitly, of that part of the past world populated by women and by illiterate and otherwise-crippled men who could not acquire enough land, shares, clubs, and stones to hurl? What of those who thus could not enter history?

"What of them indeed?" other Victorian novelists seem to shrug and ask, far too ambivalent about fully representing present reality, politically or novelistically, to care about those forgotten by history. As we have seen earlier, not all the great Victorian novelists were wholeheartedly, ardently committed to representational reform, even though they all made appropriate noises in letters, essays, and speeches. Not all writers of the age were ardently committed to representing the unrepresented, because not all writers of the age could affirm, even cautiously, a belief in the *possibility* of representation or, therefore, in the truth-serving nature of any kind of representational reform. Trollope and Thackeray, though undeniably interested in such subjects as politics and history, suggest through their treatment of those subjects that all representations of life are entirely arbitrary and, therefore, distorting media of one type or another. Representation, therefore, is just a game that takes place entirely apart from the reality that it supposedly represents. In *Oliver Twist,* Dickens had described orphans drawing straws to choose a representative, someone who, though arbitrarily chosen, would test false authority by petitioning for relief from the deadly reality of hunger. Trollope too pictures novel representatives, many of them arbitrarily chosen. However, his for the most part tell no incisive truths. Indeed, he represents representatives who have never *seen*—let alone known—some of the "rotten" boroughs and starving (often Irish) counties they represent. These men, furthermore, run on what the Radicals in George Eliot's *Felix Holt* with disgust call "paper handbills"—what Trollope calls "shibboleths"—planks in a platform promising reforms that no one has any intention of effecting. "Vote for Vavasor and the Riverbank" is the "cry with which" a character in the first of the six "Parliamentary" or "Palliser" novels goes "to the electors."[37] (The slogan is intended to imply that Vavasor, if elected, will have the Thames embanked at national expense.) "But it never will be done!" the candidate himself had protested on first hearing the "shibboleth" from its author, an agent-advisor named Scruby. "What matters that?" had been Scruby's reply (ch. 44).

Trollope is, of course, a satirist satirizing the fiction of parliamentary representation, which he shows to be, all too often, a matter of saying "that this black thing is white, or that this white thing is black."[38] But Trollope's satire, like Thackeray's, is omnidirectional and self-reflexive; it *has* to be, for Trollope's ultimate vision of the world is one in which all identities are unstable, all truths relative—and a matter of perspective. Thus, all representations are at best true for the moment, or true from the vantage point chosen by their representative, who cannot be among those truths and attempt to represent them at the same time. The "realistic" novelist is himself involved in a game, a play, of signifiers (or "shibboleths") without real significance. If he is not to be a fool, he must either: (1) accept as inevitable an "unreformed Parliament"; (2) satirize the novelist as well as Parliament (especially the novelist who claims to have some incisive truth to tell); or (3) admit that all novelists and all political representatives, whether they be "realists" or romance writers, members of the British Parliament or of the American Congress, are involved in the business of calling grey things black and grey things white.

Trollope does all three. He brilliantly satirizes the novelist, through such characters as the Dickensian Mr. Popular Sentiment in *The Warden*. He adores Parliament even as he satirizes it. The "entrance to the House of Commons," he says in the first of the "Palliser" novels, "is the only gate before which I have ever stood with envy,—sorrowing to think that my steps might never pass under it" (ch. 45). He loves it as well as laughs at it because it is a place where people *don't* quite say what they mean. By contrast, in the American Congress, the narrator of *Phineas Finn* comments, "political enmity produces private hatred," for the "leaders of political parties there really mean what they say when they abuse each other, and are in earnest when they talk as if they were about to tear each other limb from limb" (ch. 9). Trollope sees mirrored in parliamentary games a complex version of those he plays as an artist. Finally, he suggests that, if it is not fated to be false, all representation at the local or national level, whether of the political or aesthetic variety, is bound to be arbitrary, relative, and inaccurate. One man cannot represent a town, and anyway, the narrator of *Phineas Finn* asks, "Who shall say what is a town, or where shall be its limits?" (ch. 36). Someone must decide whether or not to add "bits" of the "counties" to surrounding towns, so as to "lessen" or increase their "Conservatism" or "Liberalism." But that someone, Trollope suggests in the same novel, through several analogies involving painting, will be an artist, and whatever decision is made in the name of "true" or "realistic" representation will be open to the charge of falsehood from another quarter. "In America," he writes, "the work [of portraying a people] has been done with so coarse a hand that nothing is shown in the picture but the broad plain . . . outlines of the [national] face. To give a . . . numerical majority of the people that power which the numerical majority has in the United States, would not be to achieve representation" (ch. 35). Thus—in Trollope's view, anyway—truth is lost even as it is gained by a relatively democratic system of political representation. By analogy, verity would be lost as well as gained by the novelist (or historian) who sought to represent a reality—say the reality of poor Ireland—rather than the games played in London by its "representatives." Such a novel would be more and less black, more and less white, more and less truthful, than the books in Trollope's parliamentary series.

§

Just as novelists differ in their attitudes toward the desirability— or possibility—of "achieving representation," so they write in different styles and tones, and these latter differences are tightly bound up with the former ones. Writers who, like Thackeray and Trollope, believe that truth is falsehood from some perspective—and that, if it isn't, it soon will be (their one reason why *not* to be a conservative)—revel in the linguistic slipperiness that irony exploits. By way of contrast, a Dickens (or Thomas Hardy) is more likely to write in a direct, sententious, unironic narrative manner, a manner epitomized by a passage in *Our Mutual Friend* in which we read the following words: "When we have got things to the pass that with an enormous treasure at our disposal to relieve the poor, the poor detest our mercies, it is a pass impossible of prosperity, impossible of continuance. These words have been the truth since the foundations of the universe were laid, and they will be the truth until the foundations are shaken by the builder" (ch. 41). Dickens, of course, can write ironically, but Dickens's ironies—like Hardy's—are abstract, intellectual, and *obvious*. Just as we cannot suspect the tone of the passage about England's national responsibility to "relieve the poor" to *be* ironic—just as we cannot suspect that the words are spoken by some narrator whose opinions the author detests—so we cannot suspect, even for a moment, that Dickens means what he says in the following passage from *Oliver Twist*. (Another way of saying this that some readers will prefer is that we cannot think, as we read the following passage, that the voice that *does* mean what is said is that of Dickens.) "Let it not be supposed by enemies of 'the system,'" we read just after reading of Oliver's confinement following his audacious request for more food,

> that during the period of his solitary incarceration Oliver was denied the benefit of exercise, the pleasure of society, or the advantage of religious consolation. As for exercise, it was nice cold weather, and he was allowed to perform his ablutions every morning under the pump, in a stone yard. . . . As for society, he was carried every other day into the hall where the boys dined, and there sociably flogged as a public warning and example. And so far from being denied the advantages of religious consolation, he was kicked into the same apartment every evening at prayer time, and there permitted to listen to, and console his mind with, a general supplication of the boys, in which they were entreated to be made good, virtuous, contented, and obedient, and to be guarded from the sins and vices of Oliver Twist.[39]

Dickens may believe that in a world of lies only the lies of fiction can represent the truth, but his devotion to truth prevents him from adopting, stylistically, the liar's ways. When he is not writing "straight," his ironies are so caustic that misinterpretation is all but impossible.

Consider, by way of contrast, the following passage from Thackeray's *Vanity Fair:*

> "It isn't difficult to be a country gentleman's wife," Rebecca thought. "I think I could be a good woman if I had five thousand a year. I could dawdle about in the nursery, and count the apricots on the wall. I could water plants in a green house, and pick off dead leaves from the geraniums. I could ask old women about their rheumatisms, and order half-a-crown's worth of soup for the poor. . . . I could pay off everybody, if I but had the money. This is what the conjurers here pride themselves in doing. . . . They think themselves generous if they give one child a five-pound note, and us contemptible if we are without one." (ch. 41)

Becky, apparently, thinks that, with adequate funds, she could lead the life of a "good woman," that is to say, of counting apricots on the wall and asking old women about their aches and pains. Most readers will assume—certainly a reader coming to this passage directly from Dickens would assume—that Thackeray shares these thoughts of Becky's with the reader for a perfectly obvious reason: in order to show just how limited Becky's definition of *goodness* is. But Dickens is no preparation for Thackeray, who writes passages the tone of which are treacherous, perhaps impossible, to determine. Should we be reading the passage quoted above ironically? Does the author (or narrator, if he is distinguishable from the author) really define the virtuous life as one in which plants are watered and debts paid on time? If he does, then his satirization of superficial values elsewhere in *Vanity Fair* is hypocritical to a degree. If he does not, however—if he is asking us to read Becky's self-defense ironically, as a rationalization—then there is a gap between Becky's meditation and his surprisingly sympathetic-sounding reflection on it, which follows:

> And who knows but what Rebecca was right in her speculations—and that it *was* only a question of money and fortune which made the difference between her and an honest woman? If you take temptation into account, who is to say that he is better than his neighbor? A comfortable career of prosperity, if it does not make people honest, at least keeps them so. An alderman coming from a turtle feast will not step out of his carriage to steal a leg of mutton, but put him to starve and see if he will not purloin a loaf.

Back when we read Becky Sharp's little claim that she would enjoy light housekeeping and volunteer work if only she were rich, we marveled at her self-delusion. Useless to us, now, is our realization that Becky is kidding herself. Unimportant, apparently, is the fact that ordering half-a-crown's worth of soup for the poor does not a "good" rich woman make. *This* poor woman may just have a point, Thackeray suddenly seems to want us to think; it would behoove us to wipe the grin off our face and pay attention, for a change, to what she has to say.

Once again, however, the reader has been set up to fall between incongruous commentaries. The text continues: "Becky consoled herself by so balancing the chances and equalizing the distribution of good and evil in the world." *Becky consoled herself?* The statement comes as a shock, for there has been no indication that the preceding thoughts about a congruence between honesty and prosperity have been entirely attributable (or at all attributable, for that matter) to Becky. It was surely the narrator who asked: "And who knows but what Rebecca was right in her speculations?" The subsequent question, moreover, seemed perfectly congruous: "who is to say that he is better than his neighbor?" Can we never know how to read a passage until our reading of it is completed?

The "gap," together with the non sequitur that inevitably follows it, defines the style of both Thackeray and Trollope, those writers whose faith is only in the duplicitous power of fiction, not in its power to double truth or reform reality. With Thackeray's passage on money and virtue in mind, consider this passage from Trollope's *The Warden,* noting especially the surprising intellectual space between the perspectives offered by the second and third paragraphs respectively, space visible only in retrospect from the far side:

> As Archdeacon Grantly walked across the hallowed close . . . he thought with increasing acerbity of those whose impiety would venture to disturb the goodly grace of cathedral institutions.
>
> And who has not felt the same? We believe that Mr. Horsman himself would relent and the spirit of Benjamin Hall give way were those great reformers to stroll by moonlight round the towers of some of our ancient churches. Who would not feel charity for a prebendary when walking the quiet length of that long aisle at Winchester, looking at those decent houses, that trim grassplat, and feeling, as one must, the solemn, orderly comfort of the spot. . . . Who could lie basking in the cloisters of Salisbury and gaze in Jewel's library at that

unequalled spire without feeling that bishops should sometimes be rich?

The tone of our archdeacon's mind must not astonish us; it has been the growth of centuries of self-ascendancy.[40]

"Becky consoled herself by so balancing the chances and equalizing the distribution of good and evil in the world"; "The tone of our archdeacon's mind must not astonish us," indeed. At what point in Trollope's narrative (or Thackeray's) did the voice of the narrator break off and that of Grantly's (or Becky's) self-justifying (or self-consoling) consciousness begin to speak? Was Trollope only presenting Grantly's thoughts when he asked "Who could lie basking in the cloisters of Salisbury . . . without feeling that bishops should sometimes be rich?" This seems doubtful, since the paragraph began by asking "who has not felt the same?"

Within as well as between paragraphs Trollope seems radically to alter his perspective. The sentence following the one in which Trollope directs us not to be astonished by the tone of Grantly's mind comes very close to recapturing that very tone when it asks, "Who without remorse can batter down the dead branches of a great old oak, now useless, but so beautiful?"

What do gaps, non sequiturs, and ironies (that may not be ironies at all) have to do with the subjects of representation and reform in the widest sense? A great deal, for the radical view on representation depends upon coherence and continuity, not only between representatives and their constituencies but also within acts of representation. It is incumbent upon those trying to realize radical changes in the political world to make sure that representations do not self-deconstruct, render themselves ineffectual through self-contradiction. If we return to the self-undermining passages by Thackeray and Trollope that we have just examined, moreover, we will see that both writers have larger questions of political change in mind, even as they play the games by which they confuse themselves, their texts, and especially their readers. "Becky consoled herself by so balancing the chances and equalizing the distribution of good and evil in the world." With this very sentence Thackeray throws the tone of all his previous, apparently radical questions ("And who knows but what Rebecca was right?") into question, leaving us entirely unsure about whether the author, or narrator, has no, some, or complete sympathy with Becky's radical, reformist act of redistribution. But a writer *must* have definite, consistent, determinable positions or opinions in order to be an agent of political, social, or moral reform. As long as passages—and/or portions of them—may be read equally well with or without irony, fiction will be as impotent to promote reform as Thackeray's so obviously is.

We can quickly see why Trollope's fiction is a nonreforming form by returning, briefly, to the passage in which Archdeacon Grantly strolls across a cathedral close thinking acerbically about all who would question church expenditures. The reader can only be wonderstruck, it seems to me, upon going back and rereading the statement: "We believe Mr. Horsman himself would relent and the spirit of Benjamin Hall give way were those great reformers to stroll by moonlight round the towers of some of our ancient churches." Does Trollope seriously believe that serious radical reformers would relent and reverse themselves during moonlight walks through the trappings of luxury? Would he seriously submit that Dickens—the novelist he caricatures, elsewhere in *The Warden*, as a radical writer named Mr. Popular Sentiment—would change his mind, or change it for a little while, anyway, about the wrongness of poverty in a rich land if he could just watch a prebendary walking a long aisle at Winchester? We will never know, I submit, whether Trollope offers the suggestion ironically, seriously, or in both moods serially or simultaneously, which is why Trollope's fiction can never be a reformist form in the way that Dickens's is. We will never know, because Trollope, too, is a "We." "We believe . . . Mr. Horsman . . . would relent and the spirit of Benjamin Hall give way," Trollope writes, but the spirit offering an apparent double of the world in *The Warden* is himself doubled, contradicted, within, and his two wills do not agree on what Benjamin Hall or anyone or anything else real would or should do.

Style, then, affects politics and even the possibility of effecting political attitudes in and through fiction. And, of course, political stances (which include the apolitical stance) affect style; even though two writers may use what seems a similarly ironic, sensational, melodramatic style, the irony or melodrama turns out to be different and to be put to a different end in works by writers with differing kinds or degrees of political consciousness.

Caricature, which provides high moments of entertainment in

Collins and Dickens, Thackeray and Trollope, is used by the former pair to capture the difficult-to-see, but essential, outlines of reality. In a world governed by legitimatized lies, they suggest, truth can only be reflected in mirrors that seem to censor and distort. Caricature—like mesmerism and opium and the fairy-tale romance plots Dickens so loves—is just such an agent of revelation. (Perhaps that is why Dickens, in selecting his first illustrator, chose George Cruikshank, one of the great, early caricaturists of the age of caricature; if caricaturizing texts capture reality incisively, then caricaturizing pictures may best re-present a text.)

Thackeray and Trollope, unlike Dickens, use caricature to show its potential for entertainment as well as to deny, implicitly, the possibility of representing reality through that (or any other) medium. Thus Trollope caricatures, not reality, but Dickens's style in *The Warden* by giving us a passage to read from *The Almshouse*, a radical alternative to his own novel, one written by one "Mr. Popular Sentiment." But what the caricature of Dickens attacks is, precisely, Dickens's tendency to caricature; we are shown how false caricature is through caricature. (Is Trollope being ironic? The question must be begged.)

Analogy too is handled in radically different ways by Trollope, who doesn't really believe an elected representative can really represent a borough (if Robert Dole seems to be to Ted Kennedy what Kansas is to Massachusetts, it is mere seeming), and by George Eliot, who isn't sure. Trollope's analogies involving characters in the so-called parliamentary novels inevitably mislead; any reader who thinks dashing Burgo Fitzgerald *like* dashing George Vavasor will be surprised—as surprised as they will be by how unlike Glencora and Alice, the like-seeming women romanced by Burgo and George, turn out to be. Eliot, like Trollope, invites her readers to pair characters, too, and like Trollope she undercuts her pairings, but not to the point that the very notion of analogical pairs is undermined. Analogies between Doctor Lydgate and Will Ladislaw, or between the *Three Love Problems* we are invited to think of collectively by the title of the fourth book of *Middlemarch*, are helpful to those who do not put more interpretive pressure on them than they can bear. Consequently, Eliot uses analogy to teach the uses and limits of analogies of the political, pictorial, and verbal varieties. Just after telling us that getting to know a "favourite politician in the ministry" may bring about "changes quite as rapid" as those brought about in Dorothea's impression of her new husband, Eliot begins a new paragraph: "Still, such comparisons might mislead, for no man was ever more incapable of flashy make-believe than Mr. Casaubon: he was as genuine a character as any ruminant animal, and he had not actively assisted in creating any illusions about himself" (ch. 20).

No analogy is perfect, Eliot would have us see, any more than any politician or reformed version of Parliament affords a wholly unmisleading representation. That does not mean, though, that a faulty analogy or a flashy politician may not be positively useful—or that a certain kind of reformed Parliament may not be far more fair and more beneficial than another, unreformed (or radically reformed) kind. "These ten pound householders," Mr. Brooke says, speaking of those who are to get the vote under the terms of Lord Russell's 1832 bill. "Why ten? Draw the line somewhere—yes: but why just at ten? That's a difficult question, now, if you go into it." Trollope's narrator asks a similar question ("who shall say what is a town, or where shall be its limits?") only to leave it unanswered and to suggest that it is unanswerable. Eliot's Will Ladislaw answers his liberal friend immediately: " 'Of course it is,' said Will impatiently. 'But if you are to wait till we get a logical Bill, you must put yourself forward as a revolutionist, and, then Middlemarch would not elect you, I fancy' " (ch. 41). A Parliament representing a nation down to its £10 householders may not be a "logical" analogy, but that means neither that no logical one is possible nor that the Parliament envisioned by Russell's bill is not the most logical that can be drawn in the political language of 1832.

In her earlier novel, *Adam Bede*, Eliot uses an analogy involving the earth and its moon to teach the limits of all analogical linkages. She tells us that "on a front view" of Mr. Casson, landlord of the Donnithorne Arms, his body "appeared to consist principally of two spheres bearing about the same relation to each other as the earth and the moon: that is to say, the lower sphere might be said, at a guess, to be thirteen times larger than the upper, which naturally performed the function of a mere satellite and tributary. But here the resemblance ceased, for Mr. Casson's head was not at all a melancholy looking satellite, nor was it a 'spotty globe,' as Milton has irreverently called the moon; on the contrary, no head and face could look more sleek and healthy."[41] Even Milton's art is treated as a fair but not perfect analogy to Eliot's own. By using it, Eliot aids us in understanding why the word *moon* imperfectly represents the head of rotund Mr. Casson. But Milton's language, like the word *moon,* is finally of limited use, for Milton, as Eliot suggests, does rough justice at best to that which he would double in language; there is in the moon something novel, something mysterious, something to be reverenced that finds no representation in the phrase "spotty globe." Milton, patriarchal poet whose daughters became what Dorothea Brooke surely would have become—had her husband survived longer—cannot serve as Eliot's wholly adequate representative, double, or collaborator. But then can Eliot's novel characters—can her novel itself—adequately represent the "new" woman and world? Or is *Middlemarch* too an "irreverent" distortion, a spotty globe, a badly flawed mirror like the one Hetty Sorrel must rely upon in *Adam Bede?* "Hetty objected to it because it had numerous dim blotches sprinkled over [it] and because, instead of swinging backward and forward, it was fixed in an upright position, so that she could only get one good view of her head and neck, and that was to be had only by sitting down on a low chair before her dressing table" (ch. 15).

§

The warped, spotted, and broken mirrors reflected in countless Victorian novels and alluded to in my opening paragraph are, in my view, representations of fiction in fiction. They might also stand, however, for this essay, in which I have attempted to reflect upon a variety of symbols, styles, and interlocked representational problems. Much has necessarily been left vague and dark. Some of the symbols (the Jew, the "Negro") remain to be discussed in some other place, as do some of the styles I have only alluded to (romance, for one, but also styles of novel illustration—of doubling verbal texts in visual ones). Of the more general problems concerning representation, however, one seems important to raise here, in the form of a question that readers of this essay have no doubt already formulated: Is there anything wrong with the Thackerayan, Trollopian view that fiction is but a marvelous game?

Certainly not—is there anyone who would *not* prefer Trollope to, say, Frank Norris? I do not wish to suggest that art needs to be an agent of social reform or even a mirror of abiding truths, whatever those may be. I prefer to argue, rather, that Dickens's art aspires to be both things—and that Trollope's does not. As for Thackeray's maddening, self-undercutting style, it has unquestionably demonstrated a power to endure that is itself an ironical reflection on its own singular message, which is that nothing does except treacherous language. Serious novelists of our own century, from Joyce to Pynchon, have turned the novel into an elaborate verbal puzzle that is essentially its own subject—not a representation of a world beyond itself. Perhaps that is why most of our novelists in English are not public figures campaigning, as Dickens did, against slavery and for help for pregnant teenagers. And that just may be art's gain—and our loss.

Notes

1. George Eliot, *Middlemarch*, chapter 46. Because I quote from so many novels in this essay—and because dozens of editions of each novel exist—all subsequent references to all Victorian novels shall refer to the chapter, not the page, from which the quoted passage has been taken. Future references to *Middlemarch* will be made, in parentheses, within the text.

2. For a fuller discussion of mesmerism and the fascination with it shown by Victorian writers see Fred Kaplan, *Dickens and Mesmerism: The Hidden Springs of Fiction*, (Princeton: Princeton University Press, 1975).

3. Melbourne quoted in Steven Marcus, *Dickens: From Pickwick to Dombey* (New York: Basic Books, 1965), p. 61.

4. Ibid.

5. Janice Carlisle, *The Sense of an Audience: Dickens, Thackeray, and George Eliot at Mid-Century*, p. 23; Thomas Carlyle, "Biography," in *Critical and Miscellaneous Essays: Collected and Republished* (London: Chapman and Hall, 1891), 4:60.

6. Charles Dickens, *Our Mutual Friend*, chapter 5. Future references to this novel will be made, in parentheses, within the text.

7. Macaulay makes this argument in "Southey's Colloquies on Society," collected in *Critical and Historical Essays Contributed to the "Edinburgh Review": A New Edition* (London: Longmans, Green, Reader, and Dyer, 1872), p. 117.

8. Anthony Trollope, *An Autobiography* (Oxford: Oxford University Press, 1950), p. 294.

9. This somewhat overstated claim is made by T. A. Jackson in his book, *Charles Dickens: The Progress of a Radical* (London: Lawrence and Wishart, 1936).

10. I am, for the most part, confining my remarks in this essay to major works by six great Victorian writers: Collins, Dickens, Eliot, Meredith, Thackeray, and Trollope. These are not the most overtly "political" Victorian novelists, and the novels I am discussing are not the most overtly political novels that these six novelists wrote. These two facts, however, only underscore two of the ideas underlying the whole of this essay: (1) Victorian fiction was permeated by politics; and (2) the best of Victorian fiction is implicitly, even covertly, political.

11. Edgar Johnson, *Charles Dickens: His Tragedy and Triumph* (New York: Simon and Schuster, 1952), 1:62.

12. Quoted ibid., 1:315.

13. Ibid.

14. Quoted ibid., 2:1112–13.

15. *Charles Dickens' Uncollected Writings from Household Words, 1850–1859*, ed. Harry Stone (Bloomington: Indiana University Press, 1968), p. 588.

16. From a speech to the Birmingham and Midland Institute, September 27, 1869. The passage is reprinted in Humphry House's *The Dickens World* (Oxford: Oxford University Press, 1941).

17. Jack Lindsay, *George Meredith: His Life and Work* (London: The Bodley Head, 1956), pp. 113, 115.

18. *The Letters and Private Papers of William Makepeace Thackeray*, ed. Gordon W. Ray (Cambridge, Mass.: Harvard University Press, 1946), 3:679–80.

19. Ibid., 3:682.

20. Quoted in Lewis Saul Benjamin, *The Life of William Makepeace Thackeray* (London: Hutchinson & Co., 1899), 2:4.

21. *The George Eliot Letters*, ed. Gordon S. Haight (New Haven: Yale University Press, 1955), 4:364.

22. Blackwood to Eliot, ibid., 4:398.

23. Ibid., 4:496.

24. Phyllis B. Bartlett, ed., *The Poems of George Meredith* (New Haven: Yale University Press, 1978), 1:626.

25. Trollope, *An Autobiography*, p. 292.

26. Ibid., pp. 293–94.

27. Reprinted ibid., p. 304.

28. George Henry Lewes, review of *Pendennis* in the *Leader*, December 21, 1850; reprinted in *Thackeray: The Critical Heritage*, ed. Geoffrey Tillotson and Donald Hawes (London: Routledge & Kegan Paul, 1968), p. 108.

29. Thackeray, *The Letters and Private Papers*, 3:682–83.

30. Yates quoted in Lewis Saul Benjamin, *William Makepeace Thackeray: A Biography Including Hitherto Uncollected Letters and Speeches* (London: The Bodley Head, 1910), 2:19.

31. Ibid., 2:21.

32. Carlyle quoted in David Alec Wilson, *Carlyle to Threescore and Ten (1853–1865)* (London: Kegan Paul, Trench, Trubner & Co., Ltd.), p. 90; J. Y. T. Greig, *Thackeray: A Reconsideration* (Oxford: Oxford University Press, 1950), p. 4.

33. William Makepeace Thackeray, *Vanity Fair*, chapter 19. Future references to this novel will be made, in parentheses, within the text.

34. William Nassau Molesworth, *The History of the Reform Bill of 1832* (London: Chapman and Hall, 1866), p. 338. Eliot's copy of Molesworth's book is in Dr. Williams's Library at 14 Gordon Square.

35. George Eliot, *Felix Holt, the Radical*, chapter 30. Future references to this novel will be made, in parentheses, within the text.

36. George Meredith, *Diana of the Crossways*, chapter 1. Future references to this novel will be made, in parentheses, within the text.

37. Anthony Trollope, *Can You Forgive Her?* chapter 44. Future references to this novel will be made, in parentheses, within the text.

38. Anthony Trollope, *Phineas Finn*, chapter 67. Future references to this novel will be made, in parentheses, within the text.

39. Charles Dickens, *Oliver Twist*, chapter 3.

40. Anthony Trollope, *The Warden*, chapter 5.

41. George Eliot, *Adam Bede*, chapter 2. Future references to this novel will be made, in parentheses, within the text.

Carolyn Williams

Closing the Book
The Intertextual End
of *Jane Eyre*

Asked to recall the end of *Jane Eyre*, many readers first remember the resolution of the plot, reported in Jane's conclusive address to her audience: "Reader, I married him." But that memorable line only begins the last chapter. The novel ends on quite another note, and in another voice:

> As to St. John Rivers, he left England: he went to India. He entered on the path he had marked for himself; he pursues it still. A more resolute, indefatigable pioneer never wrought amidst rocks and dangers. Firm, faithful, and devoted; full of energy, and zeal, and truth, he labours for his race: he clears their painful way to improvement: he hews down like a giant the prejudices of creed and caste that encumber it. He may be stern; he may be exacting; he may be ambitious yet; but his is the sternness of the warrior Greatheart, who guards his pilgrim convoy from the onslaught of Apollyon. His is the exaction of the apostle, who speaks but for Christ when he says— "Whosoever will come after Me, let him deny himself, and take up his cross and follow Me." His is the ambition of the high master-spirit, which aims to fill a place in the first rank of those who are redeemed from the earth—who stand without fault before the throne of God; who share the last mighty victories of the Lamb; who are called, and chosen, and faithful.
>
> St. John is unmarried: he never will marry now. Himself has hitherto sufficed to the toil; and the toil draws near its close: his glorious sun hastens to its setting. The last letter I received from him drew from my eyes human tears, and yet filled my heart with Divine joy: he anticipated his sure reward, his incorruptible crown. I know that a stranger's hand will write to me next, to say that the good and faithful servant has been called at length into the joy of his Lord. And why weep for this? No fear of death will darken St. John's last hour: his mind will be unclouded; his heart will be undaunted; his hope will be

sure; his faith steadfast. His own words are a pledge of this:—"My Master," he says "has forewarned me. Daily he announces more distinctly,—'Surely I come quickly!' and hourly I more eagerly respond,—'Amen; even so come, Lord Jesus!'"[1]

Of course this does not sound like the character "Jane Eyre," as readers over the years have complained—from formalists who have felt that the ending is "tacked on," to feminists who have felt that the novel swerves, at its end, toward the patriarchal rhetoric it had presumed to reject. Both these objections are legitimate, and yet the ending of the novel continues to evoke a powerful response, which suggests that its effect has still not been adequately explained. Precisely what makes this closing passage so problematic, so odd, and so interesting?

First and most simply, in terms of dramatic and thematic content, it focuses on the "other man," the rejected suitor, and through him it focuses on another way of life, the very way most pointedly *not* taken by Jane. Thinking about the dramatic resolution of the last chapter, we might pose the question raised by the ending this way: Why is the privileged place of closure occupied by St. John Rivers? Why does Jane end her story with "one brief glance at the fortunes of those whose names have most frequently recurred in this narrative" rather than with her last "word respecting [her] experience of married life"? Why not close on the subject of a conjugal relation so perfect that she can say "I am my husband's life as fully as he is mine" (p. 475)? After all, marriage to a character so lavishly drawn as Jane's alter ego has profound autobiographical significance: within the romantic rhetoric of the novel, Jane marries another part of herself, so to speak—her "likeness" or her "second self"—and in the marriage she thus achieves the "delightful consciousness" which "brought to life and light [her] whole nature" (p. 461).[2] Within the rhetoric of romantic congruence, in other words, another character can metaphorically reflect the central autobiographical "I"; but St. John Rivers, who has been unsympathetic in the highest degree, is not such another. Instead of turning toward the alter ego—and thus figuratively returning us to Jane's own chosen life—the novel swerves at its end into an apparent altruism that seems profoundly out of character. What could be gained by this turn toward another character, toward the world outside Jane's sequestered life—indeed, toward the other world itself?

Then again, in terms of narrative discourse—in terms of narration, that is, as opposed to plot or story—this choice at closure is even more puzzling. For the novel not only ends in an extended reference to the character of St. John Rivers but, even more surprising, it ends ostensibly in "his own words" (p. 477). Quotation of this sort has a special force in first-person narration. If one goal of a first-person narrative is to establish a particular "voice," to beguile you, "dear reader," into believing that you are hearing from this particular "person" and no other, then ending in the voice of another would be a radical gesture in any first-person novel; but ending in the voice of another seems an especially radical gesture in *Jane Eyre,* given the life history of Jane's struggle to exert the claims of a special self.

Finally, the closing paragraphs are curious because they end the novel in a web of dense intertextuality. What is the effect of so many quotations and allusions, here at the end? And what is the effect of these particular references? What is the relation of the female first person to the high canonical literature here invoked? One clue may perhaps be found in the fact that only the first intertextual reference issues directly from Jane's own narrative voice. She draws on *The Pilgrim's Progress* for a comparison when she calls St. John "the warrior Greatheart, who guards his pilgrim convoy from the onslaught of Apollyon." The second intertextual reference, from the gospel of Mark (8:34), is then offered hypothetically as the words of the exemplary, exacting apostle. Those words are ventriloquially thrown, originating in Jane's narrative voice but attributed to St. John as the apostolic inheritor. The third intertextual reference then takes us even further from Jane's voice toward St. John's. It is represented as a direct quote from St. John's "last letter." But it seems that St. John's words are not "his own words" at all. He is himself echoing the words of another. In the quotation from the gospel of Mark, St. John hypothetically would echo the words of Christ demanding self-denial and *imitatio* from anyone who would follow him. St. John's "exaction" is in large part a function of this echo-effect; he "speaks but for Christ," speaks literally *as* Christ. Then at the very last, St. John echoes the words of his namesake, St. John the Divine, in conversation with the voice of Christ. I will return, at the end of this argument, to the figure of an intertextual chain of voices. For now let us fully appreciate another aspect of this extraordinary closing gesture.

The last words of the novel are exactly the same as the last words of the Christian Bible. Jane Eyre ends the story of her life with the last words of the Revelation of St. John the Divine, excepting only its concluding benediction ("The grace of the Lord Jesus Christ be with you all. Amen."). Here are those last words:

> 7.   Behold, I come quickly. . . . 8.   And I John saw these things, and heard them. . . . 10.   And he saith unto me. . . . 12.   . . . behold, I come quickly; and my reward is with me, to give every man according as his work shall be. 13.   I am Alpha and Omega, the beginning and the end, the first and the last. . . . 16.   I Jesus have sent mine angel to testify unto you these things in the churches. I am the root and the offspring of David, and the bright and morning star. 17.   And the spirit and the bride say Come. And let him that heareth say, Come. And let him that is athirst come. . . . 20.   He which testifieth these things saith, Surely I come quickly. Amen. Even so, come, Lord Jesus. (*Revelation* 22)

For Jane to end her story by quoting these last words of the book about last things, which is itself the last book of the Book of Books—this is having the last word, with a vengeance. And yet it seems as if it is not Jane herself who has this last word, even in her own story. "I Jane" seems to have disappeared into "I John." This cannot precisely be the case, of course, since the fabric of first-person narration is never ruptured; what is conveyed is conveyed, to the last, through the fiction of that "person." What can it mean, then—but more important, *how* can it mean—for a female autobiographer to close the book of her life with the very words that close The Book, the canonical Scripture of her Protestant culture? And if she does choose to close with those words, why give them away? Why write them as the words of another? In the process of the following argument, I hope to shed light on all these questions; and in the end, I hope to show how this closing of her book might work in terms of the novel's strong, articulate, and ambivalent feminism.

§

"Contradiction"

One way to regard the ending turns on the notion that the novel ends, as it unfolds, through contradiction. As every reader has recognized, Jane's primary movement of self-definition involves opposition followed by separation; when her opposition to her surroundings becomes critical, she breaks away, to start again in another place. This characteristic movement is echoed in the narrative structure, with its alternating periods of rebellion and docile assimilation. Gilbert and Gubar have called this fundamental structure the "Angrian" dimension of the story, linking by means of their pun the fantasy of enclosure and escape characteristic of the Brontë juvenilia with the repressed anger from which this fantasy springs.[3]

The narrative voice is literally established through an episode of "contradiction," or oppositional speaking. Jane's opening and formative experience is the discovery of social difference from her Gateshead Hall cousins, her explosive rage, her violent contradiction of "Master John," and her subsequent imprisonment in the red room. This episode may be seen as formative both in the sense that it typifies Jane's experience as a character and, through the tricky economies of first-person retrospection, also in the sense that it establishes a paradigmatic event to which the narrative structure will return. Jane asserts her own sense of difference furiously, and she is punished by being locked up in such a double-binding way that her only escape is to lose consciousness. Indeed, her rage and its aftermath—loss of consciousness, remorse, physical illness—mark an "ecstasy," a division of herself from herself that establishes her self-consciousness and begins her narrative. To emphasize this point, the first of the crucial mirror scenes in the novel occurs during this opening sequence in the red room. In this scene, Jane's recognition of herself as other is visually dramatized as an emblem of identity constituted at the very moment of self-division.[4] This psychoanalytically motivated point has also its narrative force, for this opening figure—of Jane in the red room looking at her strange image in the mirror—also represents in emblematic terms what Starobinski calls the autobiographical "deviation" or "gap," the figure of narrative retrospection that marks a play of differences within the "I," between protagonist and narrator, between the "I" then and the "I" now.[5]

This recognition of self-division leads to another, externalized separation. In drawing so vehemently the boundary between herself and others, Jane definitively makes herself an outsider at Gateshead Hall—with the beneficial result that she is allowed to leave. Jane cannot, will not, play the part the Reeds have written for her; her refusal makes them want to expel her every bit as much as she wants to leave, and the matching of those desires creates a loophole through which Jane escapes to the next chapter of her story. In the course of this argument I will touch on each of Jane's points of separation, for these are the places in the narrative where the structure opens up and we can see behind the scenes to the energy driving the narrative forward. But for now it is fair to say that the entire plot of self-development in *Jane Eyre* is characterized by this rhythm: Jane taking in the scene around her, discovering the limits that differentiate her from her surroundings, and then departing, from one emblematic place to another.[6]

We can see this rhythm reflecting the stages of separation and individuation, marked out as stages of a physical journey that is at once "realistic" and allegorical.[7] We can see it that way because Jane retrospectively organizes it that way, around turning points which she describes as violent alternations between submission and rebellion. As she puts it: "I know no medium: I never in my life have known any medium in my dealings with positive, hard characters, antagonistic to my own, between absolute submission and determined revolt. I have always faithfully observed the one, up to the very moment of bursting, sometimes with volcanic vehemence, into the other" (p. 426).

In Jane's statement, "I know no medium," the stammering homonym of "know" and "no" reminds us how closely intertwined in her epistemology are the strands of introspection and negation. The structure of her autobiography—with its "progress" from place to place—works to embody Jane's retrospective conclusion that she made an advance in knowing herself each time she said "no" to something or someone else. Many commentators have pointed out that Jane's rebellious character works as a formal principle in this novel. Her "nay-saying"—that is, her statements of literal "contradiction"—are what drive the plot forward.[8] Marianne Hirsch has suggested (in a more far-reaching context) that contradiction might be seen as a female principle for binding plot and making it progress—contradiction as opposed to repetition, which she identifies as a male principle in the recent work of Peter Brooks, after the Freud of *Beyond the Pleasure Principle*.[9] Her argument is richly suggestive, though it needs qualification, for contradiction is precisely a form of repetition, in the mode of negation.[10] In contradiction, as in various forms of preterition, one does, after all, posit by the way the very thing which one presumes to negate. When Jane says to Rochester, "I am no bird; and no net ensnares me," she keeps alive the image of a bird struggling in a snare, even as she denies it as an identification of herself. This figure of negation is then replaced by an abstract, positive formulation of what the self takes itself to be. And that position is followed by a statement of the consequences, in terms of action in the plot: "I am no bird; and no net ensnares me. I am a free human being with an independent will, which I now exert to leave you" (p. 282).

By the time Jane leaves Rochester, she has developed a strong internal organ of control over the dynamics of differentiation—which muscular organ she calls her conscience, according to the conventions of her Protestant poetics. With that sense of interior control she makes subtle calibrations of identification and difference. What will the self or its text take in? What will it then divide itself against, and push out? My initial point, then, is simple: in this novel, the process of Jane's self-definition is precisely the plot, and it develops antithetically, by comparison, contradiction, and negation, in opposition or resistance at the edge of the other.

This dynamic of internalization and differentiation, essential to the structure of *Jane Eyre,* would to some extent be a function of any romantic first-person narration. In this particular narrative situation, ostensibly "other" characters often appear to some extent as epiphenomenal or phantasmic projections of the narrating "I."[11] *Great Expectations* provides another good example of a novel in which the landscape itself, inanimate objects, and all the other characters at times express Pip's projected but unconscious emotions. As in *Jane Eyre,* the total environment during each stage of Pip's journey serves as an externalized register of his current state of feeling and partial self-knowledge. Doubles—those characters whose incomplete separation from one another is their figurative rationale—graphically highlight this relation between the central self and its others. Doubles appear in all sorts of narrative situations, but they have an intensified value in first-person narration as distanced or disowned expressions of the narrating "I." Jane's vigilant sensibility makes this relation clear, as she holds every other character up to the scrutiny of comparison with herself; all the other characters to some extent seem figuratively doubled with Jane. In this respect, Bertha Mason as demonic double focuses the horrible agony of splitting, of simultaneous identification and difference—the horrible agony, in other words, of a truly internal obstacle, as Gilbert and Gubar have made clear.[12] Leaving Rochester, Jane tries to disown something that is inextricable from herself. Whether one thinks of what she tries to disown as Rochester's sinful past or her own Bertha-like rage, one can see that Jane has to give up a great deal of her sense of herself in order to accomplish the transformation. Her temporary affiliation with St. John Rivers expresses the truncated, mourning, and partial self she then becomes, and her eventual rejection of Rivers in turn moves her toward reunion not only with Rochester but with herself.

Jane Eyre, in other words, gives this typical effect of romantic first-person narration an antithetical twist: other characters, other texts—the notion of the other world itself—are introduced *in order that* they may in some sense be contradicted, so that the narrating "I" can distinguish herself from them, defining that "I" in the process. The text of this first-person "self" produces its "others" precisely in order to push them away from the center, in a very characteristic dynamic of incorporation and differentiation.[13]

§

Engendering the Narrative: Mother Nature and God the Father

How are these strategies of separation related to gender? How does the narrative "I" establish itself as a particularly female subject? How is the text "engendered"?

Of the many possible routes through this complex issue, the easiest route would follow Jane's explicitly feminist statements, especially the passage from chapter 12 that Virginia Woolf chooses for analysis in *A Room of One's Own*.[14] That passage begins with Jane's resolute desire for greater scope in practical experience and her assertion that "Anybody may blame me who likes"; it concludes both with the positive statement that "women feel just as men feel" and also with the hint, which Woolf was the first to notice, that women may feel differently: "When thus alone I not unfrequently heard Grace Poole's laugh" (pp. 140–41). This moment begins the identification between Jane and Bertha Mason which is the linchpin of the novel's feminist psycho-logic. Woolf marks the transition to Grace

Poole's laugh as an "awkward break," a stylistic clue to the female writer's deformative rage, which leads her to "write of herself where she should write of her characters."[15] In other words, this traditional line of analysis begins with Jane's explicitly feminist positions and marks their effect on the structure and style of the text. An extension of this method could easily demonstrate that the narrator sets up a gendered scheme of differentiation from other characters both male and female, and that this scheme of gender difference is in play with respect to each instance of the novel's rich intertextuality.

But in the present context—in a discussion of voice, and in order to argue for the gendered value of the novel's intertextual end—I want to look at another way the narrative seems to connect separation, gender, and narrative production. This reading will contribute to the ongoing critical discussion of gender and narrative, and at the same time it will allow us to focus not so much on structure as on the transformations accomplished in narrative time.

Jane is an orphan, of course, the quintessential figure of indeterminate identity, who must discover and construct her place in the world. Like her status incongruence as a governess on the social level of the plot, her orphanhood works on the epistemological level to open the question of her identity and "place."[16] But the romantic "I" without parents is free to imagine them, for not only the quest romance but also the family romance has been internalized.[17] Instead of discovering formerly unknown, but "real," parents (as Tom Jones does, for example,) Jane produces figurative representations of the primary, gendered others from whom the self derives and in relation to whom the self defines itself. Since Jane is at once an orphan and a first-person narrator, in other words, we may see in her narrative a succession of fantasied attempts to realize those engendering figures.

Jane's narrative engenders itself by producing figural parents from whom she differs, primal "others" who are projected in the text precisely in order to be "contradicted." She associates these primal others, these parent-figures, with different systematic principles of plotting or storytelling, and her own particular voice is generated as she steers between them. "Contradiction" is not simply a structural principle, but a mobile and productive strategy of voice in *Jane Eyre*. The narrative voice self-consciously positions itself as the separating daughter, and it enacts its own production of meaning and voice in difference from both parent-figures, Mother Nature and God the Father.[18] Jane invokes these figures at crucial moments in the story, as agents of narrative transformations; they serve as pivot points around which the narrative turns. These parent-figures, in other words, serve doubly in the construction at once of a psychology of the female subject and of a gendered scheme of narrative production or generation.

For an example, let us glance at another crucial scene of separation before focusing on Jane's transformative separation from Rochester. Early in the novel Bessie's song promises a heavenly Father who will "take to his bosom the poor orphan child."[19] And Helen Burns recommends Jane to trust in that same heavenly Father, who will receive them as true siblings in another world. On the night of Helen's death "the light of the unclouded summer moon" guides Jane to her deathbed, where the two discuss the prospects of heavenly reunion (p. 111). At that point in the plot, Jane finds Helen's invocation of another world incomprehensible. She asks the crucially skeptical questions: "Where is God? What is God?" Helen answers "God is my father." She further promises that God is Jane's father, too, and that His heaven will be their future home: "You will come to the same region of happiness: be received by the same mighty universal Parent, no doubt, dear Jane" (p. 113). But Jane remains skeptical about the existence of that other world.

Thus, Jane's separation from Helen, an alter ego at this stage of her development, takes place under the auspices of her radical skepticism. Later in the novel when she leaves Rochester, Jane seems to have come round to Helen's position. She recommends to Rochester: "'Do as I do: trust in God and yourself. Believe in heaven. Hope to meet again there'" (p. 343). But it has always been hard for readers to believe that Jane believes this herself. Where in the story since then has Jane gained the faith that she lacked at Lowood School? Barbara Hardy asked this important question about the novel in her essay on "dogmatic form."[20] She pointed out that the narrative never does enact the transformation—that is to say, the conversion—of the skeptical, querulous child into the dogmatic, Christian adult. I think this is because we are to understand that such a transformation never really occurs. In a novel so dedicated to weighing the differences between this world and the hope of another—or between the authority of the self's desire and God's law—we have to see the omission of a conversion scene, not as a flaw, but as a choice.

God as radical other is always by definition the power elsewhere, and Jane's failure to comprehend (in the sense of internalize, as well as in the sense of understand) that radical otherness is a measure of her resolute commitment to the sanctions of the self and its worldly desires. The conversion scene is missing from the novel precisely in order to leave this an open question throughout the next episodes. The metaphorics of the novel carefully rationalize the Providential dimension of the plot by casting the beloved as "idol" who stands between Jane and her God (pp. 302, 342); and Rochester himself voices this view when he admits that "Providence has checked me" (p. 319). But Rochester's marriage to Bertha Mason threatens Jane's self-definition much more than it threatens her religious scruples, as the nightmarish mirror scene in chapter 25 makes clear. There Jane confronts the specter of the other woman who is at once the obstacle between her self and its object and at the same time the disowned, angry self-reflection (pp. 311–12). This Gothic dimension of the plot reveals the internal aspects of the problem by externalizing them; and one way to understand Jane's self-division is to sense the conflict between Gothic and Providential elements of the plot's logic.

God's law, in other words, is the ostensible but not the deepest reason for Jane's separation from Rochester. She never does adopt a belief in God's law as an end in itself; nor does she accede to His radical otherness. However, she does at this point in the plot learn to invoke His name, to produce Him as a figurehead in her text, to use the notion of God's law in her narrative as a means to an end. In this strategy she subscribes, not to Helen Burns's otherworldly inter-pretation of Providence, but to Grace Poole's practical and instru-mental interpretation: "A deal of people, miss, are for trusting all to Providence; but I say Providence will not dispense with the means, though He often blesses them when they are used discreetly" (p. 185). When Jane must find the means to separate from Rochester after her aborted wedding, she finds them in the name of the Father. But the pre-Oedipal, maternal environment grounds this symbolic transformation. In this crucial place in the narrative, Jane projects first the figure of the Father, then the Mother, then the Father again to rationalize and heal over the break from Rochester, and to gener-ate more narrative.

After first invoking the Father's law, she leaves Thornfield Hall under the auspices of the Mother. The maternal symbology of the red room scene has often been noted, not only for the most obvious reasons (the whole range of uterine analogies) but also because of the presiding moonlight, and because it is the scene of Jane's threat to starve herself to death.[21] Since the novel opens with this scene, one could say that the whole articulated text literally emerges from this quintessentially pre-Oedipal place. The novel's subsequent structure bears this out: the ghastly mirror scene which again expresses Jane's self-division and prefigures her break from Rochester (through Bertha Mason's tearing the wedding veil in two) is explicitly drawn as a parallel of the mirror scene in the red room; and the moonlight on the night after Jane's departure from Thornfield is explicitly reminiscent of the moonlight in the red room (pp. 312, 346). After Jane's farewell to Rochester, the moon breaks through vapourous clouds to whisper: "My daughter, flee temptation." And Jane answers, "Mother, I will" (p. 346). She wanders away, entertaining the idea that she can figure nature as a benevolent mother, who will feed and lodge her freely: "I have no relative but the universal mother, Nature: I will seek her breast and ask repose. . . . Nature seemed to me benign and good; I thought she loved me, outcast as I was; and I, who from man could anticipate only mistrust, rejection, insult, clung to her with filial fondness. To-night, at least, I would be her guest, as I was her child: my mother would lodge me without money and without price" (pp. 349–50). But the fantasied "good mother" has its other, darker side; in the sequence that follows in chapter 28, Jane almost starves to death on this cold hillside, explicitly figured as a female landscape.[22]

In Margaret Homans's interpretation, the mother threatens to betray her daughter by leading her into the silence, objectification, and death of "the literal," starving her of actual food and depriving her also of the sustenance of narrative: that is, language and figuration. But Jane evades the literal and figures her way back into narrative.[23] I substantially agree with Homans, but I would like to read the scene in another way simultaneously. For this is the only place in the novel where the text opens itself fully to another kind of story altogether, a story as yet untold and perhaps, in its purest sense, untellable (the story of Nature as opposed to Culture, the Lacanian Imaginary as opposed to the Symbolic, the pre-Oedipal as opposed to the Oedipal). This story would be by definition untell-able in the sense that it is the story of the prelinguistic, undifferenti-ated plenitude. But our imagination of the pre-Oedipal itself is necessarily always figurative, since we have no access to the un-divided world before language except through language. Jane does quite soon return to the world of culture; but it is the Mother as much as the Father who facilitates her return. Chapter 28 is the scene of new plot in the process of generation. Mother Nature holds Jane as she strips down to her bare bones to generate another chance from within the visionary rigors of starvation. Jane's fan-tasmatic shift from "good mother" to "bad" might itself be read as a kind of figuration, as the infant imagines that the mother will punish aggressivity and separation and thus projects a betrayal *by* the mother to cover its imagined betrayal *of* the mother. Thus the heath, despite its barrenness, may paradoxically be understood in its aspect as the Kleinian "good mother" as well as "bad"—or as the "holding mother" Jessica Benjamin describes, who gives her child the sense of being figuratively held so securely that the child can risk individua-tion, can wander away, secure in the feeling (the memory, the figura-tion) of plenitude and immediacy.[24]

It is reductive to excavate the text for signs of the pre-Oedipal without also looking for the route that discourse takes as it reenters and interacts with the Oedipal plot. For it is neither the one nor the other, but the crossings and junctures of the two—pre-Oedipal and Oedipal models—through which the generation of narrative plot and voice may be described. Jane does reproduce the figure of the Father here, turning her prayer away from Nature and toward God.[25] She explicitly names "Providence" as the interventional force which both regenerates figuration and renews the plot. In other words, she writes herself back into the plot of culture, and the struggle with the Father. Jane spots a small light on the hillside, which materializes many pages later as her cousins, and this coinci-dental sighting of her earthly family may be called "Providential," after all, because the plot here is ostentatiously represented as com-ing from beyond the world of the self.[26] This providential interven-tion is, in the final analysis, not so very different from the external-izations of the Gothic plot, as we will see very clearly when we come soon to an examination of the "call" scene. Jane's inheritance from this Father is wish-fulfillment figured as the answer to prayer—the self's own wishes externalized—for Providence provides her at this point in the story with an earthly family, which leads later to her financial as well as her psychological "independence."

Just as dangerous as the apparent plotlessness of Mother Nature, however, is the overdetermined plot of God the Father. Under His auspices, the female "I" also reaches an impasse, as we are soon to see. "Providence," which may be projected as a beneficent force when Jane is in control of the naming and figuration, becomes a threatening force in the hands of another character plotting her life for her. Jane names God as the principle of separation from Rochester, only to find that she must contradict or circumvent the category "God" when it is being wielded by St. John Rivers as an indicator of his will. Even God as radical other is no exception to the dynamics of contradiction in this text. But a further act of internalization will be necessary in order for Jane to neutralize the compelling otherness of the God she has invoked. Jane will then be able to use Him as an internal marker from which to swerve away, and she can then push His words to the intertextual edges of her narrative.

With God as her Father and Nature as her Mother, Jane is caught in a very old story. To write from the position of the separating daughter is endlessly to be caught in an oscillation between two different ways of not being able to speak. Mother Nature seemed to deprive her daughter of voice and plot. But a providential Father offers language already spoken by another, and too much plot, already written for her. In this archetypal version of the family romance, the only mode of daughterly speech is "contradiction." Jane must differentiate herself from both figurative parents to become a narrating subject. After her separation from Rochester, Jane's oscillation from Father to Mother to Father again serves to heal the rift in the plot, as well as to do the work of mourning Jane's separation from her romantic alter ego.

At the point in the plot through which we will now enter the text, she imagines that she has successfully allied herself with the Father, but now comes the struggle with God's earthly representative. Jane "knows no medium," but St. John claims to be God's "medium." Her struggle with him represents the struggle with the Father and with the voice of God he presumes to convey. She has evaded the vastation of the cold breast. But now she faces cold phallic compulsion and the words of another substituted for her own.

§

Vocation and Voice

Jane's separation from Rochester is difficult indeed, but the separation from St. John is more difficult still—in terms of its narrative logic. For Jane finds herself in the apparent position of having to contradict God's will. That is essentially her dilemma, since St. John convincingly claims to be a "medium," to convey God's will and God's voice transparently. In solving this problem, Jane finds it more difficult to transform St. John than to "retransform"—the word is Jane's—her notion of God. This section of my argument will end by discussing the "call" from Rochester, which gives Jane her vocation. But in order to understand that call, we have to know more about the circumstances of its occurrence. I will discuss these circumstances in terms of plot, theme, and intertextual grounding.

In chapter 34, Jane is under duress from St. John's proposal of marriage. He claims to speak both for Nature and for God when he enjoins her to his service:

> "And what does your heart say?" demanded St. John.
> "My heart is mute—my heart is mute," I answered, struck and thrilled.
> "Then I must speak for it," continued the deep, relentless voice. "Jane, come with me to India: come as my helpmeet and fellow labourer."
> The glen and sky spun round: the hills heaved! It was as if I had heard a summons from Heaven—as if a visionary messenger, like him of Macedonia, had enounced, "Come over and help us!" But I was no apostle—I could not believe the herald—I could not receive his call.
> "Oh, St. John!" I cried, "have some mercy!"
> I appealed to one who, in the discharge of what he believed his duty, knew neither mercy nor remorse. He continued:—"God and nature intended you for a missionary's wife. . . . you are formed for labour not for love. A missionary's wife you must—shall be. You shall be mine: I claim you—not for my pleasure, but for my Sovereign's service."
> "I am not fit for it: I have no vocation," I said. (pp. 427–28)

Recent feminist theory makes clear the sense in which St. John's words may be illuminated by the pornography of sadomasochism.

This scene shares several features with that tradition, including Jane's ritually formalized pleas for mercy with no hope of mercy forthcoming; the melodrama of St. John's chilly debasement of her physical person; his intention to turn her over to another man superior to himself in status, that is, his "King"; and even including Jane's momentary thrill at the possibility of relinquishing her life to a will other than her own, through which she can hope for transcendence.[27] The titillation of St. John's attempt to get Jane into the missionary position is in part a result of the fact that his words have a primary, innocent, and even sacred import. Jane feels momentarily as if she had heard a summons from Heaven, as if a visionary messenger were promising her a part in sacred history, in a latter-day, typological reenactment of St. Paul's mission to the Macedonians (Acts 16:9). She wants her "vocation" to be authorized by a blinding call like Paul's. But she cannot recognize St. John's call on her service; she swerves almost immediately into the stance of contradiction, of antithetical self-definition: "I was no apostle . . . I could not receive his call . . . I have no vocation." On the other hand, St. John will not let her go, and he holds her with the very sanction she has recently invoked as a rationale for leaving Rochester: the representation of God's will, the aspiration to be His "medium."

The phallic character of St. John's physiognomy has often been remarked; and he has been compared to the Reverend Brocklehurst as a "pillar of patriarchy."[28] But St. John's most ostentatiously patriarchal characteristic is his pride of access, his altogether sure sense of already having the keys to the kingdom. He does not hesitate to threaten Jane in the name of God:

> "I shall be absent a fortnight—take that space of time to consider my offer; and do not forget that if you reject it, it is not me you deny but God. Through my means, he opens to you a noble career; as my wife only can you enter upon it. Refuse to be my wife, and you limit yourself for ever to a track of selfish ease and barren obscurity. Tremble lest in that case you should be numbered with those who have denied the faith, and are worse than infidels! . . . I had thought I recognized in you one of the chosen. But God sees not as man sees: *His* will be done." (pp. 434, 440)

A rough translation of this threat might run: "Do what I want you to do, or be damned."

In St. John's scheme, the glories of access to God's voice and authority are not equally available to all. St. John is very explicit about this: "I claim you—not for my pleasure, but for my Sovereign's service" (p. 428). Marriage according to St. John's terms is very clearly the institutionalized symbol of a hierarchical chain of mediation, patrilineally organized with Jane as its last term. She can briefly imagine a missionary's life for herself, but not for a moment can she imagine being a missionary's wife under these conditions. She is ready to go with him to India if she might be allowed to go "free" (p. 430), unmarried, as his "sister," in which role she could imagine them both as equal siblings of one Father. It is marriage that puts her in the subservient position, not St. John's lack of love for her in and of itself. This is all very explicit in the text; St. John wants a wife not a sister, he says, so that he can "influence [her] efficiently" and "retain [her] absolutely till death," and he uses here, appropriately enough, the language neither of romantic love *nor* of vocation, but that of wage service (p. 431). He says "I know my Leader, . . . and while He has chosen a feeble instrument to perform a great task, He will, from the boundless stores of His providence, supply the inadequacy of the means to the end. Think like me, Jane—" (p. 428). In St. John's plot, Jane would be the means to his end; as he figures himself an instrument of God, so she would be his instrument. Jane is fully aware of the dynamic at work here, which puts her in the position, as Adrienne Rich has pointed out, of Milton's Eve: "He for God only, she for God in him."[29] She asks St. John's sister Diana, in a fury of rebellion: "Would it not be strange . . . to be chained for life to a man who regarded one but as a useful tool?" (p. 441). But though St. John tries to make Jane "adequate" to his end, she in turn makes him a means to her "end" instead, as we are in the process of seeing.

We are close now to the staging of Rochester's call in the night, that deus ex machina as romantic ESP which resolves the plot in place of Providence. Interestingly enough for our purposes, this call takes place just after a scene of family Bible-reading in which St. John reads from none other than "the twenty-first chapter of Revelation," in which is recorded St. John the Divine's "vision of the new heaven and the new earth." St. John's voice is compelling as he reads of this vision: "[N]ever did his manner become so impressive . . . as when he delivered the oracles of God," Jane acknowledges. In this scene, St. John Rivers uses St. John's vision of the other world, Jane feels sure, as a pre-text to frighten her with the threat of eternal damnation if she does not go with him.

> "He that overcometh shall inherit all things; and I will be his God, and he shall be My son. But," was slowly, distinctly read, "the fearful, the unbelieving . . . shall have their part in the lake which burneth with fire and brimstone, which is the second death."
>
> Henceforward, I knew what fate St. John feared for me. (p. 442)

She comments to her readers that St. John "believed his name was already written in the Lamb's book of life." He believes himself already to be a figure in God's plot, a character in His Book. But is Jane's name written there? The son "shall inherit all things." But the daughter? In this tensely evocative scene, St. John presumes to pray for Jane, hoping for her salvation and, as its precondition, her agreement to his plot. Jane was "touched by [his prayer], and at last awed" (p. 443). If only she could feel his will as the will of God, speaking directly to her! But the trouble is—and the subtlety of the novel's feminist critique is here—the trouble is that the means are not adequate to this end. God's will, mediated through St. John, still feels like St. John's will. God's voice mediated through St. John sounds like St. John's voice.

When we return to the final paragraphs of the novel, it will be important to remember that St. John reads, in this scene, the chapter of *Revelation* directly preceding the one from which the last words of the novel are taken. This scene establishes for us the association of St. John's threatening coercion, his pride of access, and his vision of the new heaven and the new earth. It will also be important to remember that Jane is angry in this scene—she says so—though her anger is soon blocked and covered over by her conviction of St. John's sincerity, his apparent success at figuring himself as a "medium" for the words of the other.

It is at this very point that Jane almost agrees to go with St. John. "I could decide if I were but certain . . . that it is God's will I should marry you," Jane tells St. John, who instantly cries "My prayers are heard!"—so sure is he that his wishes correspond exactly with God's will (p. 444). But Jane now makes a prayer of her own, which is answered instead—and answered in such a way that her deepest wishes, not St. John's, are expressed as correspondent with God's voice. The answering call from Rochester comes, in other words, as the result of a prayer to Heaven to know God's will. And like the last two paragraphs of the novel, it is patterned on the last words of the *Revelation*. Here is the scene (and incidentally, the Mother's moonlight presides here over this crucial invocation of the Father):

> "Show me, show me the path!" I entreated of Heaven. I was excited more than I had ever been; and whether what followed was the effect of excitement the reader shall judge. . . .
> All the house was still. . . . The one candle was dying out: the room was full of moonlight. My heart beat fast and thick: I heard its throb. Suddenly it stood still to an inexpressible feeling that thrilled it through. . . . The feeling . . . acted on my senses as if their utmost activity hitherto had been but torpor, from which they were now summoned and forced to wake. They rose expectant: eye and ear waited while the flesh quivered on my bones.
> "What have you heard? What do you see? asked St. John. I saw nothing, but I heard a voice somewhere cry—
> "Jane! Jane! Jane!"—nothing more.
> "O God! what is it?" I gasped.
> I might have said, "Where is it?" for it did not seem in the room, nor in the house, nor in the garden; it did not come out of the air, not from under the earth, nor from overhead. I had heard it—where, or whence, for ever impossible to know! And it was the voice of a human being—a known, loved, well-remembered voice—that of Edward Fairfax Rochester; and it spoke in pain and woe, wildly, eerily, urgently.
> "I am coming!" I cried. "Wait for me! Oh, I will come!" (pp. 444–45)

I want to make several points about this scene, before we return to the novel's intertextual closure.

First and most simply, the call from Rochester is produced as an instance of contradiction, of Jane's antithetical self-definition, as she makes clear when she says, I "fell on my knees; and prayed in my way—a different way to St. John's, but effective in its own fashion" (p. 445). The last paragraphs of the novel, then, by extension—because they too involve a response to the same biblical intertext—may also be read as a part of this sweeping gesture of contradiction, even though they seem in the end so peaceful. Here in the call scene Jane's frustration produces an explosion, not of anger, but rather of conviction, an inner voice that provides her with a way out of this impasse, a return in the plot, and a vocation antithetical to St. John's otherworldly one. In the language of vocational service, they will serve different "Masters." (I refer of course to the fact that Jane continues to call Rochester her "Master.") Jane's discovery of her "vocation" has been figured here as a vocalized "call." After her prayer to know God's will for her life, she feels she knows His will, and it is her own.

Of course, the voice she hears in answer to her prayer to Heaven is not the voice of God, but the voice of Rochester. This is an extraordinary trope of secularization, no matter how often we consider it. The secularization turns on the substitution of a human for a divine respondent, and the internalization of the radical other as Jane's own "inner voice." "I recalled the voice I had heard," Jane writes. "Again I questioned whence it came, as vainly as before; it seemed in me—not in the external world" (p. 446). Jane surrounds the call scene with these questions, prompting us to read Rochester's call as a chiasmic figure of voice, an exchange between figuratively external (God's) and internal (Jane's) voices. In the double-crossing of this chiasmus, the voice of God is internalized as Jane's own desire and at the same moment Jane's desire is externalized as Rochester's voice, the romantic alter ego projected away from the self again. Jane's narrative voice is generated in the figural play across this boundary.[30] Indeed, the call scene produces the last turn in the plot, its resolution, and thus—according to the logic of first-person retrospective form—the achieved voice which generates the entire narration. This brilliant figure—the chiasmic exchange of voices in the call scene—wraps together the voice of Jane's romantic alter ego, the Protestant "inner voice," and the narrative voice. Jane has heard the voice of her conscience, of God's will, of her own wish-fulfillment, and of her lover's need all in one. Invocation generates both vocation and voice in this dramatized call to service.

It has always been puzzling—here again, in terms of narrative logic—that Jane doesn't tell Rochester about hearing his "call." During the scene in Ferndean garden in the penultimate chapter of the novel, Rochester tells Jane the story of calling to her and hearing her voice on the wind answering: "I am coming! Wait for me!" He had prayed to die, to be taken from this life so that he might have some hope of meeting Jane again, in the other world, according to her promise at their parting. The answer to his prayer is Jane's voice, telling him to wait, here on this earth, for her return. The story of Rochester's prayer and its answer is of course the mirror image of Jane's prayer and its answer. I should say it is the "echo," for in this scene the chiasmic figure of voice is given another twist, in the image of their disembodied voices crossing in the wind. Rochester's side of the story dramatizes the call scene by giving us two equal human voices "co-responding" on the wind, rather than the traditional hierarchy of prayer with its one human voice invoking a divine respondent. But this return to the call scene as a part of Rochester's story threatens to deflect its force away from its primary role as a turning point in the narrative of Jane's coming to voice. By keeping it a secret from Rochester, she keeps it as her story, the story of her call to voice and vocation.

Jane holds the story of her call within that figurative space between pure interiority (or wish-fulfillment) and pure exteriority (or God). She confides it only to us, her readers, and thereby holds the secret there between us, as pure *narration*. And finally, she confides it in a figure: "I listened to Mr. Rochester's narrative, but made no disclosure in return. . . . I kept these things then, and pondered them in my heart" (p. 472). In this typological figure, Jane positions herself as Mary after the Nativity (Luke 2:19), delivered of the Word. This time, however, it is not God's word, but her own name on the wind—"Jane! Jane! Jane!"—that she keeps inside.

Mediation and Immediacy

When Jane claims that her heart is mute, St. John instantly replies, "Then I must speak for it." It is against this threat of coercive mediation that Jane's heart speaks after all, and she replaces the voice of Heaven with the call of her lover and her own narrative voice, as we have seen. Aside from realizing that she must produce a voice of her own or someone else will speak for her, Jane's move of contradiction at this point in the plot represents her rejection of a role in which she would become the merest "useful tool," allowing— even wishing—St. John to mediate the voice of authority to her, hoping to achieve transcendence through him. As Jane bluntly puts it: "I was tempted to cease struggling with him—to rush down the torrent of his will into the gulf of his existence, and there lose my own. I was almost as hard beset by him now as I had been once before, in a different way, by another. I was a fool both times" (p. 443). That is Jane's explicitly formulated protest. But let us return now to the novel's intertextual closure, which reveals a deeper questioning of the traditional structure of apostolic mediation to a power elsewhere, a critique of the mediated access to authority and voice that seems too strictly reserved in the male line. I think each of the three strands of its intertextual web forms a covert protest against mediation, a protest that is at once Protestant, romantic, and feminist in its force.

Calling St. John "Greatheart," for example, is a double business. Greatheart appears only in the second part of *The Pilgrim's Progress,* as a guide for Christiana, the wife of the original pilgrim. The very structure of Bunyan's work, in other words, emphasizes the patrilineality of apostolic succession and the inevitably mediated and secondary position of woman reading within that system. Christian begins his pilgrimage as the result of reading a book of his own, while she has only a letter to initiate her pilgrimage; and that letter is from her husband's king.[31] Several critics have written of Brontë's extensive use of *The Pilgrim's Progress* as a model for Jane's "progress."[32] But the important point here—which Barry Qualls has noted—is that Bunyan's work is also a negative model, finally positioned within this text in order to be contradicted. The allusion to Greatheart seems to me not to discredit St. John, but to emphasize the fact that Jane has chosen not to be led by a "guardian angel watching the soul for which he is responsible" (p. 443). She chooses to generate her own calling, rather than to be called, through her husband, by the letter from her husband's king.

The second intertextual reference reproduces the words of Christ as if hypothetically spoken by St. John: "His is the exaction of the apostle, who speaks but for Christ when he says 'Whosoever will come after Me, let him deny himself, and take up his cross, and follow Me.'" The objective pronoun "Me" syntactically refers in this interpolated quotation both to Christ and to St. John. Their voices are represented as if in unison. St. John's apostolic "exaction," then, at once reminds us of its disciplinary rigor and of his belief that "I John" and "I Jesus" may be exactly fitted to one another, that he speaks "but for Christ," and not also for his own will to power. The whole of *Jane Eyre* is written as a protest against this arrogant belief in the perfect substitution of one voice for another, this refusal to grant the overlap or excess that would signify the difference of individual voice.

And finally, the passage from Revelation also reproduces the figure of a chain of voices in apostolic succession, as we have seen. "I John" speaks for and with "I Jesus" in the text, which St. John Rivers quotes, adding himself to the chain. His letter does not convey "his own words," as Jane calls them, but the words of another, the words of radical otherness, of God. It should be said that Jane, too, places herself at the end of that chain, but ambivalently, in her customary mode of contradiction or negation. She appropriates the words of another as a means to her own end. Let us now consider the effects generated by this complex gesture of incorporation and simultaneous negation.

When Jane turns to St. John in these last words, she honors his vocation from a safe distance, accepting and even admiring for another what is rejected for herself. These final words can be read as a "sincere" tribute to St. John's heroic vocation only if we also register the double edge, the angry refusals of the past, and her achieved safety in distance from his psychological and textual threat. In this gesture she reminds us, at the moment of closure, of her refusal to follow him (or Him). She can afford to be generous now, but this last verbal tribute is an act of altruism only in the strictly literal sense that it is expressed as a figure of otherness. According to the logic of incorporation and differentiation within, the gesture is appropriative, making a place for the other only to turn away from that place in closing her book. I am reading these last words, then, as Jane's culminating act of self-definition in the diction of contraries.

She turns the tables on the patrilineal principle of voice by pushing the insider outside, memorializing him at the edges of the text, anticipating his death, soon and far away. This is poetic justice, after all. Death was what, in a real sense, he yearned for, he who was "inexorable as death" and whose aspiration for the other world amounted to "an austere patriot's passion for his fatherland" (pp. 426–27). Meanwhile, we are to imagine Jane, Rochester, and their recapitulatory infant with his father's eyes, living on in their insular, domestic hum.

Representing the other world in a mode of negation, in other words, serves to focus the fiction of Jane's immediate, ongoing life "here and now," in England. England, which would have been empty without Rochester is now revalued as home, while St. John waits for death on the "Himalayan ridge" (p. 419). The fireside and the parlor were not his sphere. Here the difference between life and death is figured geographically, in the local color of India as a way station between England and the grave.[33] The central value of domesticity posited here is not a new thing in the novel by any means, but it gains in authority and prestige as a result of this antithetical structure. This is an anti-apocalyptic closure, in that it focuses our attention on a domestic marriage through and against the language of the apocalyptic marriage.[34] Indeed, tropes of secularization always work doubly this way: lending borrowed authority to forms of secular life and literature by analogy with the sacred forms they no longer quite represent, but still remember; carrying within themselves an implicit revision of the sacred text even as they borrow its authority for secular ends. *Jane Eyre* reenvisions marriage as a romantic institution of equal alter egos, a true alternative to marriage as an institution of male mediation, though it is certainly also the case that the novel notoriously fails to imagine a new society to contain this new vision of marriage.[35] The high value placed upon Jane's choice of romantic love and domestic marriage depends absolutely upon the hovering vision of the apocalyptic marriage, a vision entertained and then explicitly rejected. The novel uses the traditional force of the other world, the new heaven and the new earth, to mediate back to the fictive immediacy of this world, this earth, this domestic marriage.

The one thing an autobiographical narrator cannot do, after all, is to narrate her own death.[36] As we close this book, its closure deftly has us thinking about death without its being Jane's death, and thinking about the possibility of another world without its seeming to be Jane's idea. As we close her book, it is another Book that has us thinking about these last things, another voice invoking the apocalyptic marriage, the new heaven and the new earth. The only kind of eternal life that secular fiction can bestow is to leave Jane in the middle of her fictional life, and so her story ends in medias res, in the middle of worldly things, on this earth.[37] But of course immediacy is a fiction of language. The here and now can only be imagined through the mediation of figures that pretend to deny mediation. Contradicting the systematic mediation to the other world can work to imply the fictive plenitude of an immediate here and now, at home in England. Representing the voice of the other here at the end returns us to the remembered difference of Jane's particular narrative voice. Of course the ending of this novel does not sound like "Jane Eyre." But it serves graphically to mark the difference between received views and her own, between other voices and her own.

The figure of intertextuality works in this contradictory and double-binding way as well. The text in the mode of explicit intertextuality is like the first-person narrative in the voice of another. Though in a mode of negation, Jane too joins the mediating chain as its last link, by making the last words of canonical Scripture the last words of her own text. In this bold gesture, she implies a relation of apostolic succession between Christian Scripture and the literary genre of autobiography. Her life story succeeds Scripture as the authoritative text, and in this sense Jane has the last word. But in this boldly *ambivalent* gesture, she poses a profoundly radical question about voice. This radical gesture puts her narrative closure at risk, destabilizing her feminist position as well as the integrity of her narrative voice, and opening her text to the almost overwhelming influx of the other just at the moment of attempting to close its frame. Her primary claim to speak for herself is threatened by the closing invocation of a patrilineally mediated structure of authority and voice. The integrity of her text almost dissolves into the tradition she is writing (perforce) within and (by design) against. But her text has been produced from the first within these contradictions, as a sequence of transformations in which the figure of a gendered, individual subject is generated against the background of traditional authority. This first-person narrator uses the patrilineal structure of tradition and its systematics of voice to write herself into the chain, without losing the radical position she would like to construct as its last link. This is, I think, the essential effect of closing with these words, but closing in the voice of the other, and not in the voice represented as her own narrating "I." She manages to preserve the code and its authority, making it a means to her end, while disowning—or at least distancing herself from—its affiliations with a power elsewhere.

As Jane is fearful and enraged at the structures of apostolic mediation, so we may become conscious of the dynamics of canonical literary history which, like apostolic succession, has been structured as a chain of inherited authority, coded in just such intertextual references to power elsewhere. In closing her book, Jane closes with the other Book. I mean she "closes with" the other Book in a spirit of struggle, engages it, and maintains a strong sense of difference from it. And she "closes with" the other Book in the sense of using it to her own contradictory ends. These "ends" are never stable, but always mediate, involved in their means, generated only in the process of successive narrative transformations, as the female subject weaves its way between belated mediation to a power elsewhere and the silent plenitude of an impossible immediacy.

Notes

1. Charlotte Brontë, *Jane Eyre* (Harmondsworth: Penguin, 1966), p. 477. Subsequent references to the novel will be to this edition and will be cited parenthetically in the text.

2. This romantic rhetoric is most graphic in the proposal scene of chapter 23 and is symbolized there and subsequently by the horse chestnut tree, split manifestly in two, yet unified underground, at the root.

3. Sandra M. Gilbert and Susan Gubar, *The Madwoman in the Attic: The Woman Writer and the Nineteenth-Century Literary Imagination* (New Haven: Yale University Press, 1979), p. 336.

4. Jacques Lacan, "The Mirror Stage as Formative of the Function of the I," in *Ecrits: A Selection* (New York: Norton, 1977), pp. 1–7.

5. Jean Starobinski, "The Style of Autobiography," in James Olney, ed., *Autobiography: Essays Theoretical and Critical* (Princeton, N.J.: Princeton University Press, 1980), pp. 73–83.

6. Gilbert and Gubar, "A Dialogue of Self and Soul: Plain Jane's Progress," in *Madwoman*, pp. 336–71.

7. Stages of separation-individuation have been formulated by Margaret Mahler in *On Human Symbiosis and the Vicissitudes of Individuation* (New York: International Universities Press, 1968). For literary analysis inspired by Mahler's stages, see Barbara Johnson, "Mallarmé as Mother," in her *A World of Difference* (Baltimore: Johns Hopkins University Press, 1987), pp. 137–43. See also note 11, below.

8. Ellen Moers uses *Jane Eyre* as her point of departure in arguing that naysaying is a definitive gesture of the woman writer. *Literary Women* (Garden City, N.Y.: Doubleday Anchor Books, 1977), pp. 24–26.

9. Marianne Hirsch, "'The Darkest Plots': Figures of Maternal Discourse" (paper delivered at a colloquium at the Mary Ingraham Bunting Institute of Radcliffe College, Cambridge, Mass., December 1984). Peter Brooks, *Reading for the Plot: Design and Intention in Narrative* (New York: Knopf, 1984).

10. See Sigmund Freud, "Negation" (1925), in vol. 19 of *The Standard Edition of the Complete Psychological Works of Sigmund Freud* (London: Hogarth Press, 1953–74), pp. 235–40.

11. For analysis of such phantasmic projections of the first person, see Philippe Lejeune, "Autobiography in the Third Person," *New Literary History* 9, no. 1 (Autumn 1977): 27–50.

12. Gilbert and Gubar, *Madwoman*, pp. 354–62. This dimension of their reading was prefigured by Adrienne Rich in "*Jane Eyre:* The Temptations of a Motherless Woman," in *On Lies, Secrets, and Silence: Selected Prose, 1966–78* (New York: Norton, 1979), pp. 89–106.

13. The theoretical model I am using to discover and describe this dynamic in the text derives from the psychoanalysis of object relations, with its central operating

concepts of internalization, introjection and projection, primary narcissism, separation and individuation. See Melanie Klein, "The Importance of Symbol-formation in the Development of the Ego" (1930), and "Love, Guilt, and Reparation" (1937), in her *Love, Guilt and Reparation and Other Works, 1921–1945* (London: Hogarth Press, 1977); Roy Shafer, *Aspects of Internalization* (New York: International Universities Press, 1968); D. W. Winnicott, "Transitional Objects and Transitional Phenomena," *International Journal of Psychoanalysis* 34 (1953): 88–97; Winnicott, *The Maturational Processes and the Facilitating Environment* (London: Hogarth Press, 1965); and Winnicott, *Playing and Reality* (New York: Basic Books, 1971). For analysis of the literary use of object relations theory, see Meredith Skura, *The Literary Use of the Psychoanalytic Process* (New Haven: Yale University Press, 1981), pp. 186–90, and Elizabeth Wright, *Psychoanalytic Criticism: Theory in Practice* (London: Methuen, 1984), pp. 79–104.

14.   Virginia Woolf, *A Room of One's Own* (New York: Harcourt Brace Jovanovich, 1957), pp. 71–74. See also Adrienne Rich's analysis of this passage in *"Jane Eyre:* The Temptations of a Motherless Woman," pp. 97–99.

15.   Woolf, *A Room of One's Own,* p. 73.

16.   M. Jeanne Peterson, "The Victorian Governess: Status Incongruence in Family and Society," in Martha Vincinus, ed., *Suffer and Be Still: Women in the Victorian Age* (Bloomington: Indiana University Press, 1972) pp. 3–19.

17.   Harold Bloom, "The Internalization of Quest Romance," in Bloom, ed., *Romanticism and Consciousness: Essays in Criticism* (New York: Norton, 1970), pp. 3–24.

18.   This dimension of my argument is grounded in specifically feminist developments of object relations theory. The locus classicus for American critics is Nancy Chodorow, *The Reproduction of Mothering: Psychoanalysis and the Sociology of Gender* (Berkeley: University of California Press, 1978). A recent volume of essays in psychoanalytic feminist criticism marks the attempt to theorize the relation between Oedipal and pre-Oedipal models in literary analysis and the attempt to theorize a relation between feminist uses of Lacan and feminist object relations: Shirley Nelson Garner, Claire Kahane, and Madelon Sprengnether, eds., *The (M)other Tongue: Essays in Feminist Psychoanalytic Interpretation* (Ithaca, N.Y.: Cornell University Press, 1985). For analysis and critique of the position of the separating daughter within psychoanalysis and literature, see the editorial introduction to *The (M)other Tongue,* pp. 15–29; Susan Rubin Suleiman's contribution to that volume, "Writing and Motherhood," pp. 352–77; Jane Flax, "The Conflict between Nurturance and Autonomy in Mother-Daughter Relationships and within Feminism," *Feminist Studies* 4 (June 1978): 171–91; and Jane Gallop, "Reading the Mother Tongue: Psychoanalytic Feminist Criticism," *Critical Inquiry* 13, no. 2 (Winter 1987): 314–29.

19.   Gilbert and Gubar have pointed out the relevance of this song to the "patriarchal terrors of the red room and . . . patriarchal terrors to come—Lowood, Brocklehurst, St. John Rivers," in *Madwoman,* pp. 342–43.

20.   Barbara Hardy, "Dogmatic Form: Defoe, Charlotte Brontë, Thomas Hardy, and E. M. Forster," in *The Appropriate Form: An Essay on the Novel* (London: Athlone Press, 1964), pp. 51–82.

21.   On the moon as Mother, see Rich, *"Jane Eyre:* The Temptations of a Motherless Woman," pp. 101–3; and Gilbert and Gubar, *Madwoman,* pp. 340–41, 363–64.

22.   On the good object and the bad object (good mother and bad mother, good breast and bad breast), see Melanie Klein, "The Contribution to the Psychogenesis of Manic-Depressive States," in her *Love, Guilt and Reparation,* pp. 262–89; and chapters viii and ix of *The Psycho-Analysis of Children,* vol. 2 of *The Writings of Melanie Klein* (New York: The Free Press, 1984).

23.   Margaret Homans, "Dreaming of Children: Literalization in *Jane Eyre* and

Wuthering Heights," in Juliann E. Fleenor, ed., *The Female Gothic* (Montreal and London: Eden Press, 1983), pp. 257–79, especially pp. 265–71.

24. For Jessica Benjamin's specifically feminist extension of Winnicott's concepts of the "holding mother" or "holding environment," see "A Desire of One's Own: Psychoanalytic Feminism and Intersubjective Space," in *Feminist Studies/Critical Studies,* ed. Teresa de Lauretis (Bloomington: Indiana University Press, 1986), pp. 78–101.

25. Homans notes this turn in "Dreaming of Children," pp. 269–70.

26. On the providential plot in *Jane Eyre,* see Thomas Vargish, "Charlotte Brontë: The Range of Providential Intention," in *The Providential Aesthetic in Victorian Fiction* (Charlottesville: University Press of Virginia, 1985), especially pp. 58–67.

27. See Rich, *"Jane Eyre:* The Temptations of a Motherless Woman," pp. 103–4; Kaja Silverman, *"Histoire d'O:* The Construction of a Female Subject," in Carole S. Vance, ed., *Pleasure and Danger: Exploring Female Sexuality* (Boston: Routledge & Kegan Paul, 1984), pp. 320–49; and Jessica Benjamin, "Master and Slave: The Fantasy of Erotic Domination," in Ann Snitow, Christine Stansell, and Sharon Thompson, eds., *Powers of Desire: The Politics of Sexuality* (New York: Monthly Review Press, 1983) pp. 280–99. For another influential reading of the female as signifier of a male-male transaction, see Eve Kosofsky Sedgwick, *Between Men: English Literature and Male Homosocial Desire* (New York: Columbia University Press, 1985).

28. Gilbert and Gubar, *Madwoman,* p. 366.

29. Rich, *"Jane Eyre:* The Temptations of a Motherless Woman," p. 103.

30. My argument here is indebted to Barbara Johnson, "Metaphor, Metonymy, and Voice in Zora Neale Hurston's *Their Eyes Were Watching God,"* in Henry Louis Gates, Jr., ed., *Black Literature and Literary Theory* (London: Methuen, 1985), pp. 205–19. See also Ruth Bernard Yeazell, "More True than Real: Jane Eyre's 'Mysterious Summons,'" *Nineteenth-Century Fiction* 29 (1974): 127–43.

31. Judith Wilt makes this point in "Brava! And Farewell to Greatheart," a review of Gilbert and Gubar, *The Madwoman in the Attic,* in *Boundary* 2 8, no. 3 (Spring 1980): 285–99.

32. See Gilbert and Gubar, "Plain Jane's Progress," in *Madwoman,* pp. 336–71; and Barry Qualls, *The Secular Pilgrims of Victorian Fiction* (Cambridge: Cambridge University Press, 1982), pp. 43–84. On the figurative tension between vocational service to different "Masters" in Bunyan, see Michael McKeon, "Romance Transformations (II): Bunyan and the Literalization of Allegory," in *The Origins of the English Novel, 1600–1740* (Baltimore: Johns Hopkins University Press, 1987), pp. 295–314.

33. Thanks to my colleague David Suchoff, who has pointed out to me the critique of colonialism implicit in this closing view of St. John Rivers.

34. On the secularized apocalyptic marriage as a figure of romanticism, see M. H. Abrams, *Natural Supernaturalism* (New York: Norton, 1971).

35. As Carol Ohmann argues in "Historical Reality and 'Divine Appointment' in Charlotte Brontë's Fiction," *Signs* 2, no. 4 (1977): 757–78.

36. Walter Benjamin, "The Storyteller: Reflections on the Works of Nikolai Leskov," in his *Illuminations* (New York: Harcourt, Brace & World, 1968), pp. 83–110.

37. "In the middest," to use Frank Kermode's famous phrase from *The Sense of an Ending: Studies in the Theory of Fiction* (London: Oxford University Press, 1966).

David Riede

Transgression, Authority, and the Church of Literature in Carlyle

As the first and most influential of the Victorian sages, Thomas Carlyle is arguably the most important single figure in the general shift of literary authority during the nineteenth century from the romantic prophet-bard to the critic, or man of letters. His early career, in the late 1820s and 1830s, reflects with great clarity some of the complex and multitudinous causes of this general shift, causes which include a strengthening of the scientific and utilitarian outlook against the competing worldview of English and German romanticism, an emergent Evangelical ethos of socially purposeful activism, and changes in the economic conditions of literary production. In his early writings Carlyle is plainly torn between two worldviews: his profoundly religious nature drawn powerfully to romanticism, to what he called German "mysticism"; his skeptical, logical mind drawn to what he thought of as a Scotch and French ideology that combined "common sense," skepticism, and materialism. The result is writing that is generally understood in terms of romantic irony—romantic ideals are simultaneously held forth and ironically undermined; Teufelsdröckh is set forth as an inspired seer who might just be a madman.[1] But to see Carlyle simply as a romantic ironist is to miss his manifest desire to get beyond the irresolution of romanticism to a position of genuine authority, a position beyond ironic undercutting. His attitude toward Coleridge is characteristic—determined to find a fixed, unwavering, authoritative position, he was infamously harsh on the elder sage: "His talk, alas, was distinguished, like himself, by irresolution: it disliked to be troubled with conditions, abstinences, definite fulfilments;—loved to wander at its own sweet will."[2] What Carlyle sought was, precisely, resolution, an end to romantic vacillations among infinite possibilities, so it is not surprising that he participated in, and helped to form, the pre-Victorian reaction against a romantic ideology that we have come to recognize as determinedly open-ended, opposed to dogmatic certitudes. Yet all of Carlyle's assumptions regarding the oracular authority of great men were drawn from romantic notions of poetic genius, of the authority of experience and sincerity in literature, of the inspired and honest seer who depends upon the "felt indubitable certainty of Experience" (*SR* 196) to see through outworn ideological structures, who sees through the "Shows of things into Things themselves" (*SR* 205), sees through "shams" and "formulas" to the underlying "realities," "veracities," "eternal laws." His reaction to romanticism, in short, was to reify romantic possibilities, to force closure on romantic speculations, especially on those that confer a peculiar authority on the gifted seer. Consequently, he paradoxically became an antiromantic dogmatist with a lecturing platform built almost entirely of romantic planks.

Carlyle's development of an authoritarian polemic from a supposedly nonpolemical, antiauthoritarian romanticism can be explored in a number of interrelated ways. First, analysis of the relation between experience and authority in romanticism generally and in Carlyle's writings particularly reveals some of the latent ideological implications in romantic thought. But Carlyle's thought, his assumptions and rhetorical motives, should be analyzed not only in terms of his inherited romantic ideology but also in the fuller historical context of competing ideologies—his thought can be understood as an attempt, inevitably unsuccessful, to transcend ideology completely, to find an authoritative position beyond the dominant romantic and utilitarian ideologies (or what have been loosely called the "German" and "French" ideologies) of the early nineteenth century. Such analysis leads to an understanding of how Carlyle arrived at his characteristically paradoxical stance of bellowing quietism, and consequently invites questions about the rebellious, transgressive style that seems to cry out *against* rebellion and transgression. To comprehend Carlyle's strange blend of revolutionary style and conservative thought, the extent and nature of his transgression against established authority must be understood within the context of the economics of text production in the 1820s and 1830s. Finally, when Carlyle's romantic rebelliousness, evident in his transgressive style, is situated within the broad contexts of intellectual history, the economics of production, and his own later development, we can perhaps come to some tentative conclusions about the problems inherent in the development of an authoritarian romanticism, and about the extraordinary difficulties attending the idea of any kind of socially activist literature.

§

Experience into Ideology

The general assumptions about Carlyle's adoption of and later reaction against romanticism are summed up in Robert Langbaum's *The Poetry of Experience,* an important and influential study of the romantic tradition and of the continued modernity of romantic ideas. Langbaum argues that Carlyle exemplifies the characteristically romantic displacement of prior intellectual and spiritual authorities by a new subjective empiricism—a reliance on the indubitable personal truth of individual experience. Langbaum understands Carlyle in terms of a "formulation" of romanticism "that formulation itself must never be allowed to settle into dogma, but must emerge anew every day out of experience." From this romantic perspective, Carlyle's "mistake" is to forget that his assumptions have "validity only because they have been arrived at . . . through experience and self-realization."[3] That is, Carlyle's "mistake" is to become dogmatic by putting an end to the perpetual process of reformulations in experience, to harden experiential "truths" into authoritative Truth.

Langbaum's judgment that Carlyle was mistaken in wanting to move toward closure, to distinguish authoritative inspiration from madness, is itself based on a reified romantic ideology—it, in effect, repeats Carlyle's mistake of forming authoritarian rules on the basis of a supposedly antiauthoritarian ideology. Carlyle's works demonstrate in very clear ways how the adoption and reification of romantic notions help to establish certain truths of culture as bases of critical authority, a powerful discourse that could challenge the philistine society. From this point of view Carlyle was not "mistaken" in seeking definitive, authoritative truth, but was attempting to go beyond what he saw as a romantic impasse that led only to vacillation, uncertainty, and intellectual and moral chaos.[4] In other words, he was only mistaken from the romantic point of view that he was in the process of repudiating. As Janice Haney has said, Carlyle's effort was precisely to "free his text from a determinedly Romantic context" in order to turn to a more socially purposeful "emerging Victorian mode of making meaning."[5] The question that remains, however, is whether he could *succeed* in transforming romantic uncertainties into socially purposeful truths.

Carlyle's attitude toward the authority of experience very clearly demonstrates one of the major shifts in ideological perspective that occurs when romantic possibility is hardened into Victorian fact. Though he certainly was an exponent of the "felt indubitable certainty of Experience" (*SR* 196), Carlyle, like his romantic predecessors, saw experience in his early work as at best a problematic basis for authority. In the first place, though experience can never be "wholly a lie" since it is true for the individual, it may still be delusive—a "lying vision" produced by "delirium" (*SR* 147–48). In addition, Carlyle realized that however indisputably "real" experience may be, it is meaningless until *interpreted*, and useless to an author until translated into language. He therefore developed a highly idiosyncratic style in an attempt to communicate his highly idiosyncratic experience as directly as possible. The attempt and its difficulties are satirized throughout *Sartor Resartus* as the "editor" attempts to grasp the experiential reality behind Teufelsdröckh's philosophy: "'how paint to the sensual eye,' asks [Teufelsdröckh] once, 'what passes in the Holy-of-Holies of Man's Soul; in what words, known to these profane times, speak even afar-off of the unspeakable?' We ask in turn: Why perplex these times, profane as they are, with needless obscurity, by omission and by commission? Not mystical only is our Professor, but whimsical; and involves himself, now more than ever, in eye-bewildering *chiaroscuro*" (*SR* 185). But again, Carlyle would not always be content to settle for unanswered questions, and in his later writings, beginning indeed as early as the 1830s, he simply elided the issues of validating the "truth" of experience and of translating experience into expression. A passage describing Mahomet in *Heroes and Hero-Worship* is representative: "While others walk in formulas and hearsays, contented enough to dwell there, this man could not screen himself in formulas; he was alone with his own soul and the reality of things. The great Mystery of Existence . . . glared-in upon him, with its terrors, with its splendours; no hearsays could hide that unspeakable fact, 'Here am I!' Such *sincerity,* as we named it, has in very truth something of divine. The word of such a man is a Voice direct from Nature's own Heart" (*HHW* 54). The passage represents two uncritical reifications of romantic thought that are absolutely central to Carlyle's writing: the idea that the man of genius, a hero, sees through "formulas" to "realities," and the idea that experience can be translated directly into the word, that the word of man and the "voice" of nature are one and the same if only the man is sufficiently sincere.

Carlyle's romantic elision of the gap between experience and expression is an early instance of a tendency that has continued to influence postromantic thought. As Raymond Williams puts it, literary criticism has tended to forget that "literature is the process and the result of formal composition within the social and formal properties of a language. The effective suppression of this process and its circumstances, which is achieved by shifting the concept to an undifferentiated equivalence with 'immediate living experience' . . . is an extraordinary ideological feat."[6] Once experience is "translated" into language, it ceases to be experientially felt and indubitable, and can have no experiential authority for auditors or readers. Indeed, any one person's experience of reality, to use Carlyle's terms, can only be "hearsay" to anyone else. But if his writing was to have an authoritative social influence, Carlyle necessarily had to blind himself to the gap between experience and expression. The "extraordinary ideological feat" was necessary to gain a position of authority. The other, equally necessary, assumption, that certain "visionaries" or "great men" can see through "formulas and hearsays," represents Carlyle's way of getting beyond romantic uncertainties—find your great man, or hero, and take his word for what is real or true. Carlyle's solutions to the romantic impasse are clearly inadequate, but they show in a very blunt way what the problem was—in an age rife with competing "formulas and hearsays," or what we might call ideologies, how was one to transcend ideology to arrive at an authoritative position? Carlyle's early writings, like those of his romantic predecessors, assert a kind of visionary authority to examine it, question it, reexamine it, and possibly reassert it. Later, he would simply abandon these probings of tentative affirmations to adopt a transcendentalist ideology that he believed transcended ideology to arrive at the eternal truths behind enigmatic experiences.

§

Limited Ideologies and the Authority of Transgression

Carlyle could not easily transcend experience by appeal to the authority of any extant worldview because, as I have suggested, though he was powerfully drawn to English and German romantic idealism, he could see that it did not lead to the socially purposeful activism he sought. His sympathies, it seems, must have been partly with Napoleon, who confronted what we can call the "German ideology" of Teufelsdröckh in *Sartor* with a rather more forcefully activist ideology. After being "dismissed, almost thrown out of doors" by Napoleon "as an 'Ideologist,'" Teufelsdröckh observes that Napoleon himself "was among the completest Ideologists, at least Ideopraxists: in the Idea (*in der Idee*) he lived, moved and fought. The man was a Divine Missionary, though unconscious of it" (*SR* 178). The passage illustrates Carlyle's full awareness of the *need* for an ideology that provides a basis for action, or praxis. It demonstrates, in fact, why he was not willing to rest content in a state of romantic openness that could only issue in Coleridgean vacillation, not in action. Yet he could not commit himself fully either to the German ideology or to the more apparently pragmatic French ideology. In fact, all of Carlyle's early works can be read as an expression of his struggle to transcend the competing "German" and "French" ideologies, both of which he had internalized. Carlyle's deeply religious Scottish Calvinist background instilled in him a lifelong religious outlook, but the doctrinal content of that outlook had been shattered at the University of Edinburgh by the questioning spirit inherited from French philosophism and Scottish skepticism. In fact, Carlyle himself saw his Scottish milieu as an outpost of French thought, saw "Pope Voltaire" as spiritual (or antispiritual) leader of "Bishop Hume."[7] Countering the influence of the skeptical spirit, Carlyle steeped himself in German thought, serving a decade-long literary apprenticeship as a translator, reviewer, and general chronicler of Schiller, Goethe, Novalis, Richter, and others. Consequently, as he wrote to Eckermann in 1828, his British contemporaries had come to regard him as "a 'Mystic,' or a man half-drowned in the abysses of German speculation; which considering everything, is all, in my opinion, exactly as it should be" (*Letters* 4:427). But he was, indeed, only *half* drowned, and so could say sincerely at about the same time that "God knows I am no mystic, but have a clear Scotch head on my shoulders, as any man need, and too strong in logic and scepticism rather than too weak" (*Letters* 4:390).

Not surprisingly, then, all of Carlyle's writings from the 1820s through the early 1830s display an ideological battlefield on which— to speak in very broad generalizations—"French/Scottish" skepticism and "German" mysticism hold one another at bay in a state of tense irresolution. Despite his strong enthusiasm for German thought, Carlyle's skeptical Scottish head keeps him from wholly unqualified support of "mysticism" in his reviews of German writers. "Signs of the Times," for example, poises a specifically German "dynamic" ideology against a specifically French "mechanical" ideology, but despite his obvious preference for the "dynamic," the two views tend to cancel one another out, leaving Carlyle with no basis for social praxis. Consequently, the essay ends in a form of political quietism: "To reform a world, to reform a nation, no wise man will undertake" (*Works* 27:82). Even the idea of acting through prophetic writing seems to be ruled out from the opening sentence, displaced by the wish for more concrete forms of action: "It is no very good symptom either of nations or of individuals, that they deal much in vaticination. . . . Our grand business is, not to *see* what lies dimly at a distance, but to *do* what lies clearly at hand" (*Works* 27:56). Characteristically, "Characteristics" is putatively a review balancing the English materialism of Thomas Hope against the German "mysticism" of Friedrich Schlegel, and *Sartor Resartus,* of course, plays the mysticism of Teufelsdröckh off the "common sense" of an English "editor." In all of these works, by far the strongest case is made for the "German ideology," but Carlyle retains just enough skepticism to keep him from simply adopting and speaking from within what he understands to be the German point of view. Even if we accept Haney's persuasive argument that Carlyle's open-endedness is best understood in terms of Schlegel's romantic irony, it seems clear that the ironic distance from "mysticism" is the result of a "French/Scottish" perspective.

It might seem, perhaps, that the confrontation of the prevailing mechanical ideology with a dynamic or vitalist ideology would offer a dialectic that might result in a higher synthesis, in a much desired union of head and heart, body and soul, mechanism and dynamism. But such a synthesis is not possible in the terms offered—the French and German ideologies as Carlyle understood them are flatly incompatible. One, after all, is based on a mystifying, transcendental sense of wonder; the other on a resolutely demystifying materialistic empiricism. The extent of this incompatibility is painfully clear in Carlyle's remark about what he learned from each perspective: "I began with Hume and Diderot, and as long as I was with them I ran at Atheism, at blackness, at materialism of all kinds. If I read Kant, I arrived at precisely opposite conclusions, that all the world was spirit namely, that there was nothing material at all anywhere."[8] The mutual critique of *Sartor Resartus*'s German ideologue and common-sensical English editor would seem an admirable way of remaining open-minded, and it certainly does offer a brilliant and provocative work of romantic irony, but if the tension were maintained between two equally compelling systems of thought, the resulting open-endedness would leave Carlyle exactly where he did not want to be—foundering without a working faith or belief in any authoritative position. But the mystical point of view dominates the book, and in fact the final three chapters collapse the distinction between Teufelsdröckh and the editor completely. The unified point of view, moreover, seems to provide sufficient authority for an activist ideology as we learn that Teufelsdröckh may have come down from his tower to take an active part in the three-day revolution in Paris that overthrew Charles X in July 1830, and that he now may be in London, girding his loins for action.

But what action can issue from an idealist ideology except for romantic critiques of the competing materialist ideology? Philip Rosenberg, who has pointed out how difficult it is to "forge . . . a connection between thought and action," accounts for Carlyle's inability to move from ideology to ideopraxis by asserting that "It is the nature of intellect to issue in nothing," but as Rosenberg also realizes, Carlyle was not content to have "dragged his quietist impulses along with him into his career as a political essayist." Yet he seemed to have no choice but to "act" only as a writer and thinker or, as Rosenberg puts it, to take "the high road of cultural criticism."[9] Whatever Teufelsdröckh may be intending, Carlyle could find no plan for action beyond socially committed writing—he could never find a way to get beyond the point he had arrived at as early as 1823, when he noted that a man should put the knowledge he has acquired from books to "some practical use. If I could *write*, that were *my* practical use."[10] But from the mid 1830s on, his writing would at least have the rhetorical strength of resolution. From about the time he finished *Sartor Resartus,* he stopped *examining* romantic ideals and began *using* them as fixed positions to confer authority upon his own writing. That is, he began, and soon completed, the transition from romantic ironist to Victorian sage by reifying romantic speculation. Where he had been to a certain extent ironic about the authority of experience, he now became dogmatic; where he had been tentative and ambivalent about the idea of the inspired visionary's ability to bridge the gap between experience and expression with words of absolute truth, he now became absolutist. Ultimately, the result was to posit an activist ideology in which the writer himself becomes the authority, the hero, whose vision and words urge others into action. Ultimately, that is, the result was to posit the man of letters as hero, and so to take the role and speak with unhesitating authority—no more romantic vacillation, no more wavering between competing ideologies. Granted these assumptions, the visionary prophet could now see through competing ideologies—shams and formulas—to authentic truth.

The way in which a now unquestioning acceptance of romantic assumptions confers authority has been cynically hinted at by Kenneth Burke, who has commented that the Carlylean, and generally romantic, rhetoric of mystification may have a self-interested motive: "Perhaps reality would not look mysterious at all to our literary mystics, if it did not also include reverence due to their professional careerism."[11] The comment is perhaps a little harsh on Carlyle, but it does suggest the fundamental problem of the social prophet: in order to be heard at all, he must gain the ear, and the respect, of an audience that will believe him to have a genuine wisdom from "beyond the veil." And to do this, of course, the prophet must not write like other men—he must develop a style to express experience directly, and the style must be idiosyncratic in order to express the novelty of his point of view. Indeed, the language must peculiarly conform to the peculiar experience of the author in order to be "sincere"—he cannot use other people's words, other people's formulas. In an 1836 letter to Mill, Carlyle defended the peculiarities of his style on the romantic grounds that the style cannot simply express the polite usages of society but must express the inner truth of experience: "the form after all perhaps came from *within,* and was what it *best* could be, and only contradicted Blair's Lectures and use-and-wont because it could not help it" (*Letters* 6:316). In effect, Carlyle's socially activist ideology would issue in what we now recognize as "Carlylese," a startlingly original style that not only catches the ear but bellows into it. In fact, as has often been noted, Carlyle's early style is far more orthodox than his later, reflecting an early belief in quiet debate as a means to truth. As late as 1830 he was defending decorum in writing:

> I have no disposition to run *amuck* against any set of men or of opinions; but only to put forth certain Truths that I feel in me, with all sincerity. . . . Dilettantism, and mere toying with Truth, is, on the whole, a thing which I cannot practice: nevertheless real Love, real Belief, is not inconsistent with Tolerance of its opposite; nay is the only consistent there with, for your Elegant Indifference is at heart only *idle,* selfish, and quite *in*tolerant. At all events, one can and should *speak quietly;* loud hysterical vehemence, foaming, and hissing least of all beseems him that is convinced, and not only *supposes,* but *knows.* (*Letters* 5:196)

But even here the basis for Carlyle's "activist" rhetoric is becoming apparent: what is called for is sincerity and conviction; what is to be avoided is the mere elegance of the "dilettante." But though decorous, tolerant speech is suited to philosophic debate taking place above the din of social and political life, Carlyle's desire to affect society directly led him, as the English "editor" says it led Teufelsdröckh, to "descend . . . into the angry noisy Forum, with an Argument that cannot but exasperate and divide" (*SR* 15). To be heard at all above the din of battle Carlyle was already at this point developing a style that we might call, not too ungenerously, one of "loud hysterical vehemence," a style that deliberately broke the rules, breached propriety and decorum to get beyond the formulas of polite society that are reproduced in the formulas of polite writing. In 1835 he explicitly defended the necessity of breaking the rules in a letter to Sterling:

> do you reckon this really a time for Purism of Style; or that Style (mere dictionary style) has much to do with the worth or unworth of a book?

I do not: with whole ragged battallions of Scott's Novel Scotch, with Irish, German, French and even Newspaper Cockney (when "Literature" is little other than a Newspaper) storming in on us, and the whole structure of our Johnsonian English breaking up from its foundations,—revolution *there* as visible as anywhere else! (*Letters* 8:135)

The implication, clearly, is that Carlyle was joining in a revolution against decorum in language that was consonant with the revolution against the prevailing social ideology. But it is also clear that Carlyle wanted to be heard above the din of these other revolutionaries— his style would have to be even more "impure," more indecorous, than others if he were to make himself heard. The evidence of contemporary readers indicates that he succeeded. With varying degrees of disapprobation and bewilderment, reviewers commented on Carlyle's "Babylonish dialect," his "distortions and extravagancies," his "crudities," his "barbarian eloquence of language."[12]

Carlyle's style becomes what we might call a rhetoric of transgression that can make him seem quite modern to our contemporary romantic critical tradition. Geoffrey Hartman, for example, has remarked that the style of *Sartor* is, as Emerson complained, indecorous, or even, as Hartman adds, somewhat "smoky or excrementitious" and has proceeded from this observation to describe Carlyle in postmodernist critical terms. He describes the style as a "carnival" style, "an evacuated high style, an unauthorized tongue" in an "inherently excessive or transgressive" mode that "gathers counter-cultural strength" to attack the high cultural "principle of decorum."[13] Hartman's language ineluctably summons Foucault—particularly his essay "A Preface to Transgression"—and so implies, in effect, a postmodernist Carlyle. According to Foucault transgressive language defines the limits and boundaries of language, and therefore of thought, by showing where they are broken. But it does not take a postmodernist perspective to understand Carlyle's romantic purposes—John Sterling, in 1839, commented on Carlyle's style and its effect in ways that remarkably anticipate Foucault's analysis of transgressive language: "the orgasm of shaping thought and desolating emotion bursts with ruin through the steadfast bounds of science, of art, and of conscientious activity."[14] As Sterling's comment indicates, Carlyle's style itself represents a revolutionary bursting of the ideological bonds of society, a breaking through the bars of its epistemological frameworks. It represents, in effect, an activist ideology that at least aims to get beyond competing ideologies. His intention, to get beyond formulas to realities, also anticipates Foucault's still romantic assertion that "Transgression . . . affirms the limitlessness into which it leaps as it opens this zone to existence for the first time."[15] In fact, Foucault's whole discussion reads like a running commentary on *Sartor Resartus*, especially when he almost seems to echo the Carlylean turn from skepticism and denial to an "everlasting Yea": "Transgression opens onto a scintillating and constantly affirmed world, a world without shadow or twilight, without the serpentine 'no' that bites into fruits and lodges their contradiction at their core. It is the solar inversion of satanic denial." Or, in Carlyle's terms, it is the "everlasting Yea," the solar inversion of the Devil's "everlasting No." Foucault sees in transgression a liberation of language, a transcendence of dialectic in a nondiscursive language, the language of Zarathustra, with the happy result that the "obvious and garrulous identity" of the philosophical, dialectical language that "has remained unexamined from Plato to Nietzsche" now separates itself from the triumphant transgressive Dionysian language and is seen to be "gravitating in a space increasingly silent."[16] All of this corresponds, remarkably neatly, with Carlyle's own triumph over the dialectic of competing ideologies in his transgressive "Yea," his turn from the discursive language of satanic denial—or of the mechanical ideology he wants to overthrow. It even accounts for the oft-noted paradox that he spent a lifetime bellowing out a "gospel of silence."

But the important point here is to illustrate, not that Carlyle is a postmodernist, but that postmodernism still clings to a romantic ideology. The attempt to understand Carlyle's romanticism via Hartman's or Foucault's would partake of the error described by Terry Eagleton, who remarks that the task of criticism "is not to redouble the text's self-understanding, to collude with its object in a conspiracy of eloquence. Its task is to show the text as it cannot know itself, to manifest the condition of its making (inscribed in its very letter) about which it is necessarily silent."[17] Without necessarily accepting Eagleton's absolutist notion about *the* task of criticism, one can agree that it is not enough to examine a romantic ideology from a still romantic perspective—criticism ought also to explore the historical conditions that influenced the given text or body of work. Furthermore, the work can be more fully understood if located not only within the historical nexus of ideologies that inform it but also within the historical context of economic and material means of textual production.

§

Authority in the Marketplace: The "Man of Letters"

Carlyle's own economic situation is obviously of importance in this context. Having rejected the clergy, the law, medicine, and teaching as possible vocations, Carlyle determined in the 1820s to earn his bread as what he called a "man of letters," but due to the economic actualities of the literary marketplace, he was terribly ambivalent about his chosen role. In fact his letters of the 1820s and early 1830s are more preoccupied with writing as a profession than with any particular message he had to offer the world as a writer—in 1831 he was even contemplating an article on "the State of Authors at this epoch; the duties, performances, and marvellous position of the Author in our System of Society" (*Letters* 6:13). The letters reveal how his early romantic enthusiasm for the high calling of literature soon degenerated into a contempt for literature as a trade in the present age, and for his fellow men of letters. The contempt is evident in an 1824 letter to Jane Welsh: "Good Heavens! I often inwardly exclaim, and is *this* the Literary World? This rascal rout, this dirty rabble, destitute not only of high feeling or knowledge or intellect, but even of common honesty? The very best of them are ill-natured weaklings: they are not red-blooded *men* at all; they are only *things* for writing 'articles' " (*Letters* 3:234.) He felt compelled to *be* a man of letters, and yet to remain above the contemptible herd: "I will not degenerate into the wretched thing which calls itself an Author in our Capitals, and scribbles for the sake of filthy lucre in the periodicals of the day" (*Letters* 3:246). The problem was that in the present state of the trade it was exceedingly difficult to make money by publishing one's own thoughts except in the form of a review-article in one of the many periodicals of the day, and that this amounted to little more than prostituting oneself to the particular slant of any given journal: "I have said a thousand times, when you could not believe me, that the trade of Literature was worse as a trade than that of honest Street Sweeping; that I knew not how a man without some degree of prostitution could live by it" (*Letters* 5:237). As late as 1834 he was still complaining—perhaps more vehemently than ever: "To enter some Dog's-meat Bazaar; muffled up; perhaps holding your nose and say: 'Here you, Master, able Editor or whatever your name is, will you buy this mess of mine (at so much per pound), and sell it among your Dog's-meat?'—and then having dealt with the able Editor, hurry out again, and wish that it could be kept secret from all men: *this* is the nature of my connexion with Periodicals" (*Letters* 7:71). Even if a writer were, like Carlyle himself, to live in utmost poverty in order to keep from prostituting his intellect to the periodicals, he must still turn out articles at a prodigious rate in order merely to subsist. The issue came to a head for Carlyle in 1831, when he had finally achieved his ambition of writing a *book* that was not merely a review of other men's thoughts; his inability to sell *Sartor Resartus* seemed to confirm to him that the book trade was dead, "for the whole world is dancing a Tarantula Dance of Political Reform, and has no ear left for Literature" (*Letters* 5:327).[18]

The state of the marketplace and its effect on Carlyle is perhaps most clearly seen in the publication history of *Sartor Resartus*. Carlyle, who regarded *Sartor* as a "word spoken in season" (*Letters* 5:237), was willing, even eager, to speak out on political issues of the day, but he wanted to speak from a pulpit outside of the contentious, partisan journals, wanted to remain unsullied by the review business as a mere trade and to speak from an independent position befitting the high romantic ideal of the author. Ultimately, however, he was compelled to cut *Sartor* into bits and publish it in *Fraser's Magazine*, which he subsequently described as "one of the main *cloacas* of Periodical Literature, where no leading mind, I fancy, looks, if he can help it" (*Letters* 8:136). Issued from such an organ, it is no wonder that the book should seem, as Hartman says, "excrementitious." In fact some of the contemporary critics who found Carlyle's style "transgressive" were of the opinion that his excesses were a result of competing to be heard in the "angry noisy Forum" of popular journalism. Herman Merivale in the *Edinburgh Review*, for example, attributed Carlyle's "barbarian eloquence" to his having "served his apprenticeship, and acquired his peculiarities, in the school of journal and essay writing,"[19] and William Sewell, in the *Quarterly Review*, blamed his "affectations" on the same source:

His Essays have been originally, for the most part, drawn up for our periodical publications; and we need not say how much of this literature is written solely to amuse, and to amuse the most worthless class of readers—those who are incapable of regular study, and can or will read nothing but what is trifling and short, and intelligible at first sight. But to please a reader a writer must write as his readers feel; and such readers are beginning to be wearied with the monotonous mechanism of an easy style, and require something to startle and perplex, and to interest their reason with strange combinations and abrupt transitions.[20]

It is notable that these writers, describing their own forum and readership, speak of it with almost as much contempt as does Carlyle, but like Carlyle they are sufficiently ambivalent to go on writing as if for a worthy and intelligent audience.[21]

Carlyle's self-conscious ambivalence about his status as a "man of letters" is evident in his publications, which frequently allude to the state of modern literature. In "Signs of the Times," for example, he describes the burgeoning of periodical literature as symptomatic of a "mechanical age" in which individual genius is drowned out by the machinery of opinion-making:

Mark, too, how every machine must have its moving power, in some of the great currents of society; every little sect among us, Unitarians, Utilitarians, Anabaptists, Phrenologists, must have its Periodical, its monthly or quarterly Magazine. . . .

With individuals, in like manner, natural strength avails little. No individual now hopes to accomplish the poorest enterprise single-handed and without mechanical aids; he must make interest with some existing corporation, and till his field with their oxen. (*Works* 27:61)

The romantic, inspired genius cannot make himself heard except as the mouthpiece of some ideological "machine," with the result, as Carlyle notes in the same essay, that the largest "machines," the newspapers, exercise the authority that ought properly to belong to "the higher regions of literature":

The true Church of England, at this moment, lies in the Editors of its Newspapers. These preach to the people daily, weekly; admonishing kings themselves; advising peace or war, with an authority which only the first Reformers, and a long-past class of Popes, were possessed of. . . . It may be said too, that in private disposition the new Preachers somewhat resemble the Mendicant Friars of old times: outwardly full of holy zeal; inwardly not without stratagem and hunger for terrestrial things. (*Works* 27:77)

Carlyle's ambivalence should be evident—he plainly distrusts the usurped authority of the mass media, yet he must use the forum it offers if he is to attack mass culture. He can employ a transgressive style, perhaps, to mount what Hartman calls a countercultural attack on mass culture, but he must use the organs of mass culture to do it—and so he cannot get any leverage. The result, as the contemporary comments of Merivale and Sewell indicate, is that he is tarred with his own brush—writing in the journals, he is accused of journalistic vices. His transgression, as Merivale and Sewell see it, is not against the "church" of journalism, but against what Carlyle himself regarded as the true church of the "higher regions of literature."

Nevertheless, it was Carlyle's aim to work within the journalistic forum for a return to what he saw as a healthy state of literature. In "Characteristics" he argues that though "Literature is but a branch of Religion," it is currently suffering "deep-seated, wide-spread maladies" represented by the very establishment of reviewing: "Nay, is not the diseased self-conscious state of Literature disclosed in this one fact, which lies so near us here, the prevalence of Reviewing!" In the age of reviews the writer is no longer inspired by the "realities" of personal experience, but is a mere reviewer of other people's writing—often even a reviewer of reviews—experience, retailed at second or third hand, is reduced to hearsay. Carlyle objects that "your Reviewer is a mere *taster;* who tastes, and says, by the evidence of such palate, such tongue, as he has got, It is good, It is bad" (*Works* 28:24). The passage echoes Wordsworth's contemptuous dismissal of those "who will converse with us gravely about a *taste* for poetry, as they express it, as if it were a thing as indifferent as a taste for rope-dancing, or Frontiniac or sherry,"[22] and it has much the same ideological purport. In both cases the objection is, in the first place, to literary dilettantism, but beyond that, and much more importantly, it is to the whole idea of "taste" as a gentlemanly standard of judgment superior to individual experience and expression. In fact, the nature of Carlyle's "transgression" can only be fully appreciated if it is seen as a conscientious effort to overthrow the gentlemanly standard of good taste by writing in assertively "bad taste." Or, to put the matter less contentiously, it represents his effort to transcend entirely the prevailing class-based standards of taste.

The point can be better understood if we return to Carlyle's statements to Sterling and Mill that he had broken with the "purity and style" of "our whole structure of Johnsonian English" and had "contradicted Blair's Lectures and use-and-wont." Both Johnson and Blair were exponents of a style ultimately based on classical standards—that is, on a knowledge of Latin and Greek, and therefore on a gentleman's education. Johnson, for example, argued that writers ignorant of Latin and Greek "not knowing the original import of words, will use them with colloquial licentiousness, confound distinction, and forget propriety."[23] Similarly, Blair, who was for Carlyle the most prominent of a line of eighteenth-century gentlemen critics to establish and defend universal standards of taste according to polite rules of decorum and propriety, was willing to admit that "inequality of taste among men is. . . . owing in part to nature," but he added that "it is owing to education and culture still more."[24] Furthermore, in attempting to establish a "standard" of "undoubted authority," he fell back on, in effect, the classical education of a gentleman, arguing that the "universal testimony" of "the most improved nations of the earth" has established the "authority which such works [the *Iliad* and the *Aeneid*] have acquired, as standards."[25] But Carlyle, like his romantic predecessors, urged exactly the opposite points. In his praise of the working-class "Corn-Law Rhymer," Ebenezer Elliot, he not only pointedly remarked that "Genius . . . is . . . certainly of no rank," but added that at such times as the present "he that is the least educated will chiefly have to say that he is the least perverted," and he wondered "if in the way of Literature, as Thinker and Writer, it is actually, in these strange days, no special misfortune to be trained up among the Uneducated classes, and not among the Educated; but rather of two misfortunes the smaller?" (*Works* 28:139).

Clearly, then, Carlyle's deliberate "impropriety," must be understood in its historical setting as in itself constituting a political action, a deliberate attempt to "confound distinction," to attack the class structure as it was perpetuated in language by the distinction between taste and "vulgarity." The political context of Carlyle's writing reinforces the point that transgressive writing, almost regardless of its content, could be a form of political activism. As Olivia Smith has demonstrated at length, from the late eighteenth through the early nineteenth centuries the ability to write "correct," or "polite," prose was a clear reflection of social status, and therefore of political power—the clearest gauge of which is that Parliament had the power to reject any petition that it perceived to be written in "vulgar" language. The language of "taste" was the language of power and class distinction: "Refined language demonstrated that one's mind was substantially, almost constitutionally, different from the mass of mankind's. Language revealed how one perceived, which in turn revealed one's worth and social status."[26]

Carlyle's attacks on his contemporary "men of letters" as dilettantes and "dandy wits" is, like the entire chapter on "The Dandiacal Body" in *Sartor,* an attack on the underlying emptiness of class distinctions represented by finery of language as much as by finery of clothes. Language, commonly regarded as the "dress of thought," is as likely as clothing to be a sham, a screen hiding an underlying nakedness. In fact, Smith's survey of eighteenth-century language theories indicates that the prevailing standard of taste was explicitly *opposed* to language that attempted to communicate individual experience directly—a theorist such as Monboddo was representative in arguing that "Those who do not have the benefit of the artificial language [the language of the classically educated] are extremely inferior to those who do. Incapable of expressing anything other than needs and opinions, the vulgar language is 'degraded and debased by its necessary connextion with flesh and blood.'" And for Blair and others, "certain types of language: 'mere native English' or 'our northern dialect' are opposed to civilization."[27] But Carlyle insisted on the connection of his style with flesh and blood—the clothes philosopher somewhat inconsistently repudiated the idea that his style was the dress of thought: "These poor people seem to think a style can be put off or put on not like a *skin* but like a coat!" Such a skin is "the product and close kinsfellow of all that lies under it; exact type of the nature of the beast: *not* to be plucked off without flaying and death" (*Letters* 9:228).

In this historical context the "barbarian eloquence" of Carlyle's transgressive language must be understood as an attack on the entire class-based concept of civilization itself. In fact, his defense of the "lawless, untutored, as it were half-savage force" of Richter's writing is in just these terms: it defies artifice with "a natural, unarmed, Orson-like strength" that reveals the normally hidden essences of things, that "in almost monstrous fashion, yet with piercing clearness, lays bare the inmost heart and core of [the subject] to all eyes." Carlyle seems to be describing his own style as he praises the "wild vehemence" that is like "the fierce bellowing of lions amid savage forests" (*Works* 27:142). Perhaps even more significantly, he is anticipating the language he would later use to describe the uncontrollable revolutionary masses in his *The French Revolution: A History.* He did, indeed, describe the style of *The French Revolution* in similarly Jacobinical terms: "the Book is one of the *savagest* written for several centuries: it is a Book written by a *wild man,* a man disunited from the fellowship of the world he lives in; looking King and beggar in the face with an indifference of brotherhood, an indifference of contempt,—that is really very extraordinary in a Respectable country" (*Letters* 9:145). In turning from the conventional dress of "Conventionalities and Quackeries," Carlyle's style resulted in a thoroughly sansculottic book: "Such a Book is *awful:* it is itself like a kind of French Revolution,—in its way!" (*Letters* 9:184).

Carlyle is at times explicit about the nature of his attack on the distinctions of class maintained in polite language, as in his second essay on Richter: "On the whole, what a wondrous spirit of gentility does animate our British Literature at this era! We have no Men of Letters now, but only Literary Gentlemen" (*Works* 27:130). The effect of the ruling standard of gentlemanly taste, as Carlyle saw it, was that authors had become mere dandies, dressing both their thoughts and their bodies in harmless affectations that can have no political ramifications whatever:

> the literary man, once so dangerous to the quiescence of society, has now become perfectly innoxious, so that a look will quail him, and he can be tied hand and foot by a spinster's thread. Hope there is that henceforth neither Church nor State will be put in jeopardy by Literature. The old literary man, as we have said, stood on his own legs; had a whole heart within him, and might be provoked into many things. But the new literary man, on the other hand, cannot stand at all, save in stays; he must first gird up his weak sides with the whalebone of a certain fashionable, knowing, half-squirarchical air. (*Works* 27:132)

Carlyle, himself obliged to publish in the fashionable periodicals, plainly saw his task as one of restoring independence and countercultural force to the man of letters. To this end, in his early writings especially, he took pains to praise particularly those writers who were not born into the advantages of the higher classes—particularly Richter, Burns, and Johnson. In his very first major publication, *The Life of Friedrich Schiller* (1826), he pointedly and quite unnecessarily digressed for several pages to praise the impoverished man of letters "whose rank and worldly comforts depend upon [literature as a trade], who does not live to write, but writes to live." But it is among these writers, speaking the natural language of their souls, that "are to be found the brightest specimens and the chief benefactors of mankind!" (*Works* 25:42–43).

Carlyle is a kind of literary sansculottist, evolving a romantic formulation of the *true* man of letters as revolutionary prophet arising from the lower orders to restore true order. Teufelsdröckh, in many ways a prototype of the new order of seer, is described as the precise opposite of the literary dandies that Carlyle satirized in the essay on Richter and in "The Dandiacal Body": "Of good society Teufelsdröckh appears to have seen little, or has mostly forgotten what he saw. He speaks-out with a strange plainness; calls many things by their mere dictionary names" (*SR* 29). And clearly Carlyle, who often referred to his home in Ecclefechan as "Patmos," had himself in mind when he characterized Teufelsdröckh as "our wild Seer, shaggy, unkempt, like a Baptist living on locusts and wild honey" (*SR* 30). In fact, Carlyle's many defenses of impoverished men of letters, and their affinities to his descriptions of his own problems in the "trade" of literature clearly indicate that he was gradually evolving a myth of the authoritative prophet that would justify his own assumption of an authoritative, prophetic stance.

§

Authority Restored: The Church of Literature

As I have suggested, however, Carlyle was unable to speak with authority in his early works both because he was still torn between competing ideologies and because he had no forum in which to speak with complete independence. Even Teufelsdröckh, spokesman for the German or romantic element of Carlyle's mind, is ironically judged by the somewhat skeptical editor, and his transgressive style is brought into serious question: "Still the question returns on us: How could a man occasionally of keen insight, not without keen sense of propriety, who had real Thoughts to communicate, resolve to emit them in a shape bordering so closely on the absurd?" (*SR* 293). The question is evidently a genuine one, not to be dismissed as merely symptomatic of the editor's insular notions of propriety, for Carlyle's defenses of his own style to Emerson, Sterling, Mill, and others were always half apologetic. To Mill he simply said that he "could not help it"; to Emerson he prefaced his defense with an explanation: "You say well that I take up that attitude because I have no known public, and am *alone* under the Heavens, speaking into friendly or unfriendly Space; add only that I will not defend such attitude, that I call it questionable, tentative, and only the best that I in these mad times could conveniently hit upon" (*Letters* 7:265). His later comment to Sterling, however, combines apology with a rather greater degree of self-assertion: "If one has thoughts not hitherto uttered in English Books, I see nothing for it but that you must use words not found there, must *make* words,— with moderation and discretion, of course. That I have not always done it *so*, proves only that I was not strong enough; an accusation to which I for one will never plead not guilty" (*Letters* 8:134–35).

The change in tone, the increase in assertiveness, came, I believe, as a result of Carlyle's gradual reification of romantic premises in the early to mid 1830s. During the time he was writing the reviews of various writers, "Signs of the Times," "Characteristics," and *Sartor*, Carlyle was convinced that the ideological conflicts of his age of transition and the condition of the literary "trade" made absolutely authoritative writing impossible—hence the many snide comments about the usurpation of the true church of literature by the partisan and contentious organs of the mass media. As he had Teufelsdröckh say in *Sartor*, the present age of the world is one characterized by a "Church that struggles to preach and prophesy, but cannot as yet, till its Pentecost come" (*SR* 215). The frequent characterizations of Teufelsdröckh's prophetic utterances as either insane or inspired betray a genuine uncertainty about the possibility of seeing and expressing authoritative truths. After all, when he wrote the passage referring to a hoped-for Pentecost Carlyle cannot but have had in mind the fate of his much admired friend and mentor Edward Irving, who had deluded himself into believing that Pentecost *had* come to his Presbyterian congregation. Unfortunately, the divine "inspiration," the gift of tongues, revealed Irving to be not inspired at all, but insane: "My poor friend! And yet the punishment was not unjust; that he who believed without inquiry, should now believe against all light, and portentously call upon the world to admire as inspiration what is but a dancing on the verge of bottomless abysses of Madness!" (*Letters* 6:33). If Irving's inspiration was not genuine, how could Carlyle be sure that his own was? Irving, plainly, had not tempered his enthusiasm with a clear Scottish skepticism.

Nevertheless, Carlyle never doubted that the true church of literature could be restored, and as he began to harden his romantic speculations about the authority of experience and inspiration, he became more assertive about the authoritative power of the "man of letters" as prophet and priest. Even in his early works he clearly viewed romantic iconoclasm as a necessary evil, a historical phase that must eventually give way to a genuinely inspired, authoritative, affirmative mode of utterance. Soon, hopes Teufelsdröckh, will come the possibility of a new kind of "Poet and inspired Maker; who, Prometheus-like, can shape new Symbols, and bring new Fire from Heaven," but unfortunately, "Meanwhile, as the average of matters goes, we account him Legislator and wise who can so much as tell when a Symbol has grown old, and gently remove it" (*SR* 225). Indeed, like Arnold after him, Carlyle saw the death of Christianity as creating a need for a new sacred authority, a need that only literature could fill. He wrote in 1833 that "The history of Literature, especially for the last two centuries, is our proper Church History; the other church, during that time, having more and more decayed from its old functions and influence" (*Works* 28:202). As early as 1831 Carlyle was looking to a future in which the inspired author would restore spiritual values to society. He wrote to Goethe that "Literature is now nearly all in all to us; not our Speech only, but our Worship and Law-giving; our best Priest must henceforth be our Poet; the *vates* [prophet] will in the future be practically all that he ever was in theory" (*Letters* 5:220).

Carlyle was referring to his recent comments in the *Edinburgh Review* that "Literature is fast becoming all in all to us; our Church, our Senate, our whole Social Constitution. . . . The true Autocrat and Pope is that man, the real or seeming Wisest of the past age; crowned after death; who finds his Hierarchy of gifted Authors, his clergy of assiduous Journalists; whose Decretals, written not on parchment but on the living souls of men, it were an inversion of the living laws of Nature to *dis*obey" (*Works* 27:369–70). As becomes very clear in the 1832 "Death of Goethe," the age's "Pope" in this sense was Goethe, and his authority was based on a "German Ideology" in which the ideal precedes the material rather than vice versa:

> The Thought is parent of the Deed, nay is the living soul of it, the last and continual, as well as first mover of it; is the foundation and beginning and essence, therefore, of man's whole existence here be-

low. In this sense, it has been said, the Word of man (the uttered Thought of man) is still a magic formula, whereby he rules the world. . . . The true Sovereign of the world, who moulds the world like soft wax . . . is he who lovingly *sees* into the world; the "inspired Thinker," whom in these days we name Poet. (*Works* 27:377)

Significantly, when Carlyle wrote of the absolute authority of literature, he took for granted the romantic idea of the visionary seer translating his experience of "the Divine idea of the World" into the sacred Word: "The true Poet is ever, as of old, the Seer; whose eye has been gifted to discern the godlike Mystery of God's Universe, and decipher some new lines of its celestial writing" (*Works* 27:377). Nevertheless, these comments made in the early 1830s seem to enunciate a belief in past glories and a hope for the future, not a conviction of faith in the present state of literature. As we have seen, Carlyle at this time had little but contempt for his contemporary men of letters, and he certainly did not see current journalists as even subalterns in a true spiritual hierarchy.

By the mid 1830s, however, Carlyle had determined that if he were to help establish an authoritative "church of literature," he must escape from the "angry noisy Forum" of the reviews, escape from the sullied marketplace of journalism, and establish himself in the higher ecclesiastical rank of author. He wrote to Emerson that

my view is that now at last we have lived to see all manner of Poetics and Rhetorics and Sermonics, and one may say generally all manner of *Pulpits* for addressing mankind from, as good as broken and abolished: alas yes; if you have any earnest meaning, which demands to be not only listened to, but *believed* and *done,* you cannot (at least I cannot) utter it *there,* but the sound sticks in my throat, as when a Solemnity were *felt* to have become a Mummery; and so one leaves the pasteboard coulisses, and three Unities, and Blair[']s Lectures, quite behind; and feels only that there is *nothing sacred,* then, but the *Speech of Man* to believing Men! *This,* come what will, was, is and forever must be *sacred;* and will one day doubtless anew environ itself with fit Modes, with Solemnities, that are *not* Mummeries. (*Letters* 7:265)[28]

Writing for the reviews, he was obliged to speak from a false pulpit; writing in conventional style, he was obliged to speak false conventionalities. To establish the new church of literature, he must abandon the false church and the false language. As an independent author, he could take upon himself the role of the seer, penetrating to and expressing the great hidden "realities" and "veracities" of the

universe. In 1833 he took upon himself the high role of epic poet—
poet at least in his own sense of inspired seer—and set about prepar-
ing his history of the French Revolution. The extraordinary extent
of Carlyle's ambition is evident in his famous remarks to Mill:

> *Understand* me all those sectionary tumults, convention-harangues,
> guillotine holocausts, Brunswick discomfitures; exhaust me the
> meaning of it! You *cannot;* for it is a flaming *Reality;* the depths of
> Eternity look thro' the *chinks* of that so *convulsed* section of Time;—as
> thro *all* sections of Time, only to dull eyes not so visibly. To me, it often
> seems, as if the right *History* (that impossible thing I mean by History)
> of the French Revolution were the grand Poem of our Time; as if the
> man who *could* write the *truth* of that, were worth all other writers and
> singers. If I were spared alive myself, and had means, why might not I
> too prepare the way for such a thing? (*Letters* 6:446)

Carlyle's adoption of the role of historian is often cited as a "pivotal"
point in the transition from romantic transcendentalism to Victorian historicity, a key shift from faith in the authority of the
imagination to faith in the authority of facts.[29] Carlyle's own description of his undertaking, however, clearly indicates a continued loy-
alty to the romantic ideal of the author as visionary seer, and indicates, moreover, his willingness to adopt this role. But from the time
he adopts the prophetic role, he will no longer indulge in questioning it. His history will seek facts, but the most important facts for
Carlyle are not merely records of events, about which he can be
remarkably casual, but eternal facts fetched by the visionary imagination from behind the veil. Furthermore, Carlyle's turn to history
did not make his style more discreet, in an attempt at "neutral" or
"disinterested" reporting, but made it still more impure or transgressive. Indeed, it was only after Carlyle had fully taken up the role
of epic bard, when he was nearly finished with the *History,* that he
could unapologetically account for his style: "The common English
mode of writing has to do with what I call *hearsays* of things; and the
great business for me, in which alone I feel any comfort, is recording
the *presence,* bodily concrete coloured presence of things;—for
which the Nominative-and-verb, as I find it Here and Now, refuses
to stand me in due stead" (*Letters* 9:15). For my purposes, the important point here is that authority for Carlyle is not situated in history
at all, but in the author who sees beyond ideologies or hearsays into
actualities, and expresses those actualities with all the immediacy of

lived experience. Clearly authority is achieved only by taking for
granted the romantic notions that one can transcend "hearsay" in
unmediated experience and that language can communicate that
immediacy as present experience. That is, authority is based on two
premises that are no longer tenable.

Paradoxically, then, Carlyle stopped questioning and simply accepted the postulates of his romantic ideology by turning his attention away from transcendental epistemology and towards history.
From this point on, authority was no longer problematic for him.
Once he has reified romantic premises into a body of authoritarian
doctrine, he overcomes ideological struggle by simply asserting that
his ideology is, not theory, but fact. The word *fact* actually becomes,
strangely enough, more omnipresent in Carlyle's language than in
the Utilitarian Mr. Gradgrind's. In the opening pages of *Past and
Present,* for example, Carlyle contrasts romantic intuition of "the
eternal inner Facts of the Universe" and "Nature's right truth" with
what amounts to the limited ideologies of "foolish men" who "mistake transitory semblance for eternal fact, and go astray more and
more" (*PP* 14). It would be altogether too easy to compile quotations
from the later works showing the absurdity of Carlyle's equation of
doctrinaire opinion with eternal fact, but my purpose here is simply
to note how he reifies the romantic exaltation of imaginative insight
into transcendent truth to establish the ideal of the *real* (as opposed
to *sham*) man of letters as the ultimate priestly authority. And it is
worthwhile to note in passing that this seems an almost inevitable
step from Shelley's radical tribute to poets as the unacknowledged
legislators of the world, since Carlyle insists in "The Hero as Man of
Letters" that no *real* power can remain indefinitely unacknowledged.

In fact, it is in the 1840 lecture on "The Hero as Man of Letters"
that Carlyle's ideas of authority and their emergence from the "German Ideology" appear most clearly. He began the lecture with an
aphoristic affirmation of his romantic creed: "it is the spiritual always that determines the material" (*HHW* 155). Notably, this is a
precise statement of the "German Ideology" as described by Marx,
who argued that "the Germans move in the realm of the 'pure spirit,'
and make religious illusion the driving force of history."[30] But er-
roneous or not, it is precisely this notion that enables Carlyle to affirm that the true modern hero, supplanting the hero-gods, proph-

ets, poets, priests of earlier times, is the man of letters who, like all heroes, "lives in the inward sphere of things, in the True, Divine, and Eternal, which exists always, unseen to most" (*HHW* 155). The man of letters, a Shelleyan hierophant of the unseen, is a "Priest, continually unfolding the Godlike to men: Men of Letters are a perpetual Priesthood, from age to age"; the "true Literary Man" is "the light of the world; the world's Priest;—guiding it, like a Pillar of Fire, in its dark pilgrimage through the waste of Time" (*HHW* 157). This is Coleridge's "clerisy" with a vengeance, and its authority is not only spiritual but political: the inspired man of letters "becomes a power, a branch of government, with inalienable weight in law-making, in all acts of authority" (*HHW* 164). Clearly this is wishful thinking, but it makes manifest, in a garishly clear light, the authoritarian impulse behind the reification of romantic inspiration or insight. It begins to suggest what Kenneth Burke had in mind when he cynically commented on the possibly self-serving motives of literary mystics.

At this point it is worthwhile to return to the notion of transgression in writing—and to wonder how Carlyle's subversive, countercultural attack on taste, propriety, culture, and order came to end in affirmations about the writer as priest, and the literary establishment as church. Carlyle, strangely, has come to conclusions resembling those that Matthew Arnold would later arrive at by a very different route, even though Arnold was to begin by defending just the principles of taste and decorum that Carlyle had attacked. Not surprisingly, since both men were working within some of the same ideological assumptions, they were blind to similar tendencies in one another's thought—Arnold saw Carlyle as a "moral desperado,"[31] a fact that would have appalled Carlyle, who in 1832 had cried "woe to the land where, in these seasons, no prophet arises; but only censors, satirists and embittered desperadoes" (*Works* 27:435). And of course the distinction between prophet and desperado is made simply by granting or refusing to grant authoritative status to the writer's "vision" and language. For Arnold, Carlyle's language was indeed transgressive, because Carlyle had refused to take the role of disinterested social critic, had fatally mixed in the political fray, and had polluted his language. Arnold was later to wonder "Where shall we find language innocent enough, how shall we make the spotless purity of our intentions evident enough" to criticize Philistine society, and more particularly, how is Carlyle to do so "after his furious raid into this field [of political practice] with his *Latter-day Pamphlets?*"[32] Yet Carlyle differed from Arnold only in emphasis—both ultimately desired to retain a social hierarchy in which the best and wisest would rule over others, and in which a priestly language would be the mark of authority. Only in Carlyle's case the dialect of the priestly language would be very much changed—the established authority of decorous language would be overthrown and replaced.

The important point is that both writers, working towards an idea of language that would actually have authority, would actually be able to legislate over society, were conscientiously making their language *different* from conventional usage—Arnold striving for an uncommon purity, Carlyle for an uncommon impurity. They were both, as the Russian formalists say, "making it strange." They were, in other words, placing their writings within a context of "literature" that did, perhaps, achieve an ideological hegemony, an authority, as a counterculture. But this counterculture is hardly revolutionary, or subversive, or even genuinely transgressive—it is, in fact, the all but universally respected and, in practical terms, ignored high culture.

Both Carlyle and Arnold spoke authoritatively from within the most highly respected journals of the established culture, and their very acceptance suggests that neither was perceived as a genuine threat within the literary subculture. Ironically, Carlyle, like Arnold, helped to maintain a literary elitism that continues to separate high culture from popular culture—his disparagement of popular journalism, his hierarchy of authors as priests and journalists as, at best, altar boys, contributed to the separation of literature from the life of society.[33] One explanation for this, I think, is that Carlyle's language so ostentatiously calls attention to itself because he had virtually no social program to offer—only transgressive language itself, a form of literature that gives the *impression* of active intervention in society, but offers no actual program for action. Ironically, Carlyle's attempt to get beyond the "shows of the world" (*Works* 5:156), the outward garments or forms, ends in a kind of parodic formalism.

The problems inherent in Carlyle's attempts to form an activist ideology from a reified romanticism are in several ways laid bare in Joseph Mazzini's perceptive review of *The French Revolution* in the *Monthly Chronicle* (January 1840). Mazzini, an Italian freedom fighter and genuine political activist, saw that the universal approbation of the work by critics of all parties and factions indicated, not that Carlyle had succeeded in transcending limited ideological perspectives, but only that he had not posed a threat to any particular political position. The universal approval was only "a proof that the work was deemed harmless, and that men might applaud it without being thence led on to serious concessions."[34] The problem, as Mazzini saw it, was that Carlyle had no conscious "conception of humanity" to guide and inform his narrative of events, that he therefore neglected "eternal TRUTH to crawl along in . . . transitory and incomplete *reality*."[35] Certainly Carlyle did not see it this way, and would have claimed that he was forgoing transitory and incomplete *truths*—that is, formulas and shams—for eternal *reality*. But however the words are juggled, Mazzini's point is valid, and would be acceptable even to Carlyle if taken to mean that he relied upon the truth and authority of "lived experience" in preference to formulations or creeds. Mazzini recognized and praised Carlyle's extraordinary ability to represent what seemed like unmediated experience, but he praised Carlyle only as an artist, not as an authority, and certainly not as an active agent of political change. The work, he says, was

> written under the inspiration of a fancy the most vivid, and eminently poetical; excited, as we feel on the instant, by a glance at the documents of the revolutionary period. The writer—the poet, may we say—entirely passive, spell-bound, and absorbed, has mirrored on his pages the visions that haunted his brain exactly as they presented themselves, without judging, without reflecting, without even daring to look back, all terror-struck as he was. And before our eyes, as before his, in the midst of "un aria senza tempo tinto," a kind of phantasmagorial vortex, capable of giving the strongest heads a dizziness, pass in speedy flight the defunct heroes of the poem.[36]

The problem is that such a work of art does not satisfy the demand made on the historian, or even of the highest kind of artist, to interpret events, to teach and lead humanity. Carlyle's rejection of any interpretive framework sacrifices the "sacred mission" of the historian and

> gives way to the brilliant but ephemeral vocation of the *artist*—of the artist, we say, not as we understand him, the priest after his order, of the universal life, and the prophet of a great social end, but such as he is understood at the present day, the offspring and the parent of fugitive impressions, the idolator of forms and images, the repro-

ducer of transitory realities, meaningless and soul-less, brought up from the land of shades by the galvanism of imagination.[37]

A nonpartisan art, an art without overt ideological purposes, an art that lives up to the romantic polemic to be nonpolemical, ends for the political activists in sterile formalism. The ultimate aim of an art that attempts to transfer the sense of unmediated experience is, Mazzini's critique implies, aestheticism.

But though Mazzini was unable to see that the representation of literature as "immediate living experience" was in itself an "extraordinary ideological feat," he did see very clearly that every author necessarily speaks from a definite ideological perspective, even though, like Carlyle, he may vigorously deny it: "when he happens to cry out against the mania of systems, you may be sure that he is talking of systems that are not his own, for one he has, and that he obeys; were it not so, he would be no man."[38] Every author must see things from some preconceived point of view, or he will be able to make no sense of them; every author, that is to say, must have "a theory, a system, a formula, as men choose to term it. They may, indeed, regret the name, but all have the *thing*."[39] Carlyle's "formula," though seemingly at odds with his immersion in unmediated experience, is a transcendentalism that ends in fatalism—in Carlyle's "disposition to crush man by contrasting him with the Infinite." And the fatalism, in turn, leads to quietism by showing the vanity of human action.[40] Mazzini's analysis suggests, finally, that the emphasis on experience is not at all incompatible with the transcendental ideology—rather, it is the last resort of the author who wants to talk about *truth*, but can only talk about *reality*.

Mazzini's comments help us better to see that the tendency (though assuredly not the intention) of Carlyle's reliance on experience is, surprisingly enough, to situate his writing within a romantic ideology reaching from the early radicalism of Wordsworth and Coleridge to the apolitical aestheticism of the later Victorian period. As the interpretation of experience becomes more and more problematic, experience itself becomes more and more important, until finally, in a writer like Pater, the representation of experience becomes the final goal of art: "Not the fruit of experience, but experience itself, is the end." From this perspective, the "curious echo" of Carlyle's thought that Richard Stein has found in the "unlikely text" of Pater is not all that curious or surprising.[41] Despite the manifest differences between the two writers, Carlyle's ultimate quietism has, in the final analysis, an effect very like Pater's withdrawal of art into the realm of private experience—its tendencies are to transform experience into art, to render the artist absolutely authoritative in his own realm (that is, over his own experience), and finally to withdraw art from social purposiveness into its own self-enclosed world.

Carlyle himself was evidently aware of this tendency, for in his writing after *The French Revolution* he constantly emphasized the need to interpret experience. A central motif of his major historical works, *Oliver Cromwell's Letters and Speeches* and *The History of Friedrich II of Prussia,* is the plight of the editor-scholar-historian—Carlyle himself—not only to bring the old bones of the past back to life as present experience on his pages but to sift the mass of past experience for its meaning. Furthermore, of course, his late writings present his prophetic insights into reality in as programmatically ideological a form as even Mazzini could have wished. Certainly no advocate of art for art's sake, Carlyle authoritatively dictated policy to the nation: the works following *The French Revolution* abound in authoritative statements sanctioned by "fact" and "nature," but it is painfully clear that these "formulas" only masquerade as the fruits of the visionary seer's experience. Ironically, Carlyle's attempt to transcend ideological divisiveness ends in a dualistic split in his own writing, which can only offer something aspiring to the chaos of undifferentiated experience, as in *The French Revolution,* or nakedly ideological decrees supported, not by experience itself, but by formulas about experience.

In spite of his chagrin with "Literary Gentlemen" who are no longer "dangerous to the quiescence of society," Carlyle himself remained essentially a very loud political quietist, fatalistically asserting that right would eventually take care of itself. His only real "trangression," in other words, was his unique style, and the very oddness of the style helped to render it "innoxious" as "mere literature." It is, I think, an interesting example of the phenomenon that Frank Lentricchia formulates by conflating the thought of Williams and Foucault: "the refining by literary intellectuals in the late eighteenth century of the concept of 'literary' to mean 'imaginative writing' becomes an inadvertent service on behalf of the coercive and even totalitarian tendencies of modern society—a way of supervising and containing the 'literary' by keeping it enclosed in its own space, a mode of self-policing, as it were."[42] In this way the church of literature fostered by Carlyle, Arnold, and others in their different ways has worked all too well to replace Christianity—society can pay respectful lip service to the works of high culture enshrined in the universities, and go its own way.

Notes

1. See, for example, Janice Haney, "'Shadow Hunting': Romantic Irony, *Sartor Resartus*, and Victorian Romanticism," *Studies in Romanticism* 17 (1978): 313.

2. *The Works of Thomas Carlyle in Thirty Volumes* (New York: Charles Scribner's Sons, 1903), 11:56. Further quotations from this edition will be cited parenthetically in the text as *Works*. However, I have used superior modern editions for some of Carlyle's major works. Quotations from *Sartor Resartus* will be cited as *SR* and are from the edition by Charles Frederick Harrold (New York: Odyssey Press, 1937); those from *Past and Present* will be cited as *PP* and are from the edition by Richard D. Altick (New York: New York University Press, 1977); those from *On Heroes, Hero-Worship and the Heroic in History* will be cited as *HHW* and are from the edition of Carl Niemeyer (Lincoln: University of Nebraska Press, 1966).

3. Robert Langbaum, *The Poetry of Experience: The Dramatic Monologue in Modern Literary Tradition* (1957; rpt., New York: W. W. Norton, 1963), p. 20.

4. This point has been made by Gerry H. Brookes: "experience is an organic process that continues, while the certainty Carlyle desires is stable. In *The Poetry of Experience* Robert Langbaum remarks that Carlyle, like Goethe, forgets that experience which gives authority to ideas cannot be arrested. Yet by arresting it, Carlyle passes consciously beyond the Romantic phase and into a new one" (*The Rhetorical Force of Carlyle's Sartor Resartus* [Berkeley: University of California Press, 1972], pp. 120–21).

5. Haney, "'Shadow Hunting,'" p. 329.

6. Raymond Williams, *Marxism and Literature* (Oxford: Oxford University Press, 1977), p. 46.

7. *The Collected Letters of Thomas and Jane Welsh Carlyle*, 15 vols. (to date) (Durham, N.C.: Duke University Press, 1970–   ), 5:136. Subsequent quotations from the letters will be to this edition and will be cited parenthetically in the text as *Letters*. See also his comment that the "French System of Thought" is "called also the Scotch, and still familiar enough everywhere, which for want of a better title we have named the Mechanical" (*Works* 28:231).

8. J. Reay Greene, ed., *Lectures on the History of Literature, delivered by Thomas Carlyle, April to July 1838* (New York: Scribners, 1892), p. 214.

9. Philip Rosenberg, *The Seventh Hero: Thomas Carlyle and the Theory of Radical Activism* (Cambridge: Harvard University Press, 1974), pp. 54, 22, 43.

10. Thomas Carlyle, *Two Note Books*, ed. Charles Eliot Norton (New York: The Grolier Club, 1898), p. 54.

11. Kenneth Burke, *A Rhetoric of Motives* (Berkeley: University of California Press, 1969), p. 123.

12. These quotations are all from reviews reprinted in Jules Paul Seigel, ed.,

The Church of Literature and Carlyle

Thomas Carlyle: The Critical Heritage (New York: Barnes and Noble, 1971), pp. 37, 147, 47, 77.

13. Geoffrey Hartman, *Criticism in the Wilderness: The Study of Literature Today* (New Haven: Yale University Press, 1980), pp. 133, 134–37.

14. John Sterling in Seigel, ed., *Thomas Carlyle*, p. 135.

15. Michel Foucault in *Language, Counter-Memory, Practice: Selected Essays and Interviews*, trans. Donald F. Bouchard and Sherry Simon (Ithaca, N.Y.: Cornell University Press, 1977), p. 35.

16. Ibid., pp. 37, 39–42.

17. Terry Eagleton, *Criticism and Ideology: A Study in Marxist Literary Theory* (Atlantic Highlands, N.J.: Humanities Press, 1976), p. 43.

18. Carlyle's lamentations are not merely the whining of a rejected author—his sense that journals and reviews had driven independently authored books out of the marketplace is confirmed by historical scrutiny. As Lee Erickson has shown, for reasons largely related to changes in the manufacturing processes of books and paper, the first decades of the nineteenth century saw publishers become increasingly hesitant to commit themselves to idiosyncratic books (particularly books of poetry), and at the same time there was a tremendous increase in the number of journals and periodicals devoting themselves to reviewing. See Erickson, "The Poet's Corner: The Impact of Technological Changes in Printing on English Poetry, 1800–1850" in *ELH: A Journal of English Literary History* 52 (1985): 893–911. Patrick Parrinder, who notes that "the number of periodicals carrying regular reviews doubled between 1800 and 1810, and reached a peak of at least thirty-one in the early 1820s," rightly points out that "This explosion of literary reviewing must be considered a phenomenon in its own right" (p. 55). The glut of reviewing in precisely the years in which Carlyle began his literary career had, in itself, a powerful influence on inherited romantic ideas about the nature and sources of literary authority. The large audience reached by the reviews and the inherent respect commanded by their prestige tended to elevate the authority of reviewers above that of poets or philosophers. (See Parrinder, *Authors and Authority: A Study of English Literary Criticism and Its Relation to Culture* [Boston: Routledge and Kegan Paul, 1977].)

19. Herman Merivale, quoted in Seigel, ed., *Thomas Carlyle*, p. 77.

20. William Sewell, quoted ibid., p. 147.

21. For discussion of the influence of the periodical context on Carlyle's writings, see Brookes, *The Rhetorical Form*, pp. 21–22, and Ed Block, Jr., "Carlyle, Lockhart, and the Germanic Connection: The Periodical Context of Carlyle's Early Criticism," *Victorian Periodicals Review* 16 (1983): 20–27.

22. William Wordsworth and Samuel Taylor Coleridge, *Lyrical Ballads*, ed. R. L. Brent and A. R. Jones (London: Methuen and Company, 1963), p. 251.

23. Samuel Johnson, quoted in Olivia Smith, *The Politics of Language, 1791–1819* (Oxford: Oxford University Press, 1984), p. 13.

24. Hugh Blair, *Lectures on Rhetoric and Belles Lettres* (Philadelphia: T. Ellwood Zell, 1862), p. 18.

25. Ibid., pp. 23, 26.

26. Smith, *The Politics of Language*, p. 21.

27. Monboddo and Blair, quoted ibid., pp. 24, 29.

28. Even the emphasis on *speech* rather than writing indicates the nature and extent of Carlyle's transgression. He was determined to put the connection with flesh and blood, with lived experience, into his writing and so used the metaphor that would put the living, breathing voice on the page. But again, as Smith has shown,

even this romantic metaphor (which Carlyle probably adopted uncritically and unre-flectively as a simple statement) transgresses against genteel standards of propriety, since many of the rules of correct writing were formulated in the eighteenth century precisely to differentiate the correct *writing* of gentlemen from the vulgar *speech* of the uneducated.

29. See, for example, John D. Rosenberg, *Carlyle and the Burden of History* (Oxford: Oxford University Press, 1985), p. 39; Haney, "'Shadow Hunting,'" p. 333; and Albert LaValley, *Carlyle and the Idea of the Modern* (New Haven: Yale University Press, 1968), pp. 188–89.

30. Karl Marx and Frederick Engels, *The German Ideology,* ed. R. Pascal (New York: International Publishers, 1947), p. 30.

31. *The Letters of Matthew Arnold to Arthur Hugh Clough,* ed. Howard Foster Lowry (London: Oxford University Press, 1932), p. 111.

32. Arnold, "The Function of Criticism at the Present Time," in *The Complete Prose Works of Matthew Arnold,* ed. R. H. Super, 11 vols. (Ann Arbor: University of Michigan Press, 1960–77), 3:275.

33. Publication in prestigious periodicals is so closely associated with "prophetic literature" that George Landow has recently suggested that publication in "intellectual periodicals," as opposed to "journalism," is a defining characteristic of "prophetic writing" as a genre (*Elegant Jeremiahs: The Sage from Carlyle to Mailer* [Ithaca, N.Y.: Cornell University Press, 1986], pp. 20–21). The association of journalism with the lower classes in Victorian thought is commonplace—perhaps nowhere more clearly than in Arnold's characterization of such organs as the *Daily Telegraph.* Possibly the most forceful caricature of the vulgarity of journalism and journalists in Victorian fiction is Trollope's characterization of Quintus Slide, editor of *The People's Banner* in the Palliser novels.

34. Joseph Mazzini, "*The French Revolution: A History* by Thomas Carlyle," *Monthly Chronicle* 5 (January 1840): 71.

35. Ibid., pp. 82–83.

36. Ibid., p. 74.

37. Ibid., p. 72.

38. Ibid., pp. 76–77.

39. Ibid., p. 77.

40. Ibid., pp. 83, 78.

41. Richard Stein, "Midas and the Bell-Jar: Carlyle's Poetics of History," *Victorian Newsletter* 58 (1980): 9.

42. Frank Lentricchia, *Criticism and Social Change* (Chicago: University of Chicago Press, 1984), p. 54.

Herbert F. Tucker

Vocation and Equivocation
The Dialogue of Genres in Tennyson's "The Two Voices"

§

*A*lfred Tennyson's failure to publish anything of note between 1832 and 1842 constitutes one of the deafening silences of Victorian literary history. The career that eventually redeemed this apparent case of writer's block was, by any standard, a phenomenal success. From 1842 on, Tennyson's voice rang out so loud and clear that it is natural for his latter-day audience—assisted recently by scholarly amplification of a wealth of surviving manuscripts—to find the interval between his *Poems* of 1832 and of 1842 humming with imminent triumph. The chorus of attention that greeted his new work in the 1840s, and that swelled into laureate worship with the 1850s, was beyond question music to the poet's ears. Yet the critic should remember that during the 1830s Tennyson's fame was at most an unheard melody, a sound he had to imagine and fashion privately before it could be realized in public. The fact that he issued no book during the years that might be accounted a romantic poet's prime does not mean that his consciousness of the public arena for poetry had faded. On the contrary: one likely factor retarding his conversion of a set of extraordinary texts from manuscript into print was the very ambition with which he imagined his own publicity. Celebrity and canonical status like Tennyson's do not occur without premeditation; the vocation this poet projectively shaped for himself reflects an unflagging invocation to the good pleasure of the public. Courting fame in both its contemporary and its perennial aspects, during the ten years' silence between his mid-twenties and mid-thirties he undertook to become a popular poet without ceasing to be a poet who would endure.[1]

Like the bitterly disappointed if posthumously applauded Keats—whose poetic works he imitated but whose poetic career he meant to avoid imitating—Tennyson aspired to a poetry that might "be a friend / To soothe the cares and lift the thoughts of man."[2] In pursuit of this aspiration, which Tennyson fulfilled more conspicuously in his lifetime than any English poet has done since, he strove to make his writing *agreeable*. Agreeable to the ear, melodious in its strong rhythmic course, and sweetly chiming in its closes, Tennyson's verse had always been and would always be; but during the 1830s his aspiration to cultural centrality meant more. He had to cultivate those imaginative faculties that, as Keats again had said, are "capable of making all disagreeables evaporate,"[3] that render a vexing subject intellectually or aesthetically agreeable, and that, to this end, embrace a coherence making contraries, not vanish, but match, engage, and in that sense agree. Tennyson became adept in these arts; and for every "ocean-smelling osier" that critical Walter Bagehots have sniffed at in his work, there are a dozen felicities of phrase that can go far, in this debunking century, toward restoring to circumlocution and euphemism their once-good names. Even where the radical divisions underlying a poem make argumentative integrity an impossibility—as happens with any number of the texts we find most interesting today for what they tell us about the poet and his time—Tennyson more often than not managed to give his work a semblance of unity that satisfied his many readers. And if it seems that the poet sometimes held things together through nothing more than the high gloss of an extraordinary linguistic fluency, we should remember that what made all disagreeables evaporate, according to Keats, was the intensity of the art that represented them, and that artful sound meant more in the way of poetic soundness to the rhetorically exuberant century of Keats and Swinburne, De Quincey and Pater, than it means to ours.[4]

In this connection "The Two Voices" looks like an anomaly in Tennyson's oeuvre, one of the few really disagreeable poems (in each sense) that the poet ever wrote. For one thing, it exhausts the ear; and that it does so under even Tennyson's expert management seems a conclusive demonstration that no poem composed of more than a hundred and fifty rhyming tercets in the English language can long please. Now and then, as the "still small voice" clinches its one point one more time, the poetic form successfully bears the imprint of conclusive authority.[5] But a poem can conclude in the same way only so many times before losing its momentum. The prosodic quietus that "The Two Voices" repeatedly imposes seems especially inhospitable to what I take to have been Tennyson's chief purpose in writing the poem: the creation of a sustained poetic dialogue. For the halting formal procession of "The Two Voices" has a marked analogue in the substance of its dialectical argumentation.

Reserving for the moment the important fresh departure made in the last sixty lines, within the dialogue that occupies the first four hundred lines I count four distinct poetic arguments, to which summary will do little disservice. The defense of personal individuality that collapses by line 45 is defeated again in terms of the species, of human history, and thus of fame by line 117. From this second full stop until line 228, there ensues, with little internal motivation, a highly derivative crisis lyric, in which Tennyson's uncharacteristically pointless and diffuse reheating of a batch of romantic leftovers flatly reproduces, at an interpoetic level, the spiritual condition of the poetic "I," who finds consolation for lost youth in the feeble thought that others once enjoyed the supernal bliss he cannot find for himself. Then, for two hundred lines more, the two voices pick a single bone—the Wordsworthian intimation of immortality, but without the self-validating Wordsworthian drive—only to pluck at last from the embers of lukewarm debate a shrill desire for *something* that doth live:

> 'Tis life, whereof our nerves are scant,
> Oh life, not death, for which we pant;
> More life and fuller, that I want.   (ll. 397–99)

Here the poem has died if its speaker has not: the redundant phrasing and lame rhyme make one long again for the crispness of chill despair.[6]

And yet this top-heavy, indiscriminate, nearly clumsy poem has proved indispensable to students of Tennyson's career, who may account for "The Two Voices" in a variety of ways but generally agree that it must be taken into account.[7] So unsteady a text may seem more readily accessible to binary critical arguments about Tennyson's ambivalence or dialectical method than do the greater

contemporaneous poems whose rhetorical procedures it illumi-
nates. Further, its patent discontinuities suggest that, even for the
poet, this work represented more an experimental means than a
finished product: the utilitarian side of romantic craftsmanship is
here exposed to view with unusual clarity. In the following essay I
too propose to *use* the poem: to scan it as a twofold generic experiment that anticipated and indeed enabled the mixing of genres in
Tennyson's greater works of the 1840s and 1850s. I shall therefore
consign the first four hundred lines to the summary treatment
accorded them above, and shall focus instead on what seems to me
more important: on "The Two Voices" as the exploration of a road
ultimately not taken in Tennyson's career, the genre of poetic dialogue; and particularly on the last score of stanzas as a supplemen-
tary, corrective exploration of what would become the royal road of
his creative majority, the dialogue of poetic genres.

§

Nothing in the first hundred stanzas matters so much as their
failure to develop into a poem—which in turn assumes significance
alongside such facts about this text as the history of its composition
and even of its name. Christopher Ricks concludes that by June
1833 Tennyson was showing friends a substantial version of the
poem, probably three hundred lines and more, under the title
"Thoughts of a Suicide" (*Poems* 522). This early title, coming from a
writer so persistently drawn to the imagination of aftermath, carries
a teasing temporal ambiguity, one that recalls Tennyson's rejoinder
to a reviewer's charge that the author of *Maud* should be deemed
guilty of the crimes of his characters: "Fornicator I may be, adulterer
I may be, murderer I may be, suicide I am not yet." Tennyson's quip
is funny precisely because it asserts so incontrovertible a truth, yet it
is a truth that the draft title of his 1833 work in progress had made
problematic. Since the corpse of a suicide has no thoughts to speak
of, "Thoughts of a Suicide" must have presented itself as a kind of
suicide note. But in that case its title should make us wonder at what
point a man contemplating self-destruction comes to think of himself as "a suicide," to regard the deed he is pondering as a foregone
conclusion.[8]

This may look like a quibble over the obvious. But it was Tennyson's gift to estrange the obvious and return it with the force of the inevitable, and here as usual his handling of inevitability takes us beyond triviality. The temporal ambiguity built into the title "Thoughts of a Suicide" assumes considerable weight from the persistence with which the voice that counsels despair throughout the early manuscripts draws upon two related modes of Tennysonian inevitability: the appeal to Pascalian infinities of space and time that threaten to engulf the bewildered ego; and the tombstone-chiseling stroke of the tercet epigrams, repeatedly silencing the ego's claim to a place either in the argument or in the world.[9] Tennyson's draft title thus suggests the dark side of the romantic mind that becomes what it beholds and creates in its own wreck the thing it contemplates. His speaker, once a man, has become instead "a suicide," a gray shadow of his future deed. He identifies himself with the act that he envisions and that, through the operation of a self-fulfilling prophecy, has since usurped his life.

By 1842 this suggestive title needed changing, because the poem itself had changed. As in "The Palace of Art" ten years before—and with a comparable last-minute wrench—Tennyson had turned the edge of his rigorous sorrow. He had blunted the despair of his draft and converted it, if not to joy, at least to dubiety, rescuing the speaker by a picture of beatific domesticity that has since become notorious, and closing with the open question

> *wherefore rather I made choice*
> *To commune with that barren voice,*
> *Than him who said, "Rejoice! Rejoice!"*　　　　　*(ll. 460–62)*

It is a very ambivalent and anticlimactic sort of rejoicing that gets expressed in this final stanza. The simple past tense of "I made choice" arises just where a true convert would reach for a pluperfect tense that kept the tempter more firmly behind him. Tennyson's uniform choice of past tenses gives to the conclusion an air of diabolical parti pris, which disturbs the speaker's apparent restoration to life with a hint that he remains among the mortal desperadoes without knowing it. At the bottom line, this summary stanza irons the critical moment of conversion out of the poem, which thus ends with another instance of the curiously crushed temporality we have observed in its draft title. Certain notes of victory resound through the final twenty stanzas, to be sure: "The dull and bitter voice was gone" (l. 426), "And Nature's living motion lent / The pulse of hope to discontent" (ll. 449–50). But so, in counterpoint, do certain inveterate notes of "gloomy thought" (l. 459). The poem asks us to believe at the same time that a convert has been saved and that the workings of salvation have left the convert's temperament essentially untouched. Pitting ideogram against grammar, the syntax of the final stanza gives the last word to joy but semantically privileges the poem's unfinished and perhaps interminable business, the dialogue with despair. What has begun in debate and arisen to idyllic affirmation ends, instead, in equivocation.

"The Two Voices" seems one of those works whose end cycles back to its beginning, here for a resumption of fruitless dialogue that is nevertheless dignified by the speaker's explicit *choice*, this time around, "to commune with that barren voice." Bearing this equivocal structure in mind can help us understand why Tennyson called the finished poem neither "Thoughts of a Suicide" nor (to anticipate D. H. Lawrence) "Song of a Man Who Has Come Through" but simply "The Two Voices." William Brashear has suggested that the new title is a trick, accordingly to a divinely comic scenario. Having led the reader to suppose for four hundred lines that the poem represents the interior debate of a Dipsychus, or second-rate modern mind not in unity with itself, Tennyson dissolved that debate across the harmonious sabbatical panorama of lines 403–29 into a nineteenth-century reclamation of the orthodox psychomachia, wherein the traditional Christian voices of comfort and despair are seen at last to have been battling it out, to the predictable discomfiture of the latter. The true antiphon to the "still small voice" is not the speaker's, then, but the "second voice" that enters at line 427 as the speaker's good angel.[10] This ingenious reading is too good to lose altogether, but it also is too good to be wholly true: true to the untricksy sobriety the common reader rightly finds in Tennyson; true to the poem's proportions and its heavy investment in hundreds of lines of ponderous dialogue; or true even to the final movement, where, as we have seen, the orthodox ambush is itself subverted and proves to be a false bottom opening on a compromise choice to take it from the top.

One need not profess deconstruction to find the reference of Tennyson's new title unspecifiable in Brashear's sense and to construe it instead through the very notion of *equivocation,* understood fairly literally as the balancing and mutual measurement of voices in dialogue. Both as a title and as a poem, "The Two Voices" represents a major investment in dialogue; and a brief review of Tennyson's development suggests reasons why dialogue should have seemed to him especially important during the mid-1830s. If we consider how issues of personal relationship, confrontation, and aggression had given a new scope and urgency to the *Poems* of 1832—published the same year Tennyson drafted the bulk of this poem—we can imagine why he should have taken up the genre of poetic dialogue when he did. "Thoughts of a Suicide" constituted the first passage of extended dialogue Tennyson had attempted since his very early play *The Devil and the Lady* (1825?).[11] Along one major line of his subsequent development the poet had turned his hand instead to descriptive or narrative frames for voice. "Mariana" (1830) yearns aloud for dialogue in ways that refrain from it, indeed preclude it; dialogue in *The Lover's Tale* (1832; pub. 1879) is stillborn like everything else in that text; the nineteenth-century Prufrock who speaks "A Dream of Fair Women" (1832) stammers out small talk only to suffer rebukes that bind him repeatedly within his tongue-tied self.

Along this line, then, dialogue had served the poet as a note of character only through its absence or frustration. But he had also written since 1827 a series of soliloquies and dramatic monologues that exhibit a marked development, especially noteworthy in the *Poems* of 1832, away from scattered lamentation and toward direct address. With the increasing particularity of the imagined addressee in these poems had come a mounting demand, clearest in the finale to "Oenone," for the articulate murmur of reply with which dialogue might commence. This demand Tennyson first met in "Thoughts of a Suicide," and the meeting was evidently an exhilarating one. The poet's excitement, which emerges in the fact that he was circulating the new manuscript as early as June 1833, cannot well be explained solely on the strength of the several dozen stanzas that he had by then produced. Rather, the arbitrary topical potpourri of even the earliest versions directs us to the importance of the genre that contained them. Not for the first or last time in Tennyson's career, we encounter, with the circulating drafts of "The Two Voices," a significant form in quest of a plausible content. Dialogue itself constituted an experimental breakthrough for which Tennyson, and perhaps the associates with whom he quickly shared his results, had been waiting for quite some time. J. M. Kemble, at any rate, wrote at once to a friend that Tennyson's new meditations showed "a mighty stride of intellect since the Second-Rate Sensitive Mind" (quoted in *Poems* 522). The essential advance lay in Tennyson's perception that the "damnèd vacillating state" (l. 190) of the 1830 monologue to which Kemble here compared it could prove, for the dialogical poet, a blessing in disguise.

§

It takes two to dialogue. What were the two poles between which Tennyson could so vacillate as to generate his first dialogue in eight years? What *were* the two voices? One answer, highly eligible in the light of Tennyson's perennial thematic concerns, is that this text pits will against fate, the self's irresistible needs against an implacable set of environing conditions. Something like this was the poet's initial answer, I think, as he freshly attempted to write poetic dialogue with "Thoughts of a Suicide." Yet by the time that poem had become "The Two Voices," he had changed his tactics, and indeed had written the change into the revised text. For, as we shall see, "The Two Voices" moves from the philosophical dialectics of abstract debate into what might be called a dialogue between genres: the subjective genre of meditative lyric and the objective genre of descriptive idyll. For evidence that Tennyson found such generic dialogue more satisfactory than the debate of dramatically inflected voices with which he had begun, we have not just this text but the whole of the 1842 *Poems* in which it first appeared, and not just that volume but the vast balance of Tennyson's subsequent production.

One reason for this preference of generic to dramatic dialogue is simply that, for Tennyson's purposes of extending and subtilizing his poetic range, it worked. "The Two Voices" is a better poem than anything we can conjecture "Thoughts of a Suicide" to have been. And it is a better poem because Tennyson's genius was better suited to the manipulation of tonally distinct and formally perfectible poetic kinds—each discrete and complete in itself, yet each susceptible to the euphonic or discrepant resonance the other's proximity could impose—than to the mutual punctuation of rival discourses that makes voice dramatic on the page as on the stage, and that during the decade of Tennyson's silence Browning was first working to such different effect in the interests of character.[12] Tennyson's own character studies are enlightening in this connection. By the mid- 1830s, the work of drafting a major series of classical impersonations from "St. Simeon Stylites" through "Tithonus" had convinced this exceptionally self-critical poet that the central conflict between will and fate was for him *too* central to permit sustained dialogical effects: it required, indeed, the form to which we retrospectively give the apt name *monologue*. Tennyson's conversion of "Thoughts of a Suicide" into "The Two Voices" shows with exemplary explicitness much the same thing as the classical dramatic monologues on which he was concurrently working. When the self squares off against its doom, within the imaginative arena that stages all the best poetry of Tennyson, the self does not stand a chance.

Neither then does dialogue, if by that term we mean colloquy between two contending selves who can hold their interchange together because each self can hold its own (as happens in Tennyson's bourgeois eclogue of 1842, "Walking to the Mail"). The collapse of dialogical equality in this sense is amply borne out in the long first portion of "The Two Voices." When the "I" of the poem argues against self-slaughter by defending the uniqueness of the individual, the still small voice can repeatedly level these defenses from the secure vantage of an impersonal doom, drawing its daunting authority from the fatal infinities beyond selfhood. Such conditions offer Tennyson frequent opportunities to score rhetorical points, but they also disable pointed dialogue as such. Given so stacked a deck, no matter how the arguments are dealt out, the individual self is bound to lose to the doomster that runs the house. Even Tennyson's contemporaries could see as much from "Thoughts of a Suicide." By Kemble's account the voice of the self there "is thoroughly floored" (quoted in *Poems* 522), and many a subsequent reader of the revised "Two Voices" has concurred. This result is unsurprising, given the fact that the voice of despair has cornered a topic, and a cognate mood, for the expression of which Tennyson's thesaurus was so opulently endowed from the beginning of his career.

The poet's turn toward dialogue in "The Two Voices" constitutes a symmetrical reversal of the movement from dramatic exchange to brooding descriptiveness with which his career took its proper start in the composition of *The Devil and the Lady*. If we think of the poet's compositional practice as in part a reconsideration of his own development to date—a practice in which he engaged all the time, but never with more intensity than during the decade before 1842—

then we can imagine him rereading that decisive juvenile piece and finding in its patent generic fault-lines hints for the redirection of his art. These hints would inevitably have been cautionary as well as affirmative: such is the dialectic of continuity and change that makes the self-revision of a poet like Tennyson a career-making act. For a poet thus intent upon his own development, one observation must have been particularly galling: even a cursory comparison of the dialogue in *The Devil and the Lady* with that in "The Two Voices" reveals striking parallels in focus and subject matter. Both texts draw upon comparably slim budgets of deeply introverted or (what is often the same in romantic tradition) metaphysically speculative devices, so that the conversation spins itself out pretty thin pretty quickly. As an aspiring author of dialogue, then, Tennyson found himself in the 1830s much where he had been ten years before. It seems that, when he sought possible topics for dramatic conversation, in his twenties as in his teens introspection brought Tennyson face to face with something singularly abstract; and whether this something gave cause for personal terror or comfort, it must have puzzled his will to break new ground with a move into dialogue.

To judge from the revision of "Thoughts of a Suicide" into "The Two Voices," Tennyson's reaction to this unsettling confrontation with his own shortcomings was to pull up stakes and settle elsewhere. For the revised text regrounds its dialogical project, not in the rarefaction to which the poet's astringent conception of character all too evidently led, but in the more congenially abstract yet still poetically viable terrain of genre. Dissatisfied with his efforts to write dialogue, Tennyson chose instead to put his stanzas of introverted meditation into relationship with more public, symbolic or iconic kinds of poetry that also lay at his command. He struck up a dialogue, as it were, between the disappointing dialogue poem he had been writing and other established effects in his repertoire. For those other effects Tennyson turned, with results for his career that it would be hard to overestimate, to a genre he was concurrently cultivating in the mid-1830s: the domestic idyll. Having generated in "Thoughts of a Suicide" a shadowboxer's poem whose two sparring voices had degenerated into stultifying conclusiveness, Tennyson introduced a new voice, to save the soul, perhaps, but more importantly to save the poem and the mode of imaginative confrontation that the poem represented. "Thoughts of a Suicide" was rescued from the dead letter of abstruser musings when Tennyson made it a poem of two genres, and the resulting antiphony of lyric meditation and descriptive vignette is named with precision in the new title he found for it.

§

From this perspective the new voice that matters is not the angelic murmur we hear in lines 427–41 of the revised text. There is no conversing, after all, with such heavenly toned accents as it breathes—certainly there is none in the poem—and the one approach to dialogue between speaking self and rescuing evangel effectively seals the approach off: " 'What is it thou knowest, sweet voice?' I cried. / 'A hidden hope,' the voice replied" (ll. 440–41). If we read the revised "Two Voices" as a poem about dialogue, we can understand why the speaker, confronting this uncommunicative heavenly alternative, rather makes choice to commune with the barren voice, which at least talks back in ways that can be talked back to in turn. The truly new voice that prolonged Tennyson's revised text, and with it his career, is the one that received both a trial run and a ritual inauguration in this long, ignominious, essential passage:

> " 'Tis life, whereof our nerves are scant,
> Oh life, not death, for which we pant;
> More life, and fuller, that I want."
>
> I ceased, and sat as one forlorn.
> Then said the voice, in quiet scorn,
> "Behold, it is the Sabbath morn."
>
> And I arose, and I released
> The casement, and the light increased
> With freshness in the dawning east.
>
> Like softened airs that blowing steal,
> When meres begin to uncongeal,
> The sweet church bells began to peal.
>
> On to God's house the people prest:
> Passing the place where each must rest,
> Each entered like a welcome guest.
>
> One walked between his wife and child,
> With measured footfall firm and mild,
> And now and then he gravely smiled.

Herbert F. Tucker

> *The prudent partner of his blood*
> *Leaned on him, faithful, gentle, good,*
> *Wearing the rose of womanhood.*
>
> *And in their double love secure,*
> *The little maiden walked demure,*
> *Pacing with downward eyelids pure.*
>
> *These three made unity so sweet,*
> *My frozen heart began to beat,*
> *Remembering its ancient heat.*
>
> *I blest them, and they wandered on:*
> *I spoke, but answer came there none:*
> *The dull and bitter voice was gone.*　　*(ll. 397–426)*

I want to argue that what is at stake in Tennyson's cultivation of this new, idyllic voice is less a psychotherapeutic tactic than it is a poetic dialectic. But first I must anticipate a modern reader's almost certain reluctance to take this voice seriously, because that reluctance, rightly pursued, conducts to the heart of the activity that the studied serenity of this passage masks. The degree to which the pastel icon presented in these lines allergically repels us can serve to judge the poet's marksmanship in hitting the bull's-eye of literary, social, and emotional conventions that, thanks in part to Tennyson's impact upon literate Anglophone culture, remain very much in force today.[13] We know the strength of these conventions by the strength of the aversion they can still provoke at the distance of a century and a half, but our aversion need not blind us to what Tennyson did with the conventions in writing them up so memorably. If we can suspend our resistance to the scene the passage summons up long enough to read what the poet actually wrote, we shall find that resistance, or a recognizable version of it, anticipated in his speaker. If we can swallow this saccharine cliché, we shall find that its artificial sweetening wraps powerful medicine. For it discloses an ambivalent vision of communal, institutional suicide; a vision of acculturation itself as a process at once curative and lethal to the alienated mind.

The passage moves from dipsychic introversion into the bland light of conventional sentiment with a vengeance, which is to say with the poet's measured awareness of just what he is doing. Note first the lushly orchestrated transition from vocal dialogue to mute vision, as the "I" of the first three stanzas grows all eye. The hushed speaker is absorbed into the tableau before him, there to receive from the rhythm of the bells and the "measured footfall" of the holy nuclear family pacing to church a renewed impetus for the beating life he has begun the passage by desiring. The way Tennyson effects this transition with crucial devices from earlier phases in his development marks the passage as a nodal point, where the poet gathers up his past in order to project his future. In "Armageddon" and "Timbuctoo," Tennyson's very early essays in a visionary romantic mode, a seraphic guide endows the naive poet with an insight whose preternatural keenness consistently assumes synesthetic dimensions. Here, likewise, the "Behold" of the still small voice ushers in a sight that can be held. The release of the casement releases the now-silent speaker into perception of a light he describes in terms of its felt "freshness," which flows into the next tercet's musical-tactile "softened airs" and tasteful sound of "sweet church bells."[14]

What gets revealed across this four-stanza threshold, every reader will agree, is no romantic vision, but an icon encrusted with Victorian sentimentality. Moments like this occur in Tennyson with great regularity from 1842 on, and they issue a special set of challenges to the critic: to make their picturesque conventionality part of a bigger picture; to see the iconic object as in itself it really is; and to hear what, as a stereotypical but still speaking image, it has to say. A genuinely critical reading of this passage will succumb neither to mere sympathy with the Victorian ideology of domesticity nor to the mere repugnance that is, by tiresome modern reflex, its unconsidered opposite. One means of sharpening our attentiveness to the voice within Tennyson's domestic picture is to listen to the way the idyllic text contrapuntally echoes a text of a different genre, one with antithetical and potentially subversive conventions. By 1842 Tennyson was a close student of the simultaneously enabling and constraining dynamics of convention, and he knew that conventions were not to be shrugged off but just might be outmaneuvered by competing conventions. Accordingly, at this point in "The Two Voices" he summoned the aid of his favorite precursor text, the final movement of Keats's "Ode to a Nightingale." In Keats's ode the imagination of immortality ("Thou wast not born for death, immortal Bird!") conducts the speaker to a climax at which charmed casements open on "forlorn" lands—which in turn can but restore him to the disenchanted self-awareness of a mortal for whom the bell tolls (*Complete Poems*, p. 281, ll. 61–72). Now Tennyson's poem, to this point nothing if not likewise a study in solitude, offers an escape from the Keatsian trajectory by cutting it short and bailing out into a socially cushioned commonplace; its aggrandizement of institutional life occurs at the expense of the individual imagination. The desire of Tennyson's speaker for "life, not death," weak as it all too evidently is, makes him instantly "forlorn" and reduces him to a zero point from which, it seems, only institutional remedies can rouse him. The tolling bell that entered Keats's ode as a self-prescribed depressant becomes in Tennyson a welcome stimulus pealing the good news from without. Saved thus by one Victorian bulwark, the church, the speaker proceeds to give his blessing to another, the family; and with this benediction the poet freshly institutes the literary conventions of the pious domestic idyll that will have so prominent a place in his own work and in the most popular literature of his era.[15]

This escape from lonely despair, I repeat, is one that Tennyson's passage *offers;* and many a reader has been glad to take it. That it satisfied Tennyson, though, is far from clear, in view of his personal agnosticism and his imaginative proclivity for casements opening on surmise rather than certitude. Nor is it clear that the institutional escape this passage tenders is satisfactory even to Tennyson's speaker. We have just seen that the fourfold allusion to Keats's ode within these four transitional stanzas ("life, not death," "forlorn," "casement," "bells") extends a revisionary, not to say a reactionary, option for the sick sole self. At the same time, the very clustering of images from a single precursor text—unprecedented in a poem that thus far has practiced allusion only in scattered ways—impresses upon the mind the Keatsian paradigm it revises. The thematic core of this paradigm, the romantic imagination's habit of betraying us generally to the truths we think to evade and particularly to the fact of our unassisted mortality, is something Tennyson's revision has conspicuously failed to acknowledge. Indeed, the Keatsian paradigm of a chastening relapse into resisted knowledge provides a virtual model for the return of the repressed in "The Two Voices." For the fact of death remains to haunt the stanzas that follow, like a revenant restoring to consciousness what has been expressly and forcibly excluded in the initiating cry for "life, not death." Tennyson's Victorian flight into conventional edification, like Keats's high romantic flight into the purlieus of imagination, obeys the stronger and more completely romantic imperative of coming to terms with all the self can know—or, in accordance with the best romantic models, of recognizing all the self can forget. The intertextual logic at work in Tennyson's transitional stanzas anticipates what the rest of the passage amply confirms: the sweetly pealing church bells herald a vision, not a waking dream, and they will take their bitter Keatsian toll after all.

I have quoted the whole of this very familiar passage because its very familiarity threatens to keep us from understanding it. A period piece even as Tennyson penned it, it was written to be a familiar slice of conventional life; but it was also written to be more, to be unsettling in that wilder mode of familiarity we call the uncanny. To stress the paraphrasable substance of the domestic scene Tennyson here presents—people going to church, among them a representative triptych of husband, wife, and child—is to see only the convention and thus to miss the peculiar distortion that such conventional material receives at Tennyson's hands. This tableau is probably the poet's best-known early study in the domestic idyll, a nineteenth-century mode of verbal genre painting that ranks as a Victorian version of pastoral. But we should also recognize, amid the aquatints of the tableau, what our earlier attention to the passage's Keatsian residue and to its measured Tennysonian rhythms should have primed us for: the sober coloring of mortality, the still, sad music of humanity, which suffuses every detail in the scene.

These stanzas are noteworthy for a gravity that marks not just the poet's high seriousness in cleaving to contemporary canons of taste but, beyond that, his way of cleaving through them and making an otherwise two-dimensional picture of life deep with shades of the prison house, shadows of the tomb. The fifth stanza makes it sound as if the people are marching not *by* "the place where each must rest" but *into* it; the syntax weirdly implies that going to church is as good as going to the grave. Likewise, each member of the family in Tennyson's picture betrays a drag to earthward. The little maiden paces "with downward eyelids"; her mother leans on her partner, less a clinging vine than a human emblem of the "rose" whose root is ever in its grave; and between them, at the focal point, the husband

and father not only smiles "gravely" but walks with "measured foot-fall," on the downbeat to whose stroke all the people "press" with such eerie, quick automatism towards their destination. There is suicide, it seems, and then there is suicide. In revising his early manuscript, Tennyson shifted the burden of his characteristic inevitability from the dialectics of an argumentative discourse to the chiaroscuro of an ideological scene, from a vocal "quiet scorn" to a picture that "gravely smiled"; he stanched the overt thoughts of a suicide with more subtly suicidal images.

Et in Arcadia Victoriana ego. The man in the tableau can gravely smile, as befits a mature acceptance of the process of maturation, generation, and death, while he travels away from the Wordsworthian east and into the light of common day, the sabbath of community. But the speaker's response in the last two stanzas of our passage is harder to gauge. Is he acting in accordance with the vision that has been vouchsafed to him, or is he reacting against it? The penultimate stanza places the melting and beating of his heart in sympathy with the earlier uncongealing meres and with the rhythmic ground of the entire passage. Similarly, the speaker's memory of "ancient heat" is anticipated in his warm desire for social standing in lines 122–23: the "hope that warmed me in the days / While still I yearned for human praise." A closer antecedent for the "ancient heat," however, countervails this embrace of the common doom, by claiming the last refuge of romantic individualism, denial of an empirical, sharable externality:

> that other influence,
> The heat of inward evidence,
> By which he doubts against the sense.   *(ll. 283–85)*

These lines are supposed to assert belief, yet the word they find is "doubts"; as so often in Tennyson, an ostensible confession of faith expresses skepticism instead. To assign the speaker's memory of "ancient heat" to these lines is to encounter, not a social warmth, but the friction of the divided mind against itself, the rub of faith against doubt that made up a major part of the Victorians' romantic legacy and that informs the entire final movement of "The Two Voices" in spite of its patent design.

The final stanza of the poem, we remember, also prefers doubt to faith; and this preference receives an even more powerful validation at the close of our passage. Against the great thawing of the speaker's heart, which itself participates with mortal gravity in the sweet lapse to merger that prompts it, Tennyson has placed the next stanza's radical isolation: "I blest them, and they wandered on: / I spoke, but answer came there none." There is no more communing with these blessed zombies, it seems, than with the tight-lipped orthodox voice that will pronounce its occult news in the stanzas to follow. One wants to know, at this of all points in Tennyson's poem of dialogue, just what the speaker "spoke." A ritual repetition of his blessing? An ice-breaking salutation inviting further cordial speech? A mental traveler's warning to cold earth wanderers about the destination that awaits them? Tennyson's concern to make dialogue constitutive of the self emerges in the way the unresponsiveness of the speaker's addressees disqualifies his speech from the poem. We hear neither his actual words nor even a report by means of indirect discourse, only "I spoke." That is as much as we can know: the speaker dangles in a limbo that forecasts the dubiety in which the poem will conclude.

In order to see how such dubiety may have served Tennyson's ends in writing and rewriting "The Two Voices," we should observe something else about this hush at the heart of his ten years' silence. The speaker's unrevealed response to the apocalypse of bourgeois domesticity closely matches the ineffable wisdom that is asserted by the new voice of evangelist reticence: "I may not speak of what I know" (l. 435). The speaker's prosodically vexed interrogation of this voice—"'What is it thou knowest, sweet voice?' I cried"—is no more satisfactorily answered than the reader's interrogation of the speaker: "'A hidden hope,' the voice replied" (ll. 440–41). This sweet voice can extend a hidden hope because it sees "the end" and knows "the good" (l. 432). But do the end it sees and the good it knows stand in a relation of apposition or of opposition? The association of the voice with solace, heaven, and especially "blissful neighbourhood" (l. 430) has led most readers to interpret its words as ecclesiastical missives, which would bind the speaker to an acceptance of the common end, death here and the resurrection of the evangelically chosen hereafter, as a form of "unity so sweet" quite consonant with all he has just beheld.

But then, if it is the mission of this evangelical voice to proselytize, it signally fails with our speaker, who wanders on, not to church, but "into the fields" (l. 448), there to wonder at the vagaries of his own mind. And he may be right to do so: the sweet voice's persistent rhetoric of concealment points with equal plausibility to an epistemological rupture between seeing and knowing, a rupture that troubles the idyllic aesthetic of picturesque homogeneity and iconic transparence. "I see the end and know the good" opens a gap between what seems and what is, a gap the speaker inhabits when, with ancient heat, he matches inward evidence against the manifest sense of things. The speaker may find the voice encouraging because, in spite of the mortal "end" they both can see all too plainly, the voice cleaves to an antithetical "good" it knows but may not speak, and embraces a counter hope it offers but must hide. In the spirit of the revised poem as a whole, it addresses with equal plausibility the speaker's contradictory impulses to be a faithful English Protestant, on the one hand, and, on the other, to keep the romantic faith by protesting against fate and its manifold institutionalization.

Here, then, speaks a heavenly voice that equivocates like the very fiend: the sympathetic and the antithetical interpretations I have outlined are mutually exclusive. And yet, on either account, its whispers come to the speaker as good news. We might now ask, premising that in the process of revision "The Two Voices" had become an allegory of dialogue and thus of a newly dialectical mode of writing, how the speaker's silence may come as similarly good news for the poet. A comparable silence near the close of "The Palace of Art" (1832) was, without question, bad news there: the Soul, seeming to hear the "sound / Of human footsteps fall" (*Poems*, p. 417, ll. 275–76), issued a distress call but found "no murmur of reply," because in her twinned fears of otherness and of mortality she did not really desire any. In that poem the Soul's insuperable commitment to individuality consigned the poet's communitarian impulse to the status of a pietistic and thoroughly unpersuasive appendix. By the time of finishing "The Two Voices," however, Tennyson had integrated such a communitarian impulse more adequately into his text and had achieved a more compelling dialectical balance between personal identity and identification with the other, between the self's contrary demands for its own integrity and for integration with what lies beyond it. This achievement entailed his recognition that a dialectic of modes or genres might take the place of the literal poetic dialogue he had at one point felt called to write.

Hence the abandonment of dialogue proper in the idyllic finale, the farewell to conversation in lines 440–41, and the choice to "commune" rather than to speak further as the poem, appropriately, stops.

Having returned this once through a fresh attempt at dialogue to the juvenile origins of his career, Tennyson seems to have decided that once was enough. He would very seldom take dialogue up again, would grumble about its exigencies when *Idylls of the King* forced it upon him, and would bungle or at best sidestep it in the ill-fated theatrical ventures of his late years.[16] The composition of "The Two Voices" records a career choice that both affirms the poet's abilities and confesses where his genius is deficient. The "choice / To commune" commits Tennyson to the pursuit of dialogue in a figurative sense and by primarily internal means. He will henceforth give lyric voice to speakers who are dipsychic if not polypsychic, whose monologues form tense, split, shot-silk texts that are anything but monological. In his idylls, conversely, he will conduct narratives whose generating conflicts are not explicit, as dialogue might make them, but are folded between the lines and knotted by the interplay between backdrop and foreground, description and act.

§

Within this text where dialogue signally fails, an additional source of dialectical complexity lies in the one avenue for intersubjective dialogue that Tennyson keeps wide open: I mean his channel of communication with the romantic poets. Curiously, the most arresting intertextual conversation between Tennyson and an influential precursor occurs in the very passage at which dramatic conversation is most evidently stymied in the text: "I blest them, and they wandered on: / I spoke, but answer came there none." The first of these lines, as readers have noted, quotes Coleridge's "Rime of the Ancient Mariner":

> *O happy living things! no tongue*
> *Their beauty might declare:*
> *A spring of love gushed from my heart,*
> *And I blessed them unaware:*
> *Sure my kind saint took pity on me,*
> *And I blessed them unaware.*[17]

Herbert F. Tucker

The Ancient Mariner's celebrated moment of release anticipates in several ways that of Tennyson's speaker.[18] The blessing that blesses him who confers it, the gushing spring of the unfrozen heart that eases the dead weight of self-loathing, are strong in Tennyson's poem as in Coleridge's. But so, in each text, are the residual imperfections that shadow these blessings. We miss the scrupulous balance that distinguishes Tennyson at his best, and we underrate his ability to read and allude to romantic poetry, if we fail to see how the line "I spoke, but answer came there none" gives in epitome the rest of Coleridge's harrowing fable: the part not suitable for Sunday school, where for the privilege of ecstatic vision the Mariner pays and pays again the dues of voyeuristic isolation from common life, even from the sweetness of walking to the kirk with a goodly company.

It was the Ancient Mariner's open-ended schedule of payment, malarially cyclical rather than purgatorially pointed, that I think attracted Tennyson at this stage of this poem to Coleridge's famous words—and, indeed, to the image of a churchgoing community observed, as Coleridge might have said, ab extra. As a man who hath penance done, and penance more will do, the Mariner offers an apt analogue for the persona we are more than usually right here to call Tennyson's *speaker,* the figure whose principal function in this poem of dialogue is, precisely, to speak. If the Ancient Mariner stands behind the ambiguous "ancient heat" of Tennyson's vacillating speaker, he is there to emphasize vacillation as what confers strange power of speech to begin with. In Coleridge the effect of such power is to transform the Wedding Guest, or attentive reader, into an imaginative double of the Mariner, or poet, who wields and is wielded by it. Each "is of sense forlorn" ("Rime," p. 209, l. 623), having wandered too far from common sense ever to be quite sanely reintegrated into the community he has lost; yet each also finds a lost meaning or "sense forlorn" in the very language of estrangement that finds and claims him as its secret sharer. In Keats's "Nightingale" ode, likewise, *forlorn* is the very word that converts a sublime speaker into a fallen reader of his own text, who at last shares, not fancy's secrets with himself, but mortal dubieties with his fellow readers. The substance of Tennyson's allusions to these poems thus reinforces an antithetical fact of romantic allusiveness: possession by and of strange power of speech brings the speakers and listeners who feel it together, even as it leaves them forlorn. A sadder and a wiser man, Tennyson's speaker remains at large in the longing of the text, the romantic locus of Tennysonian melancholy.

To see that human longing as a poetic *prolonging* is to grasp the dialectic at which Tennyson arrived during the ten years' silence, and in no one text so conspicuously as in his experimental dialogue "The Two Voices." On one hand, the Tennysonian persona longs to merge with his fate, whether that fate takes the shape of death, which the still small voice advocates as our common destiny, or the shape of the family and church, which at first look like defenses against that destiny but in effect replace it with "unity so sweet," a fatal merger of another, institutional sort. On the other hand, and with a grip that grew stronger as it was exercised across the 1830s, the Tennysonian persona longs instead for emergence from his fate and seeks a rendezvous with destiny for oppositional purposes, which find expression in the numerous poems of crisis that date from this decade. Merger with fate and emergence from it constitute the two voices of Tennyson's career. Each voice lays claim to appreciable power of speech on its own, whether in the exhilaration and high tang of resistance or in the sweet, deep yield of acceptance. We could say schematically that each voice found its proper genre—the lyrically dramatic monologue and the socially domestic idyll, respectively—in the years during which Tennyson worked up this hybrid poem, which, of course, displays characteristics of both genres. But this scheme would require the instant qualification that both genres are themselves hybrids in their very conception. Tissues of the mutual interference between individuation and context, subjective power and subject matter, personality and history, both the monologue and the idyll provided Tennyson with occasions not just for power of speech (he had that anyhow at fifteen) but for the strange, vacillating, properly Tennysonian power that made and preserved the species of talking cure we recognize as a poetic career.

For such equivocation of genres Tennyson had abundant precedent in the works of the romantics, and the *Poems* of 1842 show him following a number of romantic leads. The satura or generic goulash of *Don Juan*, whose simmering only Byron's death could stop, reappears in the chophouse drawl and thrust of "Will Waterproof's Lyrical Monologue" and "The Vision of Sin." The erotically transcendental quests of Tennyson's earthbound major monologists are continuations of the drive that can never quite purify itself in the "lyrical drama" of Shelley's *Prometheus Unbound,* which was also a generic source for the kind of poem Browning began collecting (also in 1842) under the rubric *Dramatic Lyrics.* Arguably both Byron and Shelley had learned about the mixture of genres from the contents and sequels of the oxymoronically titled little book of *Lyrical Ballads* on which Wordsworth and Coleridge had collaborated in 1798. We grasp the originating power of the "lyrical ballad," romantic hybrid par excellence that it is, when we see how it came into being through the collision of a communal ballad tradition with a sublimely up-rooted lyrical subjectivity. Whether such a lyrical ballad took shape, like "Tintern Abbey," as a meditative "conversation poem" moving dialogically between self and other, between the one life within and the one life abroad, or whether, like the "Ancient Mariner," it employed ballad narrative to tell tales about that dialogical reciprocation, it established the way of what we now call romanticism—a way we continue to pursue, and a way in the pursuit of which Tennyson's 1842 *Poems* stand as traditionally innovative landmarks.

The penultimate stanza of "The Two Voices" describes the speaker's errant mind as "brought / To anchor by one gloomy thought" (ll. 458–59) the one relentless thought that makes a desperate man a suicide. Given the traditional iconographic association of the anchor with hope and not despair, this late image is intriguingly perverse. Moreover, the speaker reaches for this image right after asserting that he is afloat upon oceanic powers of love and fellowship, which are repeatedly rendered in liquid images: the uncongealing meres, the thawing heart, the later triad of rainbow, shower, and cloud, and most significantly the pulse of hope. Despair as anchor, hope as pulse: these images taken together help us to understand the career of a poet who was repeatedly to envision weighing anchor and taking the flood as valedictory acts portending the death of poetry. The passing of Arthur—whether as king in the *Idylls* or as giant in *In Memoriam* section 103—the transmarine quest of Galahad from "The Holy Grail," the poet's own "Crossing the Bar," all image the terminus of a career and not its course.

During the deafening silence between 1832 and 1842 Tennyson saved his voice for the sake of his vocation. In isolation he practiced dramatic ventriloquism and impassioned advocacy on a brand new scale; at a different level of vocational ambition, he also undertook the arts of what I have here called *equivocation,* the breaking and joining of inherited genres to form new ones—arts that would prove indispensable to his innovations in the long poem during the years to come. Tennyson's protracted creative retreat, then, entailed the pursuit of poetic means rather than ends, or of special effects rather than larger commitments. In the wake of Arthur Hallam's death, and of the agitation for reform that was abroad in the land during the early 1830s, Tennyson labored less to compass a destination for his craft than to secure a harbor where it might survive. Riding at anchor, he took plumb despair as the very device of his poetic trust, grounded the affirmations of faith in the postulates of doubt, and thus weathered storms of enthusiastic passion—most notably the progressive optimism of his century—which might otherwise have unmoored him from the great deep certitudes of his original melancholy. By these means he remained a poet; by these means he respected the ebb that, equally with the flood, kept Tennysonian hope a dialectical pulsation of the kind that weaves texts.

Notes

1. The poet's silent decade is discussed at greater length in my *Tennyson and the Doom of Romanticism* (Cambridge, Mass., and London: Harvard Univ. Press, 1988), pp. 177–90.

2. "Sleep and Poetry," in John Keats, *Complete Poems*, ed. Jack Stillinger (Cambridge, Mass., and London: Harvard University Press, 1982), p. 43, ll. 246–47. Subsequent references to this edition will be cited parenthetically in the text.

3. Letter of December 21, 1817, in *Letters of John Keats*, ed. Robert Gittings (Oxford: Oxford University Press, 1970), p. 42.

4. Walter Bagehot, *Collected Works*, ed. Norman St. John-Stevas, 11 vols. (Cambridge, Mass.: Harvard University Press, 1965), 2:343. Oliver Elton, *Tennyson and Matthew Arnold* ([1924; rpt., New York: Haskell, 1971], pp. 47–48), finds a peculiar condensation in Tennysonian periphrasis: "if we analyse, we never come on generality or vacancy, but always on something which is first substantially seen or definitely heard, and is then patiently brooded on until the image of it is realised in the predestined phrase." See also J. F. A. Pyre, *The Formation of Tennyson's Style* (Madison: University of Wisconsin Studies, 1921), p. 86; Bernard Groom, *On the Diction of Tennyson, Browning, and Arnold* (Oxford: Clarendon Press, 1939), pp. 101–2.

5. "The Two Voices," in *The Poems of Tennyson*, ed. Christopher Ricks (London: Longman, 1969), p. 523, l. 1. Subsequent references will be to this edition and will be cited parenthetically in the text.

6. A review of Tennyson's manuscripts suggests that the poem kept going dead in his hands. It appears from Trinity Notebook 15 that the first draft ended at line 48, then was taken up again to the closure of line 96. Trinity Notebook 22 gives evidence of two stopping places: at line 117, where the handwriting changes, and again at line 309, which is also where the Heath and Harvard manuscripts both plausibly conclude. (I thank Lord Tennyson, the Tennyson trustees, and the librarians at Trinity College and the Fitzwilliam Museum, Cambridge, and at the Houghton Library of Harvard University, for permission to examine and refer to these several notebooks.)

7. See, e.g., Edward Elton Smith, *The Two Voices: A Tennyson Study* (Lincoln:

University of Nebraska Press, 1964); Donald S. Hair, *Domestic and Heroic in Tennyson's Poetry* (Toronto: University of Toronto Press, 1981).

8. The joke about suicide is quoted in Charles Tennyson, *Alfred Tennyson* (New York: Macmillan, 1949), p. 286. Tennyson's interest in the suicide persists from the dramatic monologues he drafted on classical subjects in the early 1830s through *Maud* (1855) into "Balin and Balan" (1885). Of "Despair" (1881) he said, "I would have hypothesized the feelings of a would-be-suicide in this latter half of our nineteenth century" (*Poems* 1299). Compare his interest in the figure of the martyr, from the very early "St. Lawrence" (1825?) to the very late "St. Telemachus" (1892). I have discussed comparable temporal issues in "From Monomania to Monologue: 'St. Simeon Stylites' and the Rise of the Victorian Dramatic Monologue," *Victorian Poetry* 22 (1984): 121–37.

9. On these two modes of inevitability see, respectively, William Brashear, *The Gorgon's Head: A Study in Tragedy and Despair* (Athens: University of Georgia Press, 1977), pp. 31–36; George Saintsbury, *A History of English Prosody* (London: Macmillan, 1923), 3:96; and W. David Shaw, "The Transcendental Problem in Tennyson's Poetry of Debate," *Philological Quarterly* 46 (1967): 79–94.

10. William Brashear, "Tennyson's Third Voice: A Note," *Victorian Poetry* 2 (1964): 283–86.

11. An exception that proves the rule is a fragmentary dialogue in Trinity Notebook 20, from which Tennyson excerpted the 1832 "Song" ("Who can say?")—a text composed of rhetorical questions building to a final line that puts a full stop to poetic dialogue: "The cause is nowhere found in rhyme." For further consideration of the generic significance of *The Devil and the Lady* see my "Strange Comfort: A Reading of Tennyson's Unpublished Juvenilia," *Victorian Poetry* 21 (1983): 1–25.

12. Related phenomena in Tennyson include the pairing of contrasted studies in mood ("Mariana" and "Recollections of the Arabian Nights"), the writing of "pendent" poems that are interdependent ("Ulysses" and "Tithonus"), and the feature of the framing introduction, whether in a separate poem ("The Epic") or within a single text ("The Lotos-Eaters"). These poetic arts of juxtaposition anticipate, and in some measure appear to have dictated, the binary or dialectical strategies (my own included) whereby critics have principally sought to explain Tennyson's oeuvre. See William Cadbury, "Tennyson's 'The Palace of Art' and the Rhetoric of Structures," *Criticism* 7 (1965): 23–44; Roger B. Wilkenfeld, "The Shape of Two Voices," *Victorian Poetry* 4 (1966): 163–73.

13. Eminent, if hostile, testimony to the impact of this passage occurs in T. S. Eliot's "The Metaphysical Poets" (1921), a classic of modernist criticism written halfway between Tennyson's time and ours. Eliot quotes lines 412–23 as a touchstone for "something which had happened to the mind of England," "a dissociation of sensibility" (*Selected Essays, 1917–1932* [New York: Harcourt, 1932], pp. 246–47). We need not share Eliot's condescension in order to appreciate his insight that the stanzas in question represent an episode in cultural history: the parting of the ways between "sensation" and "reflection" that Arthur Hallam identified in Tennyson as early as 1831, and that the dialogue of genres in "The Two Voices" does not mend, but exploits.

14. Among the 1842 *Poems*, only "The Two Voices" bears a published date, and that an ominous one: "1833," the year of Arthur Hallam's death. Ricks's evidence that the poem was not completed until 1835 or even 1837 (*Poems* 522) suggests that this artificial antedating plays into the career-shaping elegiac mythology that is elaborated in *Poems* (1842), *In Memoriam*, and beyond. On Tennyson's early interest in synesthesia, see my article cited in note 11, above.

15. At the turn of the century John Addington Symonds would name idyll and lyric as "the specific channels of Victorian utterance in verse" (*Essays Speculative and Suggestive* [New York: Scribner, 1894], p. 399).

16. In a review of the first installment of *Idylls of the King*, Bagehot (*Works*, 2:197–98) noted "the remarkable similarity of the conversational powers of all the various personages" and observed, "Madame de Staël said that Coleridge was admirable in monologue, but quite incapable of dialogue. Something analogous may perhaps be said of Mr. Tennyson." For the poet's remarks see Hallam Tennyson, *Alfred Lord Tennyson: A Memoir*, 2 vols. (New York: Macmillan, 1897), 2:260.

17. "The Rime of the Ancient Mariner," in Samuel Taylor Coleridge, *Poetical Works*, ed. E. H. Coleridge (London: Oxford University Press, 1967), p. 198, ll. 282–87.

18. The fullest explication of this allusion is given in Joanna E. Rapf, "'Visionaries of Dereliction': Wordsworth and Tennyson," *Victorian Poetry* 24 (1986): 381–82.

Jerome J. McGann

Matthew Arnold and the Critical Spirit The Three Texts of *Empedocles on Etna*

§

*E*mpedocles on Etna is Arnold's most important, most interesting, and—despite his own apparent judgment of 1853, as well as the cavils of a few later readers—his most successful work of poetry. To inquire into the work's problematic success is to confront some of the central cultural issues of the Victorian period, and in particular the function of poetry and of criticism in a world which was discovering that it might be able to get on without either. Poets, critics, and students of culture have been preoccupied with Arnold's poem because the crisis in poetry and criticism which unfolds through this work has been repeated ever since. Facing the issues raised by *Empedocles* has been, for later readers, what Arnold would have called a "modern" experience.

Of course, such an experience has also meant that readers have commonly been troubled by the poem in various ways. In these troublings they have recapitulated the initial Arnoldian scene. We first locate that scene through Arnold's famous recantation of 1853, when he published his new volume of poetry, removed from it *Empedocles on Etna* (which had been the centerpiece of his previous, 1852, volume), and then made an elaborate drama of his recantation in the important Preface to his new book. There we learn that the problem with *Empedocles on Etna,* for Arnold at any rate, is that he had come to judge it, and to cast it out, precisely because it *was* a problematic poem.

At the risk of laboring what is well known to many, let me rehearse briefly Arnold's view of the matter in the 1853 Preface. He begins obliquely, by suggesting (only to dismiss) two plausible reasons which might have led him to remove the poem from his book. He has not, he says, omitted the poem "because the subject was a Sicilian Greek born between two and three thousand years ago, although many persons would think this a sufficient reason."[1] Arnold has in mind here Clough and some of his other friends, as well as the current example of poetry like that of Alexander Smith. In other words, Arnold says he is not removing the poem because he thinks its subject is dusty and irrelevant to the contemporary world and its problems. He goes on.

> Neither have I done so because I had, in my own opinion, failed in the delineation which I intended to effect. I intended to delineate the feelings of one of the last of the Greek religious philosophers . . . living on into a time when the habits of Greek thought and feeling had begun fast to change, character to dwindle, the influence of the Sophists to prevail. Into the feelings of a man so situated there entered much that we are accustomed to consider as exclusively modern. . . . What those who are familiar only with the great monuments of early Greek genius suppose to be its exclusive characteristics, have disappeared: the calm, the cheerfulness, the disinterested objectivity have disappeared: the dialogue of the mind with itself has commenced; modern problems have presented themselves; we hear already the doubts, we witness the discouragement, of Hamlet and of Faust. (*P* 591)

To the degree that *Empedocles on Etna* is an "accurate representation" of such a person and his situation, to that extent it is what he calls an "interesting" work, or one which "add[s] to our knowledge" in significant ways.

The poem fails in Arnold's eyes because something "more . . . is demanded" of poetical representations than that they be accurate and interesting. "It is not enough that the Poet should add to the knowledge of men," he says, "it is required that he should add to their happiness" (*P* 592). By this test *Empedocles on Etna* is judged a failure.

> What then are those situations, from the representation of which, though accurate, no poetical enjoyment can be derived? They are those in which the suffering finds no vent in action; in which a continuous state of mental distress is prolonged, unrelieved by incident, hope, or resistance; in which there is everything to be endured, nothing to be done. . . . To this class of situations, poetically faulty as it

appears to me, that of Empedocles, as I have endeavoured to represent him, belongs; and I have therefore excluded the Poem from the present collection. (*P* 592)

I shall recur to Arnold's analysis and judgments later in this essay. Here it is important to emphasize, first, that Arnold has not found fault with the execution of his work. Given its subject matter, given the "situation" taken up in the poem, *Empedocles on Etna* is not merely not a failure, it is a success. The problem with the poem lies rather in its conception, in what Arnold will call "the choice of . . . subjects." In taking this line Arnold is not only insisting on the moral dimension of poetical work—which is clear enough—he is saying that that moral dimension is objectively determinable.

But if we ask "What is Arnold's evidence for the moral failure of his poem?" we find a curious situation. Almost everyone who read *Empedocles* at the time, reviewers and friends alike, were enthusiastic and full of its praises; and subsequent readers have generally been of a similar mind. In truth, the moral failure of *Empedocles* appeared to Arnold's eyes alone, and to Arnold's eyes as they were seeing at a very particular time. Arnold himself was evidently of two minds about the poem, giving it with one hand in one year, and then in the next year taking it back with the other. But his own ambivalence was even more unstable, for he seems to have been of at least three minds about this troublesome work. In the 1853 volume, as well as in its second edition in 1855, Arnold printed under separate headings a number of the sections of *Empedocles*.[2] Furthermore, in 1867, "at the request of a man of genius . . . Mr. Robert Browning,"[3] he reprinted, in his volume of *New Poems,* the whole of his earlier act of moral dereliction.

According to his view of the matter in the 1853 Preface, *Empedocles* was not an "adequate" work: as Arnold later put it, *Empedocles* did not "reflect . . . completely the best general culture and intelligence of [its] age."[4] Arnold's view in 1853 was that, while it certainly reflected its age, it did not reflect from the "best" point of view. It was, rather, a symptom of its age's problems and not a solution; it was, in fact, a work in which the spirit of Empedocles, who was not adequate to his age as Sophocles or Aeschylus or Thucydides had been, overtook and infected Arnold's nineteenth-century act of rehearsal. "A second exorcism of the spirit of Empedocles"[5] therefore became necessary.

Arnold and Empedocles

In this sense, what happens to *Empedocles* in the 1853 and 1855 volumes is a rewriting of the poem. Only pieces of it are printed, as if it were a work which could be relied upon only in parts, or only in fragments. The integral text of 1852 is not printed in the pages of 1853/1855. That integral text, however, must not be thought to have disappeared from the 1853/1855 text. It hovers over that text as a powerful presence—to Arnold as well as to his readers—which could not be put by.

But in 1853 the work called *Empedocles* has undergone a change. It has been reconstituted as a superseded text—a text which does not call for revision and reprinting, but for critical commentary and selection. The 1852 work has disappeared only in the sense that it is not reprinted in 1853/1855. And in 1867, when the text changes yet again, only a superficial eye would see the latest (restored) constitution of *Empedocles* as merely a recovery of the text of 1852. An entire history of work on *Empedocles* stretches between 1852 and 1867, and Arnold's brief note to the text in the latter volume—the remark about Mr. Robert Browning—is an index to the whole of the action which *Empedocles* comprehended during that fifteen-year period.

What happens to *Empedocles* in 1853 and in 1867 must be seen— and has in fact been seen—as part of Arnold's work on *Empedocles*. The treatment of the poem in the 1853 Preface represents an effort to make up for what he judged to be the failure of the work as it stood in 1852; and the treatment in 1867 is yet another part of that effort, only in this case the effort is made to step back across the judgments of 1853 and arrive at a new accommodation with the work as it had been imagined in 1852. If 1853 passed a severe judgment on the work of 1852, 1867 solicits a critique of the judgments of 1853.

This narrative of the early textual history of *Empedocles* reminds us that the central issues taken up in both of Arnold's volumes, and epitomized in the replacement of *Empedocles* (in 1852) by "Sohrab and Rustum" (in 1853), all concerned the function of poetry in a "modern" age like the Victorian.[6] The narrative equally calls to mind the fluctuations which Arnold's ideas underwent between 1845 and 1853 as he cast about to find permanent solutions to the various problems that concerned him. The letters of those years, and particularly the letters to Clough, trace out a clear three-stage movement in his thinking. Each of these stages has a correspondent text.

Jerome J. McGann

Between 1845 and 1849 Arnold maintained—struggled to maintain, it should be said, for he had to contend with Clough on these matters—a Parnassian view of poetry; and *The Strayed Reveller, and Other Poems* (1849) is a fair exponent of his ideas at this stage. The Shakespeare of Arnold's sonnet in that volume is not Keats's chameleon poet; rather, he is a kind of Grecian Urn that teases out of thought those who seek for deep meanings or truth in poetry. "Not deep the poet sees, but wide," Arnold observes in "Resignation," and he bends his work "against the modern English habit (too much encouraged by Wordsworth) of using poetry as a channel for thinking aloud, instead of making anything."[7] To Clough he disparages what he calls "the growing Popularity of [the] strong minded writer . . . [who] talk[s] of his usefulness and imagine[s] himself a Reformer, instead of an Exhibition."[8]

In the *Empedocles* volume, however, Arnold shifts away from the ground he had taken in the 1849 book. The Parnassian poet of 1849 appears here, most dramatically, as the Callicles of the title poem, and in this posture he becomes an "Exhibition" in another sense entirely: he exhibits the limitations of a purely aesthetic approach to poetry in circumstances which are shadowed by social and psychic emergencies. Arnold's changed view is sharply defined in two letters to Clough. In February 1849, the month of publication of *The Strayed Reveller*, Arnold wrote to his friend about "form, as the sole *necessary* of Poetry as such: whereas the greatest wealth and depth of matter is merely a superfluity in the Poet *as such*" (*LC* 98–99). But in October 1852, the month of publication of the *Empedocles* volume, Arnold sent Clough his famous *magister vitae* letter. "The exuberance of expression, the charm, the richness of images, and the felicity" of Elizabethan and romantic poetry are aesthetic seductions which must be resisted, for "modern poetry can only subsist by its *contents:* by becoming a complete magister vitae as the poetry of the ancients did" (*LC* 124).[9]

It is in this letter that Arnold remarks how a complex and modern world like his own "compels . . . poetry . . . to use great plainness of speech," and to avoid the "richness" and "ornamental work" of a poetry of mere "Exhibition." "The language, style, and general proceedings of a poetry which has such an immense task to perform [i.e., supplying moral and religious wants to the age], must be very plain direct and severe." These comments might as easily be taken as

Arnold and Empedocles

a gloss on the style of Empedocles' sermon to Pausanias in act 2, scene 1, of the centerpiece poem in Arnold's new book of verse.

But the new book was not out two months before Arnold once again began to rethink his positions—to subject his latest book to a critique which had its origin in the (since rejected) Parnassianism of the 1849 volume.

> As for my poems they have weight, I think, but little or no charm
> *What Poets feel not, when they make,*
> *A pleasure in creating,*
> *The world, in its turn, will not take*
> *Pleasure in contemplating.*

"There is an oracular quatrain for you," Arnold added, "terribly true" precisely because the making of his 1852 volume had been an agony to him, no pleasure at all. "But woe was upon me if I analysed not my situation," he observed, and in this respect, once again, he had striven to go beyond what the romantics had achieved: "Werter Rene and such like none of them analyse the modern situation in its true *blankness* and *barrenness* and *unpoetrylessness*" (*LC* 26). This is what Arnold had tried to achieve in *Empedocles,* but as soon as the results were in, he felt that he had failed.

So in the 1853 volume Arnold shifted once again, this time to the position epitomized by the Preface and its illustrative instance, "Sohrab and Rustum." We now think of this as his culminant position, the initial vantage and point of view upon which all his later work, for better (in the prose writings) and for worse (in the poetry), was to proceed. But the reappearance in 1867 of the banished *Empedocles* ought to suggest how Arnold's ultimate works and ideas, like his earlier ones, may remain open to change. Nor is it without significance that *Empedocles'* return from exile should have raised a critique of Arnold's work which was structurally the same as the earlier critique raised against *Empedocles* by the 1853 volume.

That is to say, the critique of *Empedocles* in the 1853 volume is based on Arnold's argument that the function of poetry, particularly in a "modern" age, is to bring "happiness" and "joy," to resist (rather than not) the spread of angst, "mental distress," and the modern sense of fragmentariness. The resistance in poetry will stem from its formal virtues, from the impression of totality and wholeness which it conveys.

Now that argument reaches back across the *Empedocles* volume to pick up once again, in a new and stronger way, Arnold's earlier ideas about beauty, charm, and formal perfection in poetry. Indeed, Arnold's 1853 position would force a sea change on his early thought about poetry as an "Exhibition," that (in Archibald MacLeish's famous twentieth-century formulation) "Poems should not mean, but be." In 1853 Arnold would recommend the "Exhibition" in poetry of a great action rather than either some dialogue of the mind with itself or even some "true allegory of the state of one's own mind in a representative history" (*P* 598–99). In 1853 the word *Exhibition* is translated as "model": to counter "the confusion of the present times . . . [one's] attention should be fixed on excellent models" (*P* 599).

The idea of poetry as the exhibition of a great action: that is, of course, the position we most associate with Arnold—properly so, since it was the position he spent the rest of his life trying to maintain. But the voice of the "man of genius" would not be stilled in or for Arnold altogether. In 1867 Browning supplied Arnold once again with that voice of genius he had left to others, and once again *Empedocles* appeared, in the completeness—dare one say the wholeness?—of its offensive irresolutions. The very act of reprinting a work which he had so authoritatively judged, so forthrightly repudiated, reminds us of Arnold's inveterate irresolution about *Empedocles,* and allows us to glimpse the more profound and searching character of his thought. Indeed, from an Empedoclean perspective all of Arnold's public talk about poetic form, its complex order, its architectonic quality, may be seen, from the vantage of 1867, as the prose equivalent of Calliclean song: a surface of untroubled beauty, an apparition of comfort, a mask of the truth of poetry.

In 1853 Arnold wrote Clough at least two famous letters in which he reproached his older friend for his intellectual shape-shifting, for "always poking and patching and cobbling" (*LC* 130) at his ideas. "You certainly do not seem to me sufficiently to desire and earnestly strive towards—assured knowledge—activity—happiness. You are too content to *fluctuate*—to be ever learning, never coming to the knowledge of the truth. This is why, with you, I feel it necessary to stiffen myself—and hold fast my rudder" (*LC* 146). But the real truth is that Arnold needed to "stiffen" himself, not against Clough, but against himself. Whether or not Clough did not "sufficiently" desire or strive toward certain knowledge, certainly Arnold's own work was an exhibition of such a struggle parading itself as a final achievement. Arnold admitted as much in an 1858 letter to his sister "K":

> People do not understand what a temptation there is, if you cannot bear anything not *very good,* to transfer your operations to a region where form is everything. Perfection of a certain kind may there be attained, or at least approached, without knocking yourself to pieces, but to attain or approach perfection in the region of thought and feeling, and to unite this with perfection of form, demands not merely an effort and a labour, but an actual tearing of oneself to pieces, which one does not readily consent to (although one is sometimes forced to it) unless one can devote one's whole life to poetry.[10]

This is a palinode to his man of genius, to his work as a poet, a lament raised in the aftermath of the poor critical reception of *Merope,* Arnold's (alas, successful) attempt to transfer his operations to a region where form is everything. But it is a palinode which has expressed the real truth about poetry as Arnold understood it, and as he had once most deeply realized it with *Empedocles on Etna.*

The fluctuations in his treatment of *Empedocles* are an index of Arnold's strivings, and in this they mirror the nervous beauty of the poem itself, whose truth Arnold never came to the knowledge of. But in calling it back from banishment in 1867 Arnold showed that he had not altogether abandoned his original faith in the poem.

§

To proceed from the historical metaphor I have been pursuing, we will say that there are, for Arnold, at least three (and possibly four) constitutions of Empedocles—the 1852, the 1853/1855, and the 1867 version.[11]

The 1852 version is that which later readers have pursued when they emphasize the primacy in the poem of Empedocles' sermon on the mount (1.2.77–426), with its "plain direct and severe" style, over the songs of Callicles. In the integral-text *Empedocles* (i.e., the texts of 1852 and 1867), Callicles sings five intercalary lyrics. The first four are sung before Empedocles throws himself into the crater; the last comes afterwards, making up a kind of coda to the main action of the poem. The four initial songs are presented under the following rubric articulated by Pausanias:

[Empedocles] has laid the use of music by,
And all which might relax his settled gloom.
Yet thou may'st try thy playing . . .
Though from afar, distinctly; it may soothe him.   (*1.1.83–85, 89*)

Callicles' songs are thus moved into a dialogic relation with Empedocles. But the structure of the poem is such that the songs do not respond to Empedocles and his feelings, as Pausanias had hoped. Callicles has no way of knowing the precise state of Empedocles' moods, so his songs are initiated in a purely fortuitous relation to Empedocles as far as their subject matter is concerned. In the poem, therefore, it is Empedocles who responds to Callicles' songs, glossing and commenting upon them. The consequence is that the songs are repeatedly undermined by Empedocles' critical remarks.

These remarks grow increasingly critical, even deconstructive, as the action proceeds. The first song (1.2.36–76), which recalls the "wisdom" taught by Chiron to the youthful Achilles, anticipates Empedocles' sermon on the mount, which immediately follows the song. Empedocles does not comment directly on Callicles' lyric, but his "plain direct and severe" style, along with the bleak wisdom of his sermon, makes a sharp contrast with the exhibition of serenity in Callicles' song. In fact, when read against Empedocles' sermon, Callicles' first song opens itself to dark messages and overtones, its youth and serenity haunted by the horizon beyond which lay the Trojan War and Achilles' bitter immortality in Hell.

With the second of Callicles' lyrics, the Cadmus and Harmonia piece (1.2.427–60), the ironical subtext is present to the lyric immediately, not just retrospectively. This effect is produced primarily because, following directly upon Empedocles' sermon, the story of Cadmus and Harmonia need not be interpreted simply as a tale of suffering which gives way to final peace and contentment. The last three words of the lyric strike a distinctly harsh note:

Therefore they did not end their days
In sight of blood; but . . .
Placed safely in changed forms, the pair
Wholly forget their first sad life, and home,
And all the Theban woe, and stray
For ever through the glens, placid and dumb.

                    (*1.2.451–52, 457–60*)

Arnold and Empedocles

Next to the heroic self-consciousness of Empedocles, these creatures may as well come to us as a *figura* of Philistia, immersed in mere existence, uncritical, inarticulate, mindless.[12] The final three words of the lyric close out the passage on an ambiguous, if not positively critical, note. This is not an effect sought for by Callicles; it *is* an effect generated by the structure of Arnold's presentation.

Callicles' next two lyrics, the stories of the struggles between Typho and Zeus (2.1.37–88) and between Marsyas and Apollo (2.1.121–90), are explicitly deconstructed by Empedocles, and Arnold's text conspires with those acts of deconstruction by clearly opening the lyrics to negative readings. Apollo's "scornful" indifference to the horrible death of Marsyas is set alongside the sympathetic figure of Olympus who

> stands,
> *At his master's piteous cries*
> *Pressing fast with both his hands*
> *His white garment to his eyes*
> *Not to see Apollo's scorn.* (2.1.185–88)

This posture is opposed to that of Apollo, who, approached by the suppliant and worshipful Maenads, only

> *turned his beauteous face*
> *Haughtily another way,*
> *From the grassy sun-warmed place*
> *Where in proud repose he lay,*
> *With one arm over his head,*
> *Watching how the whetting sped.* (2.1159–64)

Once again, Arnold's poem does not suggest that Callicles is conscious of these ironies; his vision is all Apollonian. Indeed, Empedocles' Byronic and Promethean interpretation of the Typho lyric is beyond Callicles' imagination:

> *He fables, yet speaks truth!* . . .
> *What suffering is there not seen*
> *Of plainness oppressed by cunning,*
> *As the well-counselled Zeus oppressed*
> *The self-helping son of earth!* (2.1.89, 100–103)

This parallel between Typho and Prometheus is made explicit by Empedocles, but it is sanctioned by the text of Callicles' lyric, where the figure of Zeus, listening to Typho's agonies, calls to mind the satisfaction of Milton's God as he contemplates the fate of the fallen angels:

> *But an awful pleasure bland*
> *Spreading o'er the Thunderer's face,*
> *When the sound climbs near his seat,*
> *The Olympian council sees.*   (2.1.67–70)

To read Callicles' lyric interludes in this way is to follow the line Arnold himself sketched in his famous notes on the life of Empedocles, who is "a philosopher" capable of seeing "things as they are—the world as it is—God as he is: in their stern simplicity." But now, with his friends all dead and "the world . . . all against him," he has become "incredulous of the truth":

> He perceives still the truth of the truth, but cannot be transported and rapturously agitated by [its] grandeur: his spring and elasticity of mind are gone: he is clouded, oppressed, dispirited, without hope and energy.
>
> Before he becomes the victim of depression and overtension of mind, to the utter deadness of joy . . . and animated life, he desires to die; to be reunited with the universe. (*P* 148)

This is Arnold's 1852 way of imagining *Empedocles*, an imagination which transforms him into a Victorian type of Byron's Manfred and Prometheus, both of whom are bent upon "making Death a Victory" ("Prometheus" 59).

Arnold's way of producing this victory, however, is far more cerebral than Byron's. The crux comes when Empedocles is about to hurl himself into the volcano and be resolved back into the "elements."

> *To the elements it came from*
> *Everything will return—*
> *Our bodies to earth,*
> *Our blood to water,*
> *Heat to fire,*
> *Breath to air.*
> *They were well born, they will be well entombed—*
> *But mind? . . .*
> *But mind, but thought—*
> *If these have been the master part of us—*

Arnold and Empedocles

Where will they find their parent element?
What will receive them, who will call them home?

$$(2.1.331-38, 345-48)$$

The answer to those questions about the "parent element" is not given explicitly in the poem, but it is clear nonetheless. Empedocles' mind will be "received," "hidden," "quenched," "taken" home, and "saved" (2.1.37, 416) in language—more specifically, in poetic language that sings "The rest of immortals, / The action of men" (2.1.463–64).

But Arnold in 1852 cannot imagine that Calliclean verse could be equal to the task of "saving" someone like Empedocles. The brilliance of the final song of Callicles in the 1852 work emerges in the gap which the poem creates between the vision of Callicles and the full truth of the situation. Immediately after Empedocles commits suicide, Callicles looks up to the crater from his cool glen below and sings thus of Mount Etna:

Not here, O Apollo!
Are haunts meet for thee.
But, where Helicon breaks down
In cliff to the sea,
Where the moon-silvered inlets
Send far their light voice
Up the still vale of Thisbe,
O speed, and rejoice! $(2.1.421-28)$

So dominated by Apollo is Callicles' imagination that the immediate scene of Etna melts away to be replaced with a visionary projection of Apollo "leading / His choir," the nine Muses, up the slopes of Mount Helicon. In Callicles' lyric vision the bleak Sicilian landscape with its dangerous and powerful mountain fades out to be replaced by the serenity of Mount Helicon. And the same happens to Empedocles, who is effaced in this song by the figure of Apollo. But the 1852 *Empedocles*, thoroughly schooled in romantic resistance and Victorian moral commitments, is quite aware of Apollonian insufficiencies, so that the closing lyric is forced to say far more than its speaker is imagining.

—Whose praise do they mention?
Of what is it told?

Jerome J. McGann

> *What will be for ever;*
> *What was from of old.*
> *First hymn they the Father*
> *Of all things; and then,*
> *The rest of immortals,*
> *The action of men.* (2.1.457–64)

All of the nominatives in this list have their Apollonian equivalents, and Callicles' imagination is focused upon them. But in the Empedoclean vision the world is transformational, and "What will be for ever; / What was from of old" is "mind" itself, Empedoclean "thought" which materializes itself in the element of language, the fifth element which had no place in the understanding of the ancients, though it was glimpsed (Arnold wants us to believe) by Empedocles. Thus Arnold's poem puts enormous pressure on the lyric of Callicles, urging it toward a more troubled and more buried life. In 1852 the lyric has a secret, non-Calliclean function: to be a hymn to Empedocles, who is thereby glimpsed as one of the "immortals" now gone to his rest after his human life of "action."

This meaning in the 1852 conclusion is foreshadowed at the end of the first act of the poem when Pausanias asks Empedocles if "Thou wilt return to-morrow to the city?" (1.2.470).

> *Either to-morrow or some other day,*
> *In the sure revolutions of the world,*
> *Good friend, I shall revisit Catana.*
> *I have seen many cities in my time,*
> *Till my eyes ache with the long spectacle,*
> *And I shall doubtless see them all again;* (1.2.471–76)

Empedocles here speaks out of his doctrine of metempsychosis, but Arnold's text is supplying the old idea with a contemporary equivalent. Empedocles is reincarnated in the "mind" of Arnold's poem, in the "action" of the Victorian poet.

§

In 1853 Arnold did not reject this reading of *Empedocles;* he came to believe that it was a reading which would do his age no good, a reading which would not "animate" them to significant action. "I am glad you like the Gipsy Scholar," he writes Clough, but what does it *do* for you? Homer *animates*—Shakespeare *animates*—in its poor way I think Sohrab and Rustum *animates*—the Gipsy Scholar at best awakens a pleasing melancholy. But this is not what we want.

> *The complaining millions of men*
> *Darken and labour in pain—*

what they want is something to *animate* and *ennoble* them—not merely to add zest to their melancholy or grace to their dreams.—I believe a feeling of this kind is the basis of my nature—and of my poetics. (*LC* 146)

Of course one might well ask what could be more pleasingly melancholic than "Sohrab and Rustum?" The significance of Arnold's statement does not lie in its entire accuracy, however, but in the direction of its thought. What Arnold wants is poetry that will animate his readers with *adequate* ideas. Consequently, the critical and deconstructive thinking of his 1852 *Empedocles* is now judged "morbid," "monotonous," "painful" (*P* 592), and the transformational vision in which the poem concludes had come to seem no more than a zesty and graceful dream.

We have no need to develop an 1853/1855 "reading" of *Empedocles* because Arnold has done that for us: in the 1853 Preface, first of all, but also in the (fractured) text(s) of *Empedocles* which he published partly in the 1853 volume and partly in the new edition of that book which he published in 1855.[13]

In 1853 Arnold printed "Cadmus and Harmonia," which is lifted from *Empedocles* 1.2.427–60, and in 1855 he printed "The Philosopher and the Stars" (from *Empedocles* 2.i.276–300) as well as the four other Calliclean lyrics under the general heading "The Harp-player on Etna": "The Last Glen" (which is *Empedocles* 1.2.36–76); "Typho" (which is *Empedocles* 2.37–88); "Marsyas" (which is *Empedocles* 2.121–90); and "Apollo" (which is *Empedocles* 2.417–68, the conclusion).

In their new contexts, these poems do not mean what they mean in the 1852 volume. On the contrary, they have slipped beneath the prose judgments set forth in the 1853 Preface, where the deconstruction of Arnold's "dramatic poem" *Empedocles on Etna* produces, as a side effect, the option to encapsulate the Apollonian lyrics of Callicles. In the context of the dramatic poem the lyrics had fallen to the judgment of Empedocles—itself a partial, if also a commanding, point of view—and thence under the judgment of the whole dramatic poem. But in 1853/1855 they are set free as integral, "architectonic"—even "monumental"—pieces. The change is especially clear in the case of the most important of these texts, the closing lines of *Empedocles,* which in 1855 becomes—as the culminant text in "The Harp-player on Etna" series—"Apollo." In the 1855 printing it is all but impossible to register the presence, least of all the significance, of the overlapping images (Helicon/Etna, Apollo/Empedocles), whereas in 1852 that effect is at the very heart of what Arnold has done.

One might think that when the complete text of *Empedocles* was reprinted in 1867 (with only minor local changes), the poem had been restored to its original, 1852 condition. But this is not the case. The intervention of the 1853/1855 *Empedocles* has not been erased, as Arnold's note to the 1867 text makes explicit. As a consequence (and by an extreme paradox), the 1852 version becomes, in 1867, an even more searching and incommensurable text than it had been at the outset. This effect is paradoxical because it is a direct consequence of the 1853/1855 intervention, and because that intervention was carried out as a critical move against the poetic authority of unstable texts as such.

The 1867 *Empedocles* is a new and far more trenchant version of 1852. Line for poetical line the two texts do not look very different, but imagine reading the 1867 text under the aegis of the 1853 Preface: imagine, literally and materially, a book in which *Empedocles* was printed with the Preface inserted either immediately before it or immediately after it. Our texts of the poem normally relegate the Preface to an appendix, or they separate the two pieces by some comfortable distance. But we are wrong to enforce such separations, and the best readers of Arnold's poetry have always brought the dramatic poem and its prose rejoinder into close proximity. In doing so, however, such readers have discovered an extreme set of interpretive problems and paradoxes. That situation is what I am calling the 1867 *Empedocles,* so named because Arnold himself generated the situation by his decision to resurrect the Frankenstein monster he had first created and then destroyed.

§

Arnold's inaugural lecture in the Poetry Chair at Oxford, delivered in 1857, recurs to the same issues he raised in the 1853 Preface. But "On the Modern Element in Literature" represents an advance in the systematic element of his work. Here, for example, Arnold develops at length his ideas about poetic "adequacy" and "the critical spirit." One recurs to Greek models, Arnold argues, because Greek literature "interpreted" its world more comprehensively than any other. More than that, Greek literature achieved the "critical spirit," which he calls—the formulation is ultimately Kantian—the "rational arrangement and appreciation of facts."[14] "Disinterestedness" is the tonal mark of this critical spirit, but its object is fundamental knowledge: "to search [facts] for their law, not to wander among them at random, to judge by the rule of reason" (*CP* 24). Thinking in a critical spirit allows one a form of knowledge that stands in what Arnold calls "the true point of view" (*CP* 20, 29).

In all this one observes Arnold's desire to move beyond what he defined as Clough's situation: that is, to achieve "assured knowledge" rather than "to be ever learning, never coming to the knowledge of the truth." In the 1853 Preface he declared that he had come to the knowledge of the truth about *Empedocles;* and in his inaugural lecture he went further still and declared that he had arrived at the knowledge of what was entailed in "the knowledge of the truth" as such. He found this kind of knowledge in Greek literature, and he argued that it was—being "assured knowledge"—recoverable at any time. Greek literature is always "modern" because it has penetrated to the "law" of its subject, because it is, in short, "universal."

But if we ask "What is this ultimate and universal knowledge?" Arnold does not abide our question; or rather, we are not answered in a substantive form. Most readers of Arnold's prose have experienced its characteristic evaporation effect, if I may so call it, whereby a monumental structure ("assured knowledge") is verbally imagined, elaborated, and pursued until it finally disappears in the mist of its own words. In the end we may well feel like the superstitious Pausanias, who comes to Empedocles in search of the "secret" to the truth of Pantheia's life and Empedocles' practical curative powers, but who is given instead a stoical sermon.

The problem is not in what Arnold has written, however, but in the initial superstition with which we tend to approach his work. This superstition Arnold labored under as well, which is why his prose—a model of clarity at the surface—is so difficult to negotiate. The superstition, expressed in the simplest terms, is that there is a fundamental difference between "knowledge" and "knowing," or that one can come into the "possession" of the truth the way we imagine that we can own or possess "things." This kind of idea is properly called a superstition because it has imagined an "assured" control over circumstances: a way to triumph over the world's multitudinousness, to bring Pantheia back from the dead. In the ancient world it was called magical knowledge; in ours it is called technology.

Arnold denigrated his *Empedocles,* as well as his model in Lucretius, because both seemed "overstrained, gloom-weighted, morbid; and he who is morbid is no adequate interpreter of his age" (*CP* 34). An adequate knowledge, Arnold insists, must "animate," and not depress, the spirit; it must bring sweetness and light. But Arnold's prose (like his poetry) does not show us the objective source of this power to animate, so that in reading him we feel that we are being given words instead of things, suggestion for substance. And we feel this all the more because, although Arnold denigrates the magical pursuits of Pausanias, he himself seems to have placed a magical demand upon his own idea of knowledge: the demand for what he calls "An intellectual deliverance": "It begins when our mind begins to enter into the possession of the general ideas which are the law of this vast multitude of facts. It is perfect when we have acquired that harmonious acquiescence of mind which we feel in contemplating a grand spectacle that is intelligible to us; when we have lost that impatient irritation of mind which we feel in presence of an immense, moving, confused spectacle which, while it perpetually excites our curiosity, perpetually baffles our comprehension" (*CP* 20). There is no more famous passage in Arnold's prose, and it exhibits the evaporation effect perfectly. The argument postulates a process of knowledge, from quest to "perfect" attainment, and it asserts that a "harmonious" mind is the sign of one who possesses comprehensive knowledge. Such a mind exhibits no irritation or impatience because, of course, it has achieved full "possession of the general ideas which are the law" of the world's multitudinousness. Yet we are never told what those ideas are—not here or anywhere else; instead, we are given a picture, an "Exhibition," a "model," of a mind— Arnold's—which appears to move without impatience or irritation. We are left to infer, from the objective appearance of that mind, the objective presence of those "general ideas" which, presumably, have delivered this mind into a state of peace.

What "animates" us, in face of this passage, is not the postulated "general ideas" but the "style," that is, the (linguistic) image of a mind taking pleasure in the entertainment of its thoughts. The "general ideas" are the most phantasmal part of this passage, which has found its true "substance" in its own activity. The "general ideas" are a function of Arnold's superstitious and magical attachments to a body of "eternal truths" which would apply to all times, to all people, to all circumstances. The *idea* of such a body of ideas, that is, the commitment to them, is the motor which drives the Arnoldian mind that is working here.

Arnold's work, however, his actual writing, knows far more of the truth than has been dreamt in the philosophy of his magical and imperial intellect. In the first place, as we have already noticed, his own best prose exposes the ideological character of his magical attachments. Arnold, the thinking and writing agent: he is the substance, whereas the "general ideas" are the shadow; and Arnold's prose is aware of this. For example, when he seeks to define "the supreme characteristic of . . . the intellectual maturity of man himself," we are given an "idea," it is true. But the form which that idea is made to assume is the most telling part of the passage. The "supreme characteristic" is not that "possession" or "law" he sometimes speaks of, but a "tendency to observe facts with a critical spirit, to search for their law, not to wander among them at random." What is "supreme" here is not the "law", but the searching agent.

In his 1858 letter to his sister, Arnold defined poetic achievement as the marriage of "perfection of form" to "perfection in the region of thought and feeling"; and he lamented that the quest for such a union should have involved, for him, "an actual tearing of oneself to pieces." Arnold wanted his ideal to "animate" rather than to depress, but his own work as a poet seemed a perpetual agon. In this respect his situation exactly mirrors that of Empedocles, whose final speech (2.191–416)—particularly the latter portion (301–416)—exposes the obscurities and contradictions which he allowed his sister to glimpse in private, but which have been disguised in the public arena of Arnold's luminous and imperial prose.

Arnold represents Empedocles, at the end of the play, as crucified by his failure to maintain in himself a "Fullness of life and power of feeling" (2.259). Because he is "dead to life and joy," he "read[s] / In all things my own deadness" (2.321–22). Empedocles judges that this emotional emptiness is a function of his ferocity of mind:

Thou art
A living man no more, Empedocles!
Nothing but a devouring flame of thought—
But a naked, eternally restless mind!   *(2.327–30)*

Empedocles is in that "continuous state of mental distress" which
Arnold in his 1853 Preface called "poetically faulty" because it was
"painful, not tragic," because it was "unrelieved by incident, hope,
or resistance."

And yet Empedocles' condition does not seem quite so blank. His
suicide is an incident of some consequence, particularly in the context of Empedocles' own ideas about metempsychosis. Moreover, if
he feels the absence of that "pure natural joy" which distinguished
his youth when "neither thought / Nor outward things were closed
and dead to us" (2.240–43), we do not witness any diminishment in
the intensity of his feelings. Indeed, that intensity drives his "resistance" to his situation—his refusal to abandon the ideal he associates with his youth, when

> *we received the shock of mighty thoughts*
> *On simple minds with a pure natural joy;*
> *And if the sacred load oppressed our brain,*
> *We had the power to feel the pressure eased,*
> *The brow unbound, the thoughts flow free again,*
> *In the delightful commerce of the world.*   *(242–47)*

The older Empedocles no longer has that innocence and ease. But
in the 1852 play Arnold had greater sympathy for the older Empedocles, for the man who had "not grown easy in [his] bonds" and
who had "not denied what bonds these were" (2.396–97). This is
probably because, in 1852, Arnold had laid greater stress on Empedocles' circumstances, on "the world" for which he had no love,
and with which he felt himself at war. And we would do well to recall
the world that Arnold was recalling in his play: the time is circa 433
B.C., i.e., the action occurs on the brink of the war in which classical
Greece, at the apex of its greatness (according to Arnold's judgment), would tear itself to pieces; and the place is Sicily, i.e., the very
site where the last scenes of that tragic conflict would be played out.

Furthermore, in 1852 Arnold laid greater stress on the processes
of transformation which Empedocles' suicide evoked. His death

promised not merely an extinction of his suffering but an elemental salvation in "the sure revolutions of the world." Empedocles' doctrine of metempsychosis is most trenchantly literalized in Arnold's use of the word *elements* (2.331, 404), which in the pre-Socratic context refers to the earth, air, fire, and water of which all matter is constituted. But the mind, whose salvation so troubles Empedocles, is not embodied in those materials, and hence cannot imagine its salvation through them. Thus, when Empedocles plunges into the crater he plunges into a darkness his philosophy had not yet penetrated. But Arnold plays on the word *elements* in order to suggest that "mind" will be found "in" earth, air, fire, and water as the power which conceived them in the first place as elemental. The Empedoclean "mind" is not in any of those elements, it is in their "set." We understand this, in fact, when we recognize that the word *elements*, which *Empedocles* invokes in the context of natural philosophy, would have to call to mind the periodic table in the nineteenth-century.[15] That nineteenth-century context throws into relief the factual incorrectness of Empedocles' original elemental theory of matter, of course, but it also highlights the mental continuities stretching between fifth-century Greece and nineteenth-century Europe. Empedocles lives on into that "modern" world in his elemental thought, in his early understanding that the material world is in part a mental function. Empedocles' elemental theory is "transformed," is "saved," in the conceptual structure of modern chemistry.

In 1853, however, Arnold saw more deeply into the contradictions which his play had set in motion. It was all very well to imagine the transformation and salvation of Empedocles; the question was, would that event "animate" us or depress us? In 1853 Arnold read the concluding speech of Empedocles once again and found a problem in its transformational salvation. Even if "mind" and "thought" (2.345) are saved, and "we shall still be in them, and they in us" (2.349), the event may involve no more than a cycle of dissatisfactions:

> *and still thought and mind*
> *Will hurry us with them on their homeless march,*
> *Over the unallied unopening earth,*
> *Over the unrecognising sea; while air*
> *Will blow us fiercely back to sea and earth,*

Jerome J. McGann

> *And first repel us from its living waves.*
> *And then we shall unwillingly return*
> *Back to this meadow of calamity,*
> *This uncongenial place, this human life,*
> *And in our individual human state*
> *Go through the sad probation all again.*   *(2.358–68)*

Empedocles here turns his own theories against himself, imagining the mind in a desperate cycle of failures, swinging between an inability to control the world of nature and an incapacity to live in the world of ordinary human beings. This is the essence of his present life's experience, so that if his own ideas about transformation are correct, this is what he may expect throughout those "sure revolutions of the world."

> *And each succeeding age in which we are born*
> *Will have more peril for us than the last . . .*
> *And we shall fly for refuge to past times,*
> *Their soul of unworn youth, their breath of greatness;*
> *And the reality will pluck us back,*
> *Knead us in its hot hand, and change our nature*
> *And we shall feel our powers of effort flag,*
> *And rally them for one last fight—and fail;*
> *And we shall sink in the impossible strife,*
> *And be astray for ever.*   *(2.377–78, 383–90)*

This prospect of a cycle of final struggles and final failures seemed to Arnold in 1853 entirely too bleak and dispiriting. Arnold had fled for refuge to past times of greatness, but he found instead only the repetition of his own "reality," a Victorian face in an antique mirror.

The disappointment which is enshrined in Arnold's 1853 reading of *Empedocles* may begin to be unraveled in this passage: specifically, in that deeply Arnoldian (and Victorian) idea about seeking refuge in the greatness of the past. As Warren Anderson has observed, "Coming from a Pre-Socratic philosopher this would have no relation to any conceivable reality. It is Matthew Arnold who speaks, and in his words we see emerging a new attitude toward the Hellenic tradition."[16] But the passage in *Empedocles* is a problem because of the dramatic context. From 1853 and for the rest of his life Arnold would extol those "past times" with "Their soul of unworn youth, their breath of greatness." In this play, however, the words are not simply placed in the mouth of Empedocles, they are part of his culminant expression of despair.

In this respect, the 1853 reading of *Empedocles is deeply self-contradicted.* The play is prepared to deconstruct the theory of touch-stones at the very moment the theory is first put forth in an extended and public way, i.e., in the 1853 Preface. Arnold's glimpse of this deep antinomy in the play turned him from reading it as "tragic," as he must have read it in 1852, to reading it as "painful," as he did in 1853. In consequence, he produced an 1853 text which, by removing the offending textual presences altogether, allowed the theory of touchstones to remain intact—or at any rate, *un*attacked by his own poetic tale. Arnold's Greece could thereby remain objective and therefore possessable. As Warren Anderson acutely observed, "it is as if the Greek world were becoming externalized."[17]

The 1867 *Empedocles* is produced in full consciousness of the judgment of 1853. That is to say, the 1867 text is the text of 1853 printed in unexpurgated form, and with the suggestion that, if its "painfulness" and "morbidity" are an offense to Arnold's idea of the Higher Criticism, they may also, somehow, carry the sanction of poetic "genius." And indeed the 1867 *Empedocles* is the best text we have—the richest text, as well as the most complete. Here the "mind" and "thought" of Arnold's Empedocles is shown to be *Empedocles on Etna* itself, the "home" and "parent element" (2.345–47) of what Arnold's Empedocles was seeking.

What happens in the 1867 text is the redemption of the play from its own reified elements. No longer does the play have to meet Arnold's conceptual determinants. Its "painful" aspects, for example, restored now in their full textuality, cease to be the absolute terrors Arnold had imagined them to be. If they are terrors still, they have also been moved into a set of shifting and balanced relationships with the other affective dimensions of the work. Most crucially, perhaps, the play of 1867 translates those key terms *mind* and *thought* into operational rather than categorical equivalents. As a consequence, Empedocles' search for the ultimate "truth" behind all shifting appearances is not simply revealed to be a failure it is exposed as an illusion—like his desire to escape the cycles of pleasure and pain. Following Arnold, Empedocles had defined those cycles in desperate terms, but the 1867 text argues instead that they are supervened by a greater desperation still: by the demonic imagination of a world without such cycles and their transformations, or a world in which the transformations have turned into a vision of hell—what Blake's Urizen sought to escape when he quested for "a joy without pain . . . a solid without fluctuation."[18]

In the 1867 text the illusion of the "truth" appears as the reality of knowledge; and the "parent element" of imperiled "mind" and "thought," the salvific material which Arnold's play postulates, is "the action of men" through which mind and thought are executed. In *Empedocles* that parent element is further specified, following Arnold's adherence to the model of literature, as poetic writing. However, the 1867 play shifts the Calliclean and Apollonian model of poetry from its central position, and forces the text to accept the alternative claims of Empedoclean verse, with its commitments to dissonance, prose, and incompletion.

Thus, in 1867 we come to see that it is not the verse of Callicles which serves us for a touchstone any more than it is the verse of Empedocles. The first represents for Arnold the memorial function of writing, a mode of verse which "saves" what is valuable in the past. The second represents the executive function of writing, a mode of verse which reveals that poetry is itself one of those "actions of men" celebrated and memorialized by Callicles. They represent that ancient antinomy between poetry as formal perfection and poetry as rhetorical act. One regards the whole, the other regards the parts; and whereas in Callicles we find no irritable reaching after fact and reason, in Empedocles we witness the ceaseless Promethean engagement with the particulars of resistant circumstance.

Only in the 1867 *Empedocles on Etna* has Arnold fully articulated his understanding of the meaning of that struggle. In this third text of *Empedocles* the answer to Empedocles' question about "what" or "who" will "save" the agency of mind, in particular the mind of Empedocles, is given a clear answer. The play puts two optional answers—both traditional—to the test. In each case the deficiencies of these answers are exposed. Callicles' Apollonian music is clearly inadequate to "save" the restless energies of Empedocles; and Arnold uses the historical fact of Empedocles' fragmentary literary remains as a witness against the claims his work might have made. If Empedocles could "save" others, himself—like Jesus—he could not save.

Arnold and Empedocles

Empedocles on Etna is the "Ode to Psyche" written for a Byronic hero rather than for a gentle wood nymph. That is to say, Empedocles is "saved" in and through Arnold's belated act of poetic agency. In this sense the play argues that mind is saved through further acts of mind. But it is crucial to see that "mind" in the play is gradually shown to be forever incapable of "assured knowledge." This is so, first of all, because the hero of the drama is a figure who is himself "ever learning, never coming to the knowledge of the truth." But it is also true because the hero's belated pale-mouthed prophet, Matthew Arnold, cannot bring his own thought about Empedocles into "the true point of view." He cannot do this because his play has not, like its own 1853/55 text, removed altogether its Empedoclean elements.

What this means, most crucially, is that *Empedocles* is an argumentative and rhetorical poem. It argues that there must be a poetic form, a form of wholeness, which will be adequate to the Empedoclean and Byronic spirit. It is a poem that reaches after fact and reason. But in doing so, it has condemned itself to that process of irresolution which Arnold lamented: to be ever learning, to be never in possession of an assured knowledge. In this sense, what it celebrates is, not "assured knowledge," but the endurance of the activity of knowing as that activity is carried out in poetry.

Thus we may see the appropriateness, the perfection in a way, of the final, 1867 text of the work. This is a text whose meaning Arnold himself did not and could not fully understand. We know that he did not because he produces the text only at the intervention of an external agency, the "poetic genius" that came to him in the figure of Robert Browning. We know that he could not because the produced texts—all three of them—are self-contradicted. The poem is "irritable" at its core because it reaches after facts and reasons for an activity—poetry—which it has imagined as ideally free of such questing and questioning.

The 1867 text is the "best text," however, because in it the play's contradictions and inadequacies are least disguised—or rather, most fully realized. In this text is summarized the entire history of the poem's irritabilities. The text shows that the "parent element" of Empedoclean "mind" and "thought" is language conceived as one of the primary "actions of men." The text further argues that the parent element is, in this particular case, originally embodied in those acts of Matthew Arnold called *Empedocles on Etna*. But those acts are irritable and unsatisfied, and have left behind them an irritating and unsatisfactory legacy. Yet in that history of unsuccess we recognize the poem's achievement. *Empedocles on Etna*, more than any of Arnold's other works, stands in "the true point of view" because it has "externalized itself" even in its act of externalizing, of fictionalizing, its subjects. It is a work which, having at last agreed to include itself in its subject matter, has finally demanded that all things must be called into question. That is not "the critical spirit" as Arnold defined it in his prose, yet it is, particularly for a man like Arnold, truly a remarkable achievement.

Notes

1. *The Poems of Matthew Arnold*, ed. Kenneth Allott (London: Longman, 1965), pp. 590–91. I will use this edition (hereafter cited in the text as *P*, followed by the page number) for all quotations from the poetry and from the Preface to the 1853 volume.

2. These were all the songs of Callicles, plus one section from Empedocles's discourse. The text of *1853* printed only the Cadmus and Harmonia lyric; *1855*, the second edition of *1853*, printed the remainder of the fragments. See discussion that follows.

3. These are Arnold's words in his note to the 1867 printing of the poem.

4. This is in an 1857 letter to his brother Tom quoted in R. L. Lowe, "Two Arnold Letters," *Modern Philology* 52 (1955): 263. The texts of Arnold's letters quoted herein are taken from various currently available published sources, but they have been corrected against the texts that will be printed in the forthcoming edition of the complete letters edited by Cecil Y. Lang.

5. Dwight Culler, *Imaginative Reason: The Poetry of Matthew Arnold* (New Haven: Yale University Press, 1966), p. 155.

6. For a discussion of "Sohrab and Rustum" which is related to this treatment of *Empedocles*, see my *Social Values and Poetic Acts* (Cambridge, Mass.: Harvard University Press, 1987), pp. 82–92.

7. *Unpublished Letters of Matthew Arnold*, ed. Arnold Whitridge (New Haven: Yale University Press, 1923), p. 17; see also Culler, *Imaginative Reason*, pp. 74–78.

8. *The Letters of Matthew Arnold to Arthur Hugh Clough*, ed. Howard Foster Lowry (London: Oxford University Press, 1932), p. 59. Hereafter cited in the text as *LC*, followed by the page number.

9. In the same letter Arnold shows, however, that in placing his new emphasis on the importance of "contents" and meaning, he has not altogether abandoned his earlier formal imperatives. Because "poetry . . . has . . . an immense task to perform," he says, "it must not lose itself in parts and episodes and ornamental work, but must press forwards to the whole" (*LC* 59). This remark clearly anticipates the formulations about poetic wholeness that he would begin to develop more fully in the Preface to the 1853 volume.

10. *Letters of Matthew Arnold, 1848–1888*, ed. G. W. E. Russell (London: Macmillan, 1901), 1:84.

11. The fourth possible version is the 1855 edition of the 1853 *Poems;* for in the

1855 edition Arnold printed all five of the lyrics of Callicles from *Empedocles,* whereas in 1853 he only printed "Cadmus and Harmonia."

12.   See the *OED* for "dumb," where one finds that the word has denoted "lacking in understanding" since the fifteenth century at least.

13.   The volume was titled *Poems* (Second Series [1855]).

14.   The text here is from that collected in *Matthew Arnold: On the Classical Tradition,* ed. R. H. Super (Ann Arbor: University of Michigan Press, 1960), p. 25. Hereafter cited in text as *CP* followed by the page number.

15.   About sixty elements had been distinguished in Arnold's time.

16.   See Warren D. Anderson, *Matthew Arnold and the Classical Tradition* (Ann Arbor: University of Michigan Press, 1971), p. 43.

17.   Ibid.

18.   *The [First] Book of Urizen,* plate 4 (see *William Blake: The Book of Urizen,* ed. Kay Parkhurst Easson and Roger R. Easson [Boulder, Col.: Shambala Press, 1978], p. 38).

J. Hillis Miller

Praeterita and the Pathetic Fallacy

*I*n two previous essays on Ruskin I have argued, in the first, that the pathetic fallacy, so forcefully denounced in a famous section of *Modern Painters* 3, is in fact a dyslogistic name for prosopopoeia, the ascription of a name, a face, and a voice to the absent, the inanimate, or the dead, and, in the second, that Ruskin's preface of 1885 to *Praeterita* proposes ways to perform the exceedingly difficult act of avoiding prosopopoeia in an autobiography.[1] If Paul de Man is right, and he *is* right, to say that "prosopopoeia is the trope of autobiography, by which one's name . . . is made as intelligible and memorable as a face,"[2] then it would seem impossible to avoid committing in an autobiography the idolatrous sin of the pathetic fallacy in the peculiarly narcissistic form of the creation of an effigy in words of one's past self and then ascribing to it a name, a face, a voice: animation, in short. Nevertheless, the project outlined in the preface is in fact carried out by many elements in text proper. In this brief essay I shall attempt to sketch these out and then identify a fundamental problem with Ruskin's attempt to avoid prosopopoeia in his autobiography.

In spite of the fact that *Praeterita* brings to life for the reader many persons—not only the young Ruskin himself, but his parents, relatives, teachers, acquaintances, and so on—there is still much emphasis on scenes; on landscape, mountains, rivers, flowers; and on the architecture Ruskin studied with such loving care. Moreover, both the things and the people are treated with a kind of distancing condescension. They are held at arm's length to be scrutinized and described, as a geologist inspects a rock: "My entire delight was in observing without being myself noticed,—if I could have been invisible, all the better. I was absolutely interested in men and their ways, as I was interested in marmots and chamois, in tomtits and trout. If only they would stay still and let me look at them, and not get into their holes and up their heights! . . .—this was the essential love *of Nature* in me, this the root of all that I have usefully become, and the light of all that I have rightly learned."[3]

One pervading stylistic tone of *Praeterita* is comic irony. This is especially evident in the old Ruskin's treatment of his foolish, arrogant, proud, ignorant young self, but it is present in his treatment of others too. One example out of the superabundance of possible ones is what Ruskin says of his father's plans for him: "His ideal of my future,—now entirely formed in conviction of my genius,—was that I should enter at college into the best society, take all the prizes every year, and a double first to finish with; marry Lady Clara Vere de Vere; write poetry as good as Byron's, only pious; preach sermons as good as Bossuet's, only Protestant; be made, at forty, Bishop of Winchester, and at fifty, Primate of England" (p. 185).

This ironic condescending distance of the old Ruskin who writes *Praeterita* from his young self about whom he writes and from the associates of that young self is reinforced by a constant stream of depersonifying figures. The old Ruskin continually speaks of the young Ruskin as something less than a person. His early life, for example, is said to have been "days of mere rivulet-singing, in my poor little watercress life" (p. 151). Of his foolish infatuation with the daughter of his father's business partner, he says: "while in company I sate jealously miserable like a stock fish (in truth, I imagine, looking like nothing so much as a skate in an aquarium trying to get up the glass)" (p. 180). Of this childish love, he says his mother "was rather annoyed at the whole business, as she would have been if one of her chimneys had begun smoking,—but had not the slightest notion her house was on fire." The callow youth John Ruskin in love is said to have lived in a "daily swelling foam of furious conceit" (p. 181). At that time of his life, he says, "There was really no more capacity nor intelligence in me than in a just fledged owlet, or just open-eyed puppy, disconsolate at the existence of the moon" (pp. 183–84). Of himself a little later, at Oxford, he says, "I had been received as a good-humoured and inoffensive little cur, contemptuously, yet kindly, among dogs of race at the gentlemen-commoners' table" (p. 195). Of all his missed opportunities at Oxford he says: "Alas! there I stood—or tottered—partly irresolute, partly idiotic, in the midst of them: nothing that I can think of among men, or birds, or beasts, quite the image of me except poor little Shepherdess Agnes's picture of the 'Duckling Astray'" (p. 199). Later still he speaks of his "chrysalid torpor" (p. 227) or of himself as "a little floppy and soppy tadpole,—little more than a stomach with a tail to it, flattening and wriggling itself up the crystal ripples and in the pure sands of the spring-head of youth" (pp. 279–80). These figures are eloquent and funny, but the effect of their recurrence is to depersonify the young Ruskin. This functions as an indirect way of asserting the personality of the presently speaking, writing, and judging "I," the grownup frog or butterfly who looks back from the height of achieved wisdom on the foolish tadpole or crysalis he once was.

These last two images also suggest a model of sudden discontinuous transformative growing up. Like many autobiographers—for example, like the Rousseau of the *Confessions*—Ruskin appropriates from Augustine and from the general tradition of religious autobiography the motif of decisive conversion. But, like Rousseau again, Ruskin contradicts this motif's implication of a once and for all change, as of Saul into Paul or of Augustine the sinful rhetorician into the prospective Christian saint, by multiplying the moments of conversion and spreading them out over a long temporal sequence. Like Rousseau, Ruskin locates the decisive moment of change first here and then there, as though one could be converted and converted again, in defiance of the logic of conversion that defines it as a river that can be crossed only once. On each occassion, Ruskin says something like: "Forever after I was different," or "From this experience I date my commitment to so and so." Here are three examples, out of a great many that punctuate the *Praeterita* like so many little inaugural moments dividing the past from the future, each one implicitly contradicting the claim of all the others to be such a moment. Of his first glimpse of the Alps, from Schaffhausen, in 1833, Ruskin says, "I went down that evening from the garden-terrace of Schaffhausen with my destiny fixed in all of it that was to be sacred and useful" (p. 116). Then of his first view of the Jura two years later he says: "but the Col de la Faucille, on that day of 1835, opened to me in distant vision the Holy Land of my future work and true home in this world" (p. 167). The third example, a decisive moment in the long record in *Praeterita* of the gradual erosion of Ruskin's belief in the evangelical Protestantism he had learned from his mother, makes explicit Ruskin's awareness that his life did not organize itself around a single moment of conversion. Nevertheless, the passage singles out a moment of 1858, when Ruskin turned to Veronese's *Solomon and the Queen of Sheba* in the gallery at Turin from the shabby Protestant service he had attended earlier that day, as being particularly decisive. The moment was a kind of living oxymoron, a conversion not really a conversion because he was already converted: "Of course that hour's meditation in the gallery of Turin only concluded the courses of thought which had been leading me to such end through many years. There was no sudden conversion possible to me, either by preacher, picture or dulcimer. But, that day, my evangelical beliefs were put away, to be debated no more" (p. 496).

This contradictory notion of a conversion experience that can be repeated over and over in a different form throughout life is itself contradicted again by Ruskin's insistence, throughout *Praeterita*, on another fundamental Protestant idea. This is the notion that he was born with a fixed character that remained essentially the same throughout all the vicissitudes and changes of his life. There are many affirmations of this in *Praeterita*. One follows the often-cited passage from the last chapter of *Praeterita* 1 in which Ruskin asserts that he differed from other children even of his own type in mixing in hyperbolic plenitude three incompatible but inalterable constituents: "I had, in my little clay pitcher, vialfuls, as it were, of Wordsworth's reverence, Shelley's sensitiveness, Turner's accuracy, all in one" (p. 220). A passage just after this in the manuscript, cut in the published version, asserts that his character was a mixture of "pervicacity [*sic* in Cook and Wedderburn, possibly a misreading of 'pervivacity?'] and unchangeableness" (p. 608). The two terms are expanded in a forceful double image (another depersonifying one, like the image of the chemicals mixed in a clay vial): "So that the aspect of my life to its outward beholder is of an extremely desultory force—at its best—confusedly iridescent—unexpectedly and wanderingly sparkling or extinct like a ragged bit of tinder. Only by much attention—if any one cares to give it,—nor then without some clue of personal word, like this I am writing,—could the spectator of me at all imagine what an obstinate little black powder of adamant the faltering sparks glowed through the grain of" (pp. 608–9). The published text then picks this up with a resounding assertion that he was not converted at all but remained inalterably fixed throughout: "But so stubborn and chemically inalterable the laws of the prescription were, that now, looking back from 1886 to that brook shore of 1837, whence I could see the whole of my youth, I find myself in nothing whatsoever *changed*" (p. 220).

In the preface of 1885 Ruskin proposes to describe in *Praeterita* his "personal character" (p. 11). *Praeterita* itself does this in a way that is faithful to the avoidance of prosopopoeia by speaking habitually of that "character" as though it were a thing, not a person, as in this image of the chemical prescription. That character, however, was a chemical mixture of a peculiar kind that could change but not change, change once and for all and yet go on changing decisively again, while still remaining stubbornly and obstinately the same. The drama of *Praeterita*, or its strange narrative logic, is the representation along a temporal line of more and more episodes that bring into the open or exemplify this double contradiction.

There is, however, one more topic related to the rejection of prosopopoeia that must be discussed here. This is the question of Ruskin's notorious loss of religious belief. The loss is often said to be the secret drama of *Praeterita*, as it was of the lives of so many eminent Victorians. I have already cited the famous passage in which Ruskin turns his back on the Protestant chapel and chooses rather Veronese's Solomon and Sheba glowing "in full afternoon light" (p. 495). As with everything else in *Praeterita*, things are not so simple here either. Ruskin both lost his religious faith and did not lose it. Wordsworth's reverence, for which a snowdrop was "part of the Sermon on the Mount" (p. 220), was as much a fixed part of his character as Turner's accuracy that saw things exactly as they were, without evasion by a single metaphor. This penchant for "accuracy," as I have shown, led Ruskin to hatred of the personifying pathetic fallacy, especially in its narcissistic form: "With Shelley, I loved blue sky and blue eyes, but never in the least confused the heavens with my own poor little Psychidion" (p.220). The passage about his conversion to the religion of art, to the profane beauty of Sheba, or rather of one of her maid's of honor, or rather of Veronese's painting of the maid of honor, glowing in the afternoon sun (see p. 497), ends with a claim that this aesthetic enjoyment is a form of reverence, a form of faith: "And as the perfect colour and sound gradually asserted their power on me, they seemed finally to fasten me in the old article of Jewish faith, that things done delightfully and rightly were always done by the help and in the Spirit of God" (p. 496). The religion of art is still a religion, though Ruskin's defense of it here paradoxically invokes, not Christianity, but the Jewish faith, based on the Hebrew Bible, the faith that of course especially abjures graven images.

What does this deconversion that was not really a deconversion have to do with the renunciation of prosopopoeia? The answer is easy to see. The whole complex structure of Ruskin's assumptions about prosopopoeia falls to the ground or into the abyss if the underlying supporting assumption of the existence and omnipotence of God vanishes. The renunciation of the pathetic fallacy as idolatry depends on the assumption that only God has the right to give personality or to take it away. The assertion that the pathetic fallacy is justified in the language of those in a condition of prophetic exaltation, as Ruskin says in "On the Pathetic Fallacy," depends on the assumption that God and his workings in the world are so far above man as to be namable only in catachrestic personifications. Ruskin's project in the preface to *Praeterita* and his practice in the text itself transfer this structure from the proper naming of mountains, flowers, and the sea to the use of prosopopoeia as the fundamental trope of autobiography. But insofar as *Praeterita* tells the story of Ruskin's gradual loss of religious faith, the text pulls out from under itself its own basic presupposition. Without the support of religious faith, prosopopoeia in autobiography becomes no longer a complex prolepsis of the hoped-for resurrection after death but nothing more nor less than a figure both inevitable and in error whereby language ascribes a name, a face, and a voice to what does not, in fact, have them. This subjection to a linguistic rather than a religious predicament includes the personification of his past self by an autobiographer, along with the locutions of the lying poet who says the foam is cruel and crawls. *Praeterita,* like other works by Ruskin, is haunted throughout by this possibility. That he was unwilling or unable to choose unequivocally either possibility is evidence that "reverence" remained to the end as much a part of his "character" as a passion for truth-telling "accuracy." It is also testimony to Ruskin's recognition of the high stakes involved in the position one takes or allows one's language to take on apparently so narrow and "rhetorical" a question as the status of the figure of speech called prosopopoeia.

Notes

1. For the first essay, see my "Catachresis, Prosopopoeia, and the Pathetic Fallacy: The Rhetoric of Ruskin," in *Poetry and Epistemology,* ed. Roland Hagenbüchle and Laura Skandera (Regensburg: Verlag Friedrich Pustet, 1986), pp. 398–407. The second essay, "Prosopopoeia and *Praeterita,*" is forthcoming in a Festscrift for Jerome Hamilton Buckley, ed. John Maynard and Donald Stone (Cambridge: Cambridge University Press, 1989).

2. Paul de Man, "Autobiography as De-Facement," *The Rhetoric of Romanticism* (New York: Columbia University Press, 1984), p. 76.

3. John Ruskin, *Works,* library edition, ed. E. T. Cook and Alexander Wedderburn, vol. 35 (London: George Allen, 1908), p. 166. Page numbers for further quotations from this volume will be cited in the text.

William E. Fredeman

Pictures at an Exhibition Late-Victorian and Modern Perspectives on Pre-Raphaelitism

*T*he death, in 1919, of William Michael Rossetti, the last of the Pre-Raphaelite brothers, the secretary of the Brotherhood, and the editor of the *Germ,* marked the end of an era. Four decades later, a descendant of another brother, in a memoir that the *Times* reviewer described as "a most accomplished and sweetly satisfying performance," offered a succinct résumé of Rossetti's role in the formation and function of this unique movement in English art. The occasion is a Sunday "at home" hosted by the second Mrs. Holman Hunt—a deceased wife's sister—and her young granddaughter, Diana. After tea, the guests—among them Edward Marsh, Dean Inge, and an American lady, a Miss Clair van der Zuite—are divided into two groups for the tour of the pictures and house, furnished apparently with the bric-a-brac and costumes from every painting ever executed by the master. "That's a sketch of Leigh Hunt and *this* is Dante Gabriel Rossetti," announces the young tour guide:

> He was the villain of the piece.
> "My! What wonderful eyes!" cried the Yankee Lady. "He's always been my idol. Wasn't it he and Burne-Jones who started it all. Pre-Raphaelism I mean?"
> "Oh no, you've got it all wrong!" I was shocked, and thankful Grand couldn't hear. I had always hated Rossetti. It was his fault Helen gave us macaroni—slimy white worms. Grandpa had never eaten it before he met those sly Italians. Arthur called them Wops.

"He looks so romantic!" gushed the Yankee Lady, craning forward to see.

"He didn't really look a bit like that. He was dirty and horrid, his hair was always greasy and he spilt soup and spaghetti all down his clothes. They weren't even his! He borrowed everyone else's, even Bruno's. He never gave them back, and what's more he was a cheat!"

"Come now, I think that's a little hard," protested someone.

"Yes he was. He was Grandpa's pupil and never paid the rent and sent his picture—Grandpa'd painted most of it—to an exhibition, without telling him and Johnnie Millais, although he'd said he wouldn't until theirs were ready too. He ate Grandpa out of house and home and gave noisy parties, and shouted at the models. It was Grandpa and Johnnie who started it all and it was pre-Raphaeli*tism* with a T."

There was a sympathetic murmur.

"Poor Grandpa got thrown out because he hadn't any money and Mr. Ruskin turned against him because he was Johnnie's friend. Everything went wrong and it was all Rossetti's fault because he told lies and took all the credit."

"Well, that's a most interesting theory," said Mr. Edward Marsh. "Our small guide feels very strongly."

To these astonishing revelations, the American lady responds: "I feel mighty confused but I just can't wait to tell the folks at home. My, it's like living in the past!"[1]

§

If this amusing episode has a familiar ring, the redolence is not accidental: for Diana Holman-Hunt's recollections, while difficult to classify generically save as fiction imitating fiction, are essentially a recycling of the biases and disgruntlements of her grandpa's two volumes of recollections of the Brotherhood and the movement. On the eve of their publication (5 December 1905),[2] Hunt, disabled by asthma and afflicted by partial blindness, sent the following note to his old friend and fellow Pre-Raphaelite Brother, William Michael Rossetti:

Tomorrow I am told my book on Pre-Raphaelitism is to come out.

I cannot pretend that you will approve of my treatment of the subject for it is entirely in opposition to the theory for which you are specially responsible.

The fact that the world appeared to be satisfied with your story, although I daily had reason to see the harm it caused me, left me disinclined to enter the list against you for this I could see was necessary if I championed my view of the truth.

I know that you have not said a word opposed to your own understanding of the case and personal considerations would not have induced me to come into the arena but fresh publications were always appearing in the same tenor, so not private interest alone, but understanding of the cardinal purpose of Pre-Raphaelitism was being more and more distorted and for this I could not but feel heavily responsible. The conviction of your own good faith assured me that you would respect the independence of an opposite witness and I could not fear that you would regard my independent course as necessarily hostile to my long standing esteem and affection for you.

Advancing age to both of us has prevented meetings between us of late years or I should explain myself by word of mouth. Now I am obliged to be content with this letter although it is a colder form for the expression of friendship, the moreso in having to be written by another hand.

William noted in his diary that in responding to this letter, he had forewarned Hunt that he might possibly insert into his own forthcoming *Reminiscences* "some rejoinder to his allegations," but he added, in deference to their long friendship, "Don't at all want to do this if it can be helped."[3]

Hunt's autobiography is characterized by a tone that can only be described as militantly petulant, especially in those sections treating the formation and activities of the PRB. In the three final retrospective chapters, he argues violently, often vindictively, for the primacy of his and Millais's roles in the Pre-Raphaelite saga and for his having been Rossetti's chief mentor in painting. Particularly chagrined by the increasing prominence given to Rossetti in domestic and foreign critical studies of the movement, Hunt indicts both William Michael Rossetti and Frederic George Stephens, whom he labels the two nonartistic "sleeping brothers," as the culprits responsible both for misreporting the aims of the Brotherhood, which, he avers, they never understood, and for promulgating the claims of Ford Madox Brown's influence and Rossetti's leadership.

As Helen Rossetti Angeli noted in her impartial survey of Hunt's postmortem attacks on Rossetti,[4] there is ample evidence that Rossetti himself never advanced his own cause as the founder of the Pre-Raphaelites, as Hunt maintains. Indeed, in a letter written to Ernest Chesneau on 7 November 1868, on the occasion of the publication of that critic's *Les nations rivales dans l'art*—the central section from which William Michael printed in his *Memoir* of his brother—Rossetti rebutted unequivocally Chesneau's description of him as "Chef de l'Ecole Pré-Raphaélites," arguing to the point that

> when I find a painter so absolutely original as Holman Hunt described as being my "disciple," it is impossible for me not to feel humiliated in the presence of the truth, or to refrain from assuring you of the contrary with the utmost energy. The qualities of realism, emotional but extremely painstaking (*minutieux*), which gave the *cachet* to the style known as Pre-Raphaelite, are to be found principally in all the work of Holman Hunt, in a great part of that of Madox Brown, in certain examples of Hughes' work, and in the admirable work of Millais' youth. It was our *camaraderie*, rather than any actual collaboration of style, which united my name to theirs in the days of enthusiasm of twenty years ago.[5]

As a matter of fact, rather than puffing his own role in the movement, Rossetti tended in late life to pooh-pooh the entire episode. Denying to Hall Caine the existence of an English school of painting, he said:

> [Brown is] more French than English; Hunt and Jones have no more claim to the name than I have. As for all the prattle about pre-Raphaelitism, I confess I am weary of it, and long have been. Why should we go on talking about the visionary vanities of half-a-dozen boys? We've all grown out of them, I hope, by now. . . . What you call the movement was serious enough, but the banding together under the title was all a joke. We had at that time a phenomenal antipathy to the Academy, and in sheer love of being outlawed signed our pictures with the well-known initials.[6]

Given the generosity of Hunt's treatment of Rossetti in his two 1886 *Contemporary Review* articles on the Brotherhood, subtitled "A Fight for Art," and in the encomia of his dedicatory address presented at the opening of the Rossetti Fountain in Cheyne Walk in 1887, his attacks in *Pre-Raphaelitism* appear both gratuitous and inconsistent, though readers familiar with J. G. Millais's life of his father (1898) will recognize distant echoes in Hunt's later recollections. "As to Rossetti," Millais says,

> the fact is he was never a Pre-Raphaelite at heart. Himself a man of great originality, and a free thinker in matters of Art, he was captivated by the independent spirit of the Brotherhood, and readily cast in his lot with them. But it was only for a time. By degrees, their methods palled upon his taste, and not caring any longer to uphold

them before the public, he broke with his old associates, determined to follow the peculiar bent of his genius, which taught him *not* to go to Nature for his inspirations, but to follow rather the flights of his own fancy. His subsequent career is sufficient evidence of that. Only two years after he first joined the Brotherhood, Mr. Hunt, who taught him all the technique he ever knew, got him to come down to Knole to paint a background straight from Nature whilst he overlooked and helped him. After two days, however, Rossetti was heartily sick of Nature, and bolted back to London and its artificial life.[7]

That Hunt was one of J. G. Millais's principal sources discolors some sections of the Millais memoir, but in content and tone it is a far more dispassionate and far less egoistic account of the life of its subject; and its personal assessments, while unequivocal, are characterized by a restraint and temperance that contrast dramatically with the invidious bluster of Hunt's character assassinations.

Proponents of William Holman Hunt have always been embarrassed by the portrait of him that emerges from *Pre-Raphaelitism*, and to date no historian of the movement has advanced a successful explanation for the marked reversal and unexpected antipathy that mars his verbal portraits of the PRBs, especially that of Rossetti. The "Round Table" of the PRB had, after all, dissolved more than half a century before Hunt launched his attack, and it is hardly credible that he could for so many years have harbored in private such intense grudges and jealousies against a fellow Brother, to whom at one time he had been so attached. Rossetti and Millais were, from the evidence of the early correspondence, never close, as Millais's son points out in a footnote.[8] But Hunt and Dante Gabriel were fast friends, who shared models, and digs, and the general *cameraderie* that Rossetti speaks of. When Hunt embarked for the Holy Land in 1854, he took with him a daguerreotype of Rossetti's first major picture, *The Girlhood of Mary Virgin*. Facing the picture in the case, which is reproduced in *Pre-Raphaelitism*, is a slip with the inscription, "To. W. Holman Hunt from D.G.R. / Christmas 1853," followed by four lines from Henry Taylor's *Philip van Artevelde* transcribed in Rossetti's hand:

> There's that betwixt us been, which men remember
> Till they forget themselves, till all's forgot,
> Till the deep sleep falls on them in that bed
> From which no morrow's mischief knocks them up.[9]

Reviewing his emotions on his departure from England fifty years earlier, Hunt remembers: "My thoughts in connection with the past were led to the Pre-Raphaelite Brotherhood, from which we had hoped so much, and which, it could not be ignored, was now, at least in part, a failure. The old comradeship was kept up as far as possible by letter, and renewed on my return. I for long cherished the hope that again as old men, with all the fever of distracting life abated, we might have other Pre-Raphaelite meetings."[10] This passage, poignantly reminiscent of Arnold's "longing like despair," forces the question, and the remainder of this paper will be devoted to providing explanations for the seemingly inexplicable shift in views and values advanced in Hunt's history of Pre-Raphaelitism. The answer, which is complicated, involves a death, a pair of exhibitions, a spate of publications, the good offices of a devoted brother, and a radical redefinition of one of the major movements in English art in the nineteenth century—all focused on the year 1883.

§

In a perverse sense, and of course in a totally different context, Malcolm's report of Cawdor's death in *Macbeth* is equally true of Dante Gabriel Rossetti:

Nothing in his life
Became him like the leaving it; he died
As one that had been studied in his death. (1.4.7–9)

When William Michael entered in his diary that on Easter Sunday, 9 April 1882, "My dear Gabriel, the pride and glory of our family" had expired around 9:31 P.M., he may have imagined that he was locking forever the door to Rossetti's House of Life; but in fact he was only closing for the summer a residence whose ghostly occupant would consume nearly all his literary energies until his own death in the middle of his ninetieth year. Concluding his entry for 26 April, recording Gabriel's death and the details of his funeral, he added: "Propose to resume this diary pretty soon, but not quite now." Clearly, even William, by temperament and disposition far more placid and detached than his brother, had been temporarily traumatized and exhausted by the weight of responsibility he had been forced to assume in the last years and final months of Rossetti's life.

At the time of his death, Rossetti was known to the British public almost exclusively as a poet. After a series of delays, involving the disinterment of his wife's coffin to retrieve the manuscripts he had misguidedly buried with her in 1862—surely, one of the most sensational events in publishing history—his *Poems* (1870) attracted a paean of critical acclaim, vitiated two years later by Robert Buchanan's infamous attack in *The Fleshly School of Poetry,* the appearance of which nearly killed Rossetti in the summer of 1872. If he had before been reluctant to go public with his poems and pictures, in the last decade he became a virtual recluse in his house at 16 Cheyne Walk, alienated from most of his old friends and even from his family, broken in health, hopelessly and increasingly addicted to obscenely large doses of chloral that provided his only anodyne for insomnia, and attended by a series of companions, nurses, doctors, keepers, and studio assistants, who did what they could to keep him constructively engaged—principally in turning out potboilers for his private patrons, on whom he depended for his livelihood.[11] These were the years of George Hake, Henry Treffry Dunn, and Theodore Watts, and of the young Hall Caine, who would use his association with the dying poet-artist to launch his own career. The decade, obviously, was not unrelievedly black: Rossetti's muse began to stir in the late seventies, and he lived to see well reviewed the revised and new volumes of his poems, published in 1881–82, and to read a few months before the end Buchanan's retraction of his "Fleshly" attack in his novel, *God and the Man,* which he dedicated "To An Old Enemy":[12]

> *I would have snatch'd a bay leaf from thy brow,*
> > *Wronging the chaplet on an honoured head;*
> *In peace and charity I bring thee now*
> > *A lily-flower instead.*

William's diary picks up again on the ninth of August. By then, Rossetti had been given an abundant send-off in the popular press, with obituaries in all the major London and provincial newspapers and in journals as far away as Italy and the United States; Frederic George Stephens and Watts had jointly eulogized him in the *Athenaeum;* and the Chelsea sale of the household effects at 16 Cheyne Walk, including his books and a few original artworks—among them the celebrated Blake manuscript and sketchbook—had brought nearly £3,000 into the family coffers, a sum that would only partially offset the liabilities of his estate.[13]

With his mother and Christina, William was the chief legatee, and, naturally, he inherited the task of executor. Alive, Rossetti was the untidiest of men, so it is not surprising that his affairs were left in a complete state of disarray; but even William, who knew him better than anyone, was unprepared for the accumulation of unpaid bills: £50 to one chemist (Bell) for chloral, £52 to another (Dinneford) for the same commodity; an outstanding debt to Clarence Fry, the photographer, for a disputed sum that was finally settled for £350; a £200 IOU held by Theodore Watts, which he generously relinquished to William, while still claiming £43 for the sawdusting of Rossetti's studio some years before.[14]

But these were only the dribbles. Rossetti's old habit of demanding cash advances against unpainted pictures commissioned by his patrons left him owing £400 to William Graham and almost £1600 to Leonard Valpy; and Lee and Pemberton, the house agents for Lord Cadagon, demanded £300 for repairs to 16 Cheyne Walk before they would negotiate a termination of the lease. Old friends and associates, too, came forward for settlements: William paid out £185 to Treffry Dunn, Rossetti's former studio assistant; and, after a long dispute and the discovery that she had received, for various services rendered, £1110 since 31 March 1875, he settled with Fanny Cornforth, now Mrs. Schott, a £300 undated IOU for £65. When the will was probated on 19 January, the affidavit declared liabilities, including funeral expenses, of £2762 against assets totalling only £5300, but the £2538 balance did not take into account most of the items listed above. Following the sale of the remaining works, which realized £3417, at Christie's in May 1883, and after settling all encumbrances, including taxes, commissions, and legal fees, William and his family realized no more than £3000, hardly a princely sum from a painter many regarded as a king.[15]

William's attention to the mundane and practical details of life hardly occupied his full attention, and at this juncture, it is important to maintain a kind of stream-of-consciousness awareness of several events that are going on simultaneously, in all of which William is operating as a behind-the-scenes impressario. The wide obituary coverage has already been mentioned.[16] Beyond the publicity and notoriety provided by these death notices, two facts are notable. First, similarities of detail and even of phraseology suggest that they derive from a common text, probably from a release prepared at Birchington by William, Watts, and Hall Caine and telegraphed to the major papers. Some twenty notices appeared between 11 and 15 April, and it would not then (or now) be uncommon for family and friends to compile at least the vital statistics on which obituaries could be based. More interestingly, however, many of the obituaries draw pointed attention to Rossetti's role as both poet and painter, underscoring the fact that, because he never himself exhibited his works or allowed his patrons to do so, his reputation as an artist rested essentially on viva voce reporting, from sources that could not be regarded as wholly dispassionate.[17] The notice in the *Morning Post* for 12 April, after citing Rossetti's association with the Pre-Raphaelites, contains the startling announcement that "The Fine Art Society proposes to hold at once an exhibition of Mr. Rossetti's work similar to the Millais exhibition which was held last year. The society will be glad to have the co-operation of possessors of important examples of the deceased artist's work." It seems highly unlikely that a proposal for an exhibition could have been set in motion within three days of Dante Gabriel's death, unless of course, arrangements had begun before 9 April without his awareness; it is equally impossible, however, that any gallery would have made such an announcement without the knowledge and approval of William Michael.

Unfortunately, there is no surviving evidence to settle the point, and William, as already noted, had during this period deserted his diary. That no further references appear to the Fine Art Society exhibition is doubtless owing to the successful negotiations concluded over the summer with Lord Leighton to include Rossetti in the winter exhibition at the Royal Academy. On 19 August, William notes in his diary that he had received a letter inviting him to call on Leighton "to clear up some details concerning Gabriel's works, in view of the forthcoming exhibition at the R.A." The next day, he and Watts went to Leighton's newly completed mansion in Holland Park Road, where William expressed to him his "opinion that the exhibition ought to include all Gabriel's leading pictures of his best style, so far as procurable, along with a fair typical representation of all periods and modes in the development of his art." While the president of the Royal Academy seemed in the main agreeable to this proposal, William felt that Leighton "views with some disfavour the general run of Gabriel's pictures produced within the last 4 or 5 years."[18] It was not until December that H. Virtue Tebbs proposed an exhibition at the Burlington Fine Arts Club to supplement the one at the Royal Academy (R.A.), and while William was initially lukewarm to the proposal, he obviously decided that it would be in the best interests of Gabriel's memory and reputation to cooperate.

While these arrangements for the two exhibitions were underway during the fall of 1882, William was engaged in other projects designed to expedite and enhance public recognition of Rossetti's place in the history of nineteenth-century art and literature. By the date of the first new entry in his diary (13 August), he had begun reading through the letters written to him by Gabriel with a view to publishing an annotated edition of them with a memoir by Watts.[19] He also began to gather a collection of photographs of Rossetti's works which could be offered for sale; and by the end of 1883, he was negotiating with Elliot Stock to write a critical introduction to a reprint of the *Germ*. To the rash of writers poised to pounce on Rossetti's remains almost as soon as the ceremonies in Birchington churchyard were concluded, William lent varying degrees of assistance. The work on Rossetti's art proposed by the former Pre-Raphaelite Brother F. G. Stephens, and announced in the catalogue of the Burlington Club exhibition, was not finally published until 1894, but four books on Rossetti actually appeared before the end of 1882—by William Tirebuck, Hall Caine, William Sharp, and Carlo Placci.[20]

With the first, published in October, subtitled *His Work and Influence,* William had no involvement. Watts was furious that his proprietary claims were being usurped, and, calling Tirebuck an "ass" and his book a "baby-like production," warned William that "a lot of fellows will scribble about him and vulgarize his name"; but William could not but be gratified that the unknown author had referred to Dante Gabriel as "the most influential of the much-talked-of Brotherhood."[21] With Caine's and Sharp's volumes—the first a personal memoir with excerpts from Rossetti's private correspondence, later to be more accurately entitled by its author, *My Story*[22]—William had direct input, reading the proofs and making suggestions (in the case of Caine, *demands*) for revision. While William was not pleased by the tone of Caine's *Recollections,* published in early November, he was highly interested in the exhaustive artistic catalogue that Sharp proposed to append to his volume, principally because it would prepare the ground for the forthcoming exhibitions and for his own sale of Rossetti's works in the spring. Sharp's volume balances Rossetti's performances as both poet and artist, and though one critic, Franz Hueffer, labeled it "a painstaking but ponderous and ill-constructed monograph,"[23] it was nevertheless the first extended discussion of Rossetti's art; and the brief section discussing his "Reasons for not Exhibiting," containing a partial listing of previously exhibited works, offered a convenient counter to the charge in some quarters that Rossetti's prominence stemmed from what Buchanan and others in regard to the reception of his poems in 1870 called "coterie glory."[24] Furthermore, in identifying William's brother and father-in-law, Ford Madox Brown, as respectively the "father" and the "grandfather" of the PRB, Sharp gave greater prominence to the two artists' roles in that larger movement of the "English Renaissance" that writers like Pater, Walter Hamilton, and Oscar Wilde saw as having been directly influenced by the Pre-Raphaelites.[25] Whatever the quality of these early books, they generated reviews which kept Rossetti's name before the public in a way it had never been before, and set the stage for the events of the following year.

On New Year's day 1883, the Fourteenth Winter Exhibition of the Royal Academy opened in Burlington House, with Gallery V given over to eighty-three works by Dante Gabriel Rossetti, who shared the limelight with another non-member of the Royal Academy, John Linnell, to whom Galleries I and II had been assigned. William had expressed early disappointment (in November) at the size of the proposed Royal Academy display, and the organizers of the Burlington Club exhibition were motivated in part by the decision of the Royal Academy Hanging Committee to restrict the numbers of works shown by refusing replicas and studies. At the private showing on 29 December 1882, over half the works (forty-six) were mounted on screens, and the overall effect was one of such crowding that in response to the strictures of Franz Hueffer, the influential music critic on the *Times,* and, incidentally, the brother-in-law of William Michael, who reviewed the exhibition on the next day, the Committee redistributed the screened pictures in Gallery VI.[26] On 13 January 1883, the exhibition in the rooms of the Burlington Fine Arts Club opened, with the one hundred fifty-two works on display introduced in a splendid catalogue prefaced by H. Virtue Tebbs, Rossetti's patron and friend, who had been his legal representative at the exhumation of Elizabeth Siddal in 1869.

Together, the two exhibitions included 235 works by Rossetti— 60 percent of the 395 listed in Sharp's incomplete catalogue, just over 30 percent of the 766 identified by the most recent compiler of Rossetti's works, Virginia Surtees.[27] Drawn from the collections of all Rossetti's most important patrons—G. P. Boyce, William Graham, the various members of the Ionides family, James Leathart, F. R. Leyland, George Rae, William Turner, and Leonard Valpy, the exhibitions were deficient mainly in the number of pictures they contained which belonged to the family, 211 of which (53 not in Surtees) would be sold in the remaining works sale in May. If the Royal Academy exhibition, with 33 oils and 30 watercolors, had a higher proportion of the major pictures that today are regarded as among Rossetti's best, or best-known, or most important works— *The Girlhood of Mary Virgin* (no. 286), *Found* (287), *Ecce Ancilla Domini* (288), *Dante's Dream* (318), *Beata Beatrix* (293), *The Seed of David* (296), and *Proserpine* (314)—the Burlington show was a far more representative collection. Not only did it have almost as many oils (25) and major watercolors (34), but the chronological coverage was far greater, with 12 works from the 1840s (as opposed to 1 at the R.A.), 35 against 3 at the R.A. from the 1850s, 63 from the 1860s (as opposed to 11 at the R.A.), and 42 from the 1870s and 1880s, against the R.A.'s 23. In addition, Rossetti's success as a portrait painter could be far more readily documented from the 34 portraits shown at the Burlington exhibition than from the three hung at Burlington House.

Needless to say, the critics came out in force:[28] at last, an evaluation of Rossetti as an artist could be made firsthand, and, while the responses were not uniformly laudatory, only that in the *National Review*, written by David Hannay—who was the son of Rossetti's old friend from PRB days, James Hannay, and "the sugar plum of the universe," as Rossetti called Hannay's wife—was totally negative. By refusing to exhibit during his lifetime, Hannay declares, Rossetti "served his reputation well": his drawing Hannay finds feeble, his scope confined and limited, his subjects (eight-tenths of whom are women) monotonous, his development as an artist wholly static, and his message meaningless; only on his superiority as a colorist is

Hannay willing to concede a point, and that grudgingly: "When he had everything his own way (and why should he not when the canvas, the paint, the purchaser, and the critic, all belonged to him?) he could produce a rich piece of colouring." Decrying Ruskin's claim that it is the "poetic meaning" in Rossetti's work that sets it apart, Hannay exposes his own critical limitations in his conclusion: "Yesterday it was Blake, the day before it was Botticelli, who was seized hold of, lifted up for a sign, and overpraised till their really fine qualities seemed in danger of suffering from ridicule by comparison. To-day it is Dante Gabriel Rossetti, and to-morrow it will be another. . . . But it is only *l'arte robuste* to which Théophile Gautier promises immortality."[29] More characteristic were critiques by William Sharp, Harry Quilter, J. Beavington Atkinson, J. Comyns Carr, F. G. Stephens, and a host of others in the newspaper press, who, while they may have exaggerated Rossetti's significance, and even in some instances praised him for qualities which he neither possessed nor pretended to, nevertheless entrenched his position as a leader in nineteenth-century art. Such a work was *A Dream of Fair Women* by the Rev. Alfred Gurney, who chose to read works such as *The Blessed Damozel, Astarte Syriaca, Proserpine,* and *Mnemosyne* as portraits of beauty which manifest a "sacramental intelligence."[30]

For his part, William Michael had every reason to be pleased with the exhibitions. On his fourth visit to the Royal Academy (4 January), he noted that "the collection seems to be decidedly attractive to the public: the casual remarks which I hear in the room evidence pleasure and interest, without anything like favouring partisanship or *parti-pris.*" After attending on the final day (10 March), he was gratified to find the crowd "considerable" with "two or three times (as usual) as many persons in Gabriel's rooms as in any other." The Burlington Club exhibition, accessible only by members' tickets, attracted a total of 12,000 viewers and it had to be extended by four days to accommodate all those who wanted to see it. It was, said William, "a very interesting display, well calculated to maintain and enhance his reputation"; on 17 March, the day the exhibition was scheduled to close, William estimated there were 200 people in the rooms. William was even cordial to the unofficial third exhibition opened in late May by Fanny Schott and her husband. He entered in his diary on 22 May: "Went to see the so-called 'Rossetti Gallery' at 1A Old Bond Street got up by Schott out of the works by Gabriel which remained in the hands of Mrs. S.—some strictly her property, others no doubt not so in reality, but allowed unchallenged to pass as if they were. The collection is considerably eked out with photographs, etc., but does certainly contain a fair number of thoroughly fine things. The catalogue, Watts tells me, is Howell's work."[31]

The 211 lots in the sale of the remaining works at Christie's on 12 May—consisting mainly of studies for the works that had appeared in the two principal exhibitions but supplemented by a number of finished oils—brought generally high prices, as the *Times* reviewer noted (14 May); the sale, including one picture belonging to J. P. Seddon and five that were owing to Valpy, brought £4692. But the sale served another purpose beyond establishing price guidelines for future works by Rossetti that might come on the market: because the lots were arranged strictly in chronological order, they constituted in essence a fourth exhibition for the three days they were on view before going under the hammer. In all, over five hundred works by the artist who had exhibited only about thirty pictures before his death and only a half dozen in the last decade of his life had been available for public scrutiny in the spring of 1883. Collectively, nearly two-thirds of his total corpus had been on view. And while Holman Hunt belittles the size of Rossetti's canon on the grounds that it is inflated by his lifelong habit of making studies for his paintings, a practice Hunt and Millais abandoned early in their careers, the cumulative effect of the exhibitions of 1883 was clearly impressive. Rossetti has never since had such exposure: the 1973 retrospective exhibition at the Royal Academy, the largest since 1883, contained 274 original works. So popular was his art with the public that there was considerable pressure put, both in the press and on William Michael Rossetti privately, to mount a combined exhibition. That "ideal" exhibition was never mounted, but the net effect of the three (or four) exhibitions that were held was to place Rossetti at the forefront of those artists identified as belonging to the Pre-Raphaelite movement.[32]

§

1883, then, was a bumper year for Rossetti. Prior to his death, besides reviews and a dozen notices of his pictures, most of them written by F. G. Stephens and published in the *Athenaeum*, there had been fewer than ten separate articles written on him, and no books, save *The Fleshly School of Poetry*. By the end of 1883, his bibliography had grown by five books and some twenty-five articles, plus obituaries, notices of exhibitions, and reviews. Ruskin, in this year, singled him out over Holman Hunt in his Oxford lectures on *The Art of England* as "the chief intellectual force in the establishment of the modern romantic school in England";[33] and Pater, in a long review-essay, identified in his poems qualities of "crisis" and "mystic isolation" belonging to "some revival of the old mythopoeic age" amounting to a "new order of phenomenon" and the creation of a "new ideal" in poetry.[34] By the end of the century, publications on Rossetti would constitute a small library that would dwarf the combined writings on all the other Pre-Raphaelites.[35]

Clearly, the accident of being the first of the major Pre-Raphaelites to die proved fortuitous for Rossetti's reputation. Watts almost said as much in his not particularly informative 1883 essay, "The Truth about Rossetti":

> This mysterious artist, who refused to appear with his fellows in an open court of criticism, but whose admirers, nevertheless claimed for him all the honours of having appeared there and of having won the brightest crown—who and what was he? What *droits du seigneur* had he that exempted him from the common sanctions of the domain of art? But it is vain to contest any man's claims by challenging the pretentions of his admirers, and such quarrels as this are never adjusted save, alas! by that one high Power who knows no favouritism and who adjusts everything. Death is indeed a peacemaker and gives, at last, every man his due. Let this be the balm for every unhappy critic-ridden poet and painter, that even artistic and literary criticism knows its duty, knows how to be just, and perhaps generous, if the man whose works come up for judgment will first do *his* duty by dying.[36]

Of course, Rossetti dead could hardly capitalize on the advantage that jumping the gun on Millais and Hunt had given him. Luckily, he found in William Michael the best press agent a brother ever had; and William was not only dedicated to Rossetti's memory and reputation, he was also destined to outlive the six other members of the Brotherhood. Holman Hunt's specific charges that William distorted Rossetti's role in the PRB are totally unfounded: William's advocacy won out by virtue of his sheer indefatigability. Beginning in 1884 with a long retrospective review of the 1883 exhibitions in the *Art Journal,* William started in 1886 to produce—in addition to the publication of Rossetti's *Collected Works* with a memoir—volume after volume of editions, letters, memoirs and diaries, chronologies, and bibliographies[37] which not only served to keep alive public interest in Rossetti but also provided the documentary resources for other writers, foreign and domestic, who were conducting their own independent studies of the Pre-Raphaelites, in which Rossetti assumed an increasingly escalating degree of prominence.[38]

In the two decades prior to the appearance of Hunt's *Pre-Raphaelitism,* there were scarcely any voices of sufficient counter-weight to offset the received opinion on Rossetti established by the exhibitions of 1883. One by one the members of the first and second brotherhoods and the "associates" died off—Woolner in 1892, Brown in 1893, Millais and Morris in 1896, Burne-Jones in 1898: each death stimulated publications and, in some instances, sales and exhibitions, but Rossetti's position remained unassailable; indeed, in the case of Burne-Jones, Rossetti was credited as being the supreme influence on his art. Through it all, at his home at Draycott Lodge, Fulham, an aging, failing, and embittered Holman Hunt could only fume and fulminate at what he regarded as the injustice of Rossetti's triumph. He and Millais had won their own particular degrees of fame—Millais as president of the Royal Academy, Hunt as the greatest religious painter of the age, a recognition signaled by his Honorary D.C.L. from Oxford and the Order of Merit—but for Hunt these were pyrrhic victories so long as Rossetti's name continued to be identified, as it was, for example, in Harry Quilter's history of Pre-Raphaelitism (1892), not only with the founding of the movement, but as, in fact, synonymous with the name itself. "Nothing dies so hard as a word," Quilter says, "particularly a word which nobody understands, and there is little doubt but that the one in question will survive all of us; but a day will surely come when it will be seen that the essence of what is now known as pre-Raphaelitism was not the influence of a school or a principle, but simply the influence of one man, and that man, Dante Gabriel Rossetti."[39]

Quilter's definition of Pre-Raphaelitism as a phenomenon exclusively identified with Rossetti has, of course, no credibility among modern critics or art or literary historians. But from the mid-eighties until well into the present century, the emphasis on Rossetti

Pictures at an Exhibition

promoted by the exhibitions of 1883 and the publications they inspired—reinforced by the expropriation of Rossetti by Pater, Wilde, and the fin de siècle as the paterfamilias of aestheticism— altered radically the definition of Pre-Raphaelitism for several generations of students. Rossetti may no longer be regarded as the sole Pre-Raphaelite—though he figured more prominently than either Hunt or Millais in the 1984 Tate Gallery retrospective exhibition— but his paintings and poems still describe, in the strictest mathematical sense, the critical parameters of the term.[40]

Notes

(The abbreviations DGR and WMR are often employed in the notes, owing to the frequent recurrence of Dante Gabriel and William Michael Rossetti's names. PRB is used throughout text and notes to signify the Pre-Raphaelite Brotherhood.)

1. Diana Holman Hunt, *My Grandmothers and I* (New York: Norton, 1961), pp. 117–18.

2. William Holman Hunt, *Pre-Raphaelitism and the Pre-Raphaelite Brotherhood*, 2 vols. (London: Macmillan, 1905). Subsequent references are to the two-volume second edition (London: Chapman & Hall, 1913), which was substantially revised by his widow from his own notes three years after Hunt's death.

3. Hunt's unpublished letter and WMR's diary are both in the Angeli Papers, from which all the manuscripts cited in this article are printed with the generous permission of Mrs. Imogen Dennis and Mrs. Anne Yandle, the Head of Special Collections in the University of British Columbia (U.B.C.) Library.

4. Helen Rossetti Angeli in her chapter on Hunt in *Dante Gabriel Rossetti: His Friends and Enemies* (London: Hamish Hamilton, 1949), pp. 59–73.

5. William Michael Rossetti, *Dante Gabriel Rossetti: His Family-Letters with a Memoir*, 2 vols. (London: Ellis & Elvey, 1895), 1:129. Mrs. Angeli's translation of Chesneau's letter to DGR, quoted in French in the *Memoir*, appears on pp. 61–62 of her book on DGR.

6. Quoted in T. Hall Caine, *Recollections of Dante Gabriel Rossetti* (London: Stock, 1882), pp. 219–20.

7. J. G. Millais, *The Life and Letters of John Everett Millais*, 2 vols. (London: Methuen, 1899). The quotation is from the abridged one-volume 3d ed. (1905), pp. 28–29.

8. Ibid., p. 28.

9. Hunt, *Pre-Raphaelitism*, vol. 1, facing p. 269.

10. Ibid., 1:268. In *Some Reminiscences*, 2 vols. (London: Brown Langham, 1906) WMR discusses the alienation that existed late in life among the original members of the PRB.: "It is a sad and indeed a humiliating reflection that, after the early days of *cameraderie* and of genuine brotherliness had run their course, followed by a less brief period of amity and goodwill, keen antipathies severed the quondam P.R.B.'s. I here omit Collinson, who, after having voluntarily retired from the band, was practically lost sight of by the other members, though none of them took a serious dislike to him. Woolner became hostile to Hunt, Dante Rossetti, and Millais. Hunt became hostile to Woolner and Stephens, and in a minor degree to Dante Rossetti. Stephens became hostile to Hunt. Dante Rossetti became hostile to Woolner, and to a minor degree to Hunt and Millais. Millais, being an enormously successful man while others were only

William E. Fredeman

commonly successful, did not perhaps become strictly hostile to any one; he kept aloof however from Dante Rossetti, and I infer from Woolner. In all these instances I know something about the causes of the alienation, and in my memoir of Dante Rossetti I have stated the facts concerning him and Woolner; but it is no business of mine to expound the details here, nor to endeavour to apportion acquittal or blame. I will however avow my belief that, with a moderate spirit of conciliation and of making allowance for diverging points of view, most of these acerbities would have been avoided or healed" (1:75).

11.   For Rossetti's own opinions of his paintings, particularly the later works, see " 'What Is Wrong with Rossetti?': A Centenary Reassessment" (pp. xxii–xxiii), my introduction to *Centennial Essays on Dante Gabriel Rossetti,* a special Rossetti double issue of *Victorian Poetry* (1982) guest-edited by W. E. Fredeman.

12.   Robert Buchanan, *God and the Man,* 3 vols. (London: Chatto and Windus, 1881). Only the first stanza of the dedication is quoted. In a new edition of 1882, Buchanan added two new stanzas dedicating the book specifically to Rossetti. The following paragraph also appears in the Preface: "Since this work was first published, the 'Old Enemy' to whom it was dedicated has passed away. Although his name did not appear on the front of the book, as it would certainly have done had I possessed more moral courage, it is a melancholy pleasure to me to reflect that he understood the dedication and accepted it in the spirit in which it was offered. That I should ever have underrated his exquisite work, is simply a proof of the incompetency of all criticism, however honest, which is conceived adversely, hastily, and from an unsympathetic point of view; but that I should have ranked myself for the time being with the Philistines, and encouraged them to resist an ennobling and refining literary influence (of which they stood, and stand, so mournfully in need), must remain to me a matter of permanent regret" (p. vi).

13.   WMR's marked copy of the catalogue with extensive annotations was given to me in 1963 by Helen Rossetti Angeli.

14.   Of these two claims, WMR wrote in his diary (12 December 1882): "The higgledy-piggledy transactions between Watts and Gabriel, whereby liabilities of never-defined amount were incurred by G., and then a cheque drawn at random for a large sum—£100, 50, or what—were, from a professional point of view, to my way of thinking very unsatisfactory."

15.   These figures, never before published, are calculated from information provided in WMR's diary. They have been rounded off for citation in this paper. The regal references to Rossetti are attributed to P. B. Marston and Whistler in various sources.

16.   WMR later assembled the obituaries in a scrapbook, together with a large number of reviews, notices, and other press cuttings, most of which are annotated with the source and date. I have drawn on this scrapbook, given me by Helen Rossetti Angeli in 1963, for many of the facts provided in this paper.

17.   While it is generally true that Rossetti refrained from exhibiting, it is not the fact that none of his works had ever been seen. He had shown his pictures during Pre-Raphaelite Brotherhood days at the Free Exhibition (1849), the National Institution (1850), and at the Old Water Colour Society (1852). In 1857, he sent seven works to the Pre-Raphaelite Exhibition in Russell Place. The following year, he had three works at the Liverpool Academy, and two others appeared there in 1861 and 1864. He contributed to at least two of the annual exhibitions (1855 and 1860) of the Hogarth Club, of which he was a member. A handful of other works were sent at various times to exhibitions in Manchester, Edinburgh, and Glasgow between 1862

and 1879. The last picture to be shown publicly during his lifetime was *Dante's Dream*, on the occasion of its purchase by the Walker Art Gallery in Liverpool in 1881. In November 1882, about ten of his works were on display at the Royal Institute, Manchester. In all, discounting pictures exhibited on more than one occasion, only about thirty separate works had been seen by the public prior to the exhibitions of 1883.

18.   The four letters from Leighton to WMR in the Angeli-Dennis Papers all deal with the Royal Academy exhibition. William clearly wanted a larger exhibition than Leighton was willing to mount. In his first letter (19 November) Leighton rejects the idea of showing duplicates; in this and in successive correspondence he remains polite but firm in opposing the enlargement of the exhibition, of letting it, as he says, "dribble over to another room."

19.   The subject of Watts's promised biography is thoroughly surveyed in my *Prelude to the Last Decade: Dante Gabriel Rossetti in the Summer of 1872* (Manchester: John Rylands Library, 1971). The year after the publication of WMR's *Family Letters with a Memoir* (1895), Watts writes to the *Spectator* of his continued intention to produce a biography of his friend.

20.   Of the four books in 1882, all save T. Hall Caine's were entitled *Dante Gabriel Rossetti*, but two had subtitles distinguishing their approach. William Tirebuck's *Dante Gabriel Rossetti: His Work and Influence*, like Caine's *Recollections of Dante Gabriel Rossetti*, was published by Stock; William Sharp's *Dante Gabriel Rossetti: A Record and a Study* was published by Macmillan; and Carlo Placci's book by Rassegna Nazionale in Florence.

21.   Tirebuck, *Dante Gabriel Rossetti*, p. 30. Watts-Dunton's remarks are taken from an unpublished letter dated 24 July 1882 in the Angeli Papers at U.B.C.

22.   Caine twice revised his 1882 *Recollections:* in 1909 as *My Story* (New York: Appleton) and under its original title for the centenary of DGR's birth (London: Cassell, 1928).

23.   Franz Hueffer twice reviewed the exhibit. His comment on Sharp appears in his first review, 30 December 1882, which was reprinted in "Exhibitions of Rossetti's Pictures," in *Italian and Other Studies* (London: Stock, 1882), p. 85.

24.   From an anonymous article in the *Saturday Review* 33 (24 February 1872): 399–40; excerpted by Robert Buchanan in *The Fleshly School of Poetry* (London: Strahan, 1872), pp. 94–96.

25.   Pater's essay on Rossetti appeared in the second edition of volume 4 of T. H. Ward's *The English Poets* (London: Macmillan, 1883) and was reprinted in his *Appreciations* (London: Macmillan, 1889). Walter Hamilton's *The Aesthetic Movement in England* (London: Stock, 1882), which went through three editions in the same year, was devoted, in the main, to the Pre-Raphaelites. The title of the book is explained in the Preface: "it describes what might be more correctly styled, A Renaissance of Medieval Art and Culture." Wilde's lecture on "The English Renaissance," given in America in January 1882, is reported in a chapter in Hamilton's volume.

26.   In Hueffer's second *Times* notice of the exhibition (13 January), he acknowledged the expansion into Gallery VI, adding that "the immense change . . . makes the original mistake on the part of the Hanging Committee all the more unaccountable" (reprinted in *Italian and Other Studies*, p. 93). In some quarters, Leighton was held personally accountable for attempting to minimize Rossetti's art, a view, judging from a letter from Leighton dated 25 January, that WMR did not subscribe to: "Thank you for your kind words. I never for a moment doubted your faith in my sincerity. It was not a pretty revelation that people could be found to say openly that an exhibition to which I had devoted so much thought and care was a deliberate plot to stab poor

Rossetti in the back, in other words that I am a very low blackguard indeed; fortunately, as I told my informant, a thought so ignoble could only soil those who uttered it." (Partially printed in Leonée Ormond and Richard Ormond, *Lord Leighton* [New Haven: Yale University Press, 1975], p. 104.)

27. Virginia Surtees, *The Paintings and Drawings of Dante Gabriel Rossetti (1828–1882): A Catalogue Raisonné*, 2 vols. (Oxford: Clarendon Press, 1971).

28. For notices and articles dealing with the 1883 exhibitions, see W. E. Fredeman, *Pre-Raphaelitism: A Bibliocritical Study* (Cambridge: Harvard University Press, 1965), 21.7–21.16 and 30.2–30.10.

29. David Hannay's review, entitled "The Paintings of Mr. Rossetti" (*National Review* 1 [March 1883]: 126–34), is devastatingly negative—"I, for my own part, see, first of all [in DGR's pictures], monotony; the same face, the same stare, nearly the same attitude, on every wall" (p. 128). His major strictures are quoted in the text, but his discussion of the symbolic level in Rossetti's painting, "the suggested poetic meaning," poses many interesting questions that have a distinct relevance to so many modern readings of Rossetti's art. The quotations cited in the text are from pages 131 and 134.

30. Reverend Alfred Gurney, *A Dream of Fair Women* (London: Kegan Paul, Trench, 1883).

31. Many of the artifacts in Fanny Cornforth Schott's possession were sold to Samuel Bancroft, Jr., and are now in the Delaware Art Museum. The fullest account of Fanny is in Paull Franklin Baum's introduction to his *Dante Gabriel Rossetti's Letters to Fanny Cornforth* (Baltimore: Johns Hopkins University Press, 1940); but see also Jan Marsh's *The Pre-Raphaelite Sisterhood* (London: St. Martin's Press, 1985).

32. WMR entered in his diary after his first visit to the Burlington Fine Arts Club exhibition (13 January), that someone had suggested to him the desirability of combining the two exhibitions and showing them at the "height of the next London season." WMR wrote at once to Charles Deschamps, who had offered to mount an exhibition before the arrangements had been made with the Royal Academy, but although there are several subsequent references to WMR's correspondence on the subject, nothing came of the proposal. On 27 February, Robert Collinson, the former director of the Figure and Painting Schools at South Kensington, made a similar proposal in a letter to the *Times*, arguing that the timing of the exhibitions, in terms of both available light and the number of visitors to London from the provinces, prohibits proper exposure of the pictures. "To art students," he continued, "these pictures are a most valuable lesson as examples of magnificent colour, draughtsmanship, and design, and for the deep earnestness and poetic inspiration pervading them all." Had Rossetti exhibited at the Grosvenor Gallery or the Royal Academy, he reasons, the cause would be less urgent, "but his works are now presented for the first and, probably, the last time"; a combined exhibition, he predicts, "would attract a vast public who have heard of Rossetti's fame at a distance and are deploring that when the season for their annual visit to the metropolis arrives the opportunity will be past forever."

33. *The Works of John Ruskin*, ed. E. T. Cook and Alexander Wedderburn, 39 vols. (London: Allen, 1903–12), 33:269.

34. Pater, *Appreciations*, pp. 228–42.

35. One of the values of comparative enumerative bibliography is in tracing the relative receptions of artists and writers at any given time.

36. Theodore Watts, "The Truth about Rossetti," *Nineteenth Century* 13 (March 1883): 406.

37.   Beside the 1886 *Collected Works* and a number of simple reprints, WMR published other important editions of the works in 1891, 1904, and 1911, the latter still the standard edition. His books on Rossetti and related topics include: *Dante Gabriel Rossetti as Designer and Writer* (London: Cassell, 1889); *Family-Letters with a Memoir*, 2 vols. (London: Ellis & Elvey, 1895); *Ruskin: Rossetti: Pre-Raphaelitism* (London: Allen, 1899); *The Germ*, reprint with a separately printed Preface (London: Stock, 1901); *Praeraphaelite Diaries and Letters* (London: Hurst & Blackett, 1900), *Rossetti Papers* (London: Sands, 1903), *A Bibliography of Dante Gabriel Rossetti* (London: Ellis, 1905); *Dante Gabriel Rossetti: Classified Lists of His Writings* (London: privately printed, 1906); and *Some Reminiscences*, 2 vols. (London: Brown, Langham, 1906).

38.   Besides the titles already mentioned, the following book- or monograph-length works on Rossetti published before the turn of the century are listed in Fredeman, *Pre-Raphaelitism* (numbers in parentheses): L. J. Swinburne (30.11), Joseph Knight (25.11), H. C. Marillier (30.24), P. W. Nicholson (32.5), F. G. Stephens (30.17), Esther Wood (30.18), and Ford M. Hueffer (30.21). Percy Bate, author of the first full-scale Victorian history of Pre-Raphaelitism (London: Bell, 1899) actually does not overemphasize the role of Rossetti and, in fact, regards Ford Madox Brown as the "founder" of the movement.

39.   Harry Quilter, "A Chapter in the History of Pre-Raphaelitism," in *Preferences in Art, Life, and Literature* (London: Swann Sonnenschein, 1892), p. 66. Section 9, entitled "The Painting and the Poetry of Dante Gabriel Rossetti," is a reprint of Quilter's article "The Art of Rossetti," *Contemporary Review* 43 (February 1883): 190–203.

40.   *The Pre-Raphaelites* [catalogue of the exhibition] (London: Tate Gallery, 7 March–28 May 1984). In the Introduction to this handsome, scholarly, and profusely illustrated catalogue, the Tate's former director, Alan Bowness, acknowledges that Rossetti gave Pre-Raphaelitism a "new lease of life" in the 1860s and uses the term *clandestine* to describe the gradual growth of Rossetti's reputation. Acknowledging that Rossetti was "perhaps . . . always the organizer and driving spirit of the Brotherhood" and the main impetus behind the second wave of the movement, he credits him with full responsibility for bringing Pre-Raphaelitism international recognition as a major force in the European symbolist movement. "But," he concludes, "it was only one kind of Pre-Raphaelite painting that was so admired in the nineties, whereas ultimately it is the sheer variety of the work that impresses. . . . What group of English painters can match them?"

Daniel Albright

Lyrical Antibiography

Nowadays most readers are comfortable with the notion that biography is a species of fiction; that a biographer, if he agrees to observe some principle of non-contradiction of contemporary written sources, is free to invent, to ascribe any sort of convenient and striking identity to his subject. In this abyss of freedom the biographer toils patiently and with such good humor as he can muster. The autobiographer, of course, has always enjoyed such a reputation for fancifulness and complicated, ingenious self-delusion. Among the many resources dubious to the historian but available to the biographer or the autobiographer is the lyric mode; and I have asked myself whether the lyric mode is likely to be useful for biographical purposes, whether it will be compatible with the usual modes of biographical discourse, and whether a coherent image or shadow of a personality can be produced by strictly lyrical means. Many of the examples discussed here are taken from Victorian poets, who often used the lyric mode with biographical or autobiographical intention, as a kind of intimate publicity.

Occasionally one comes across a plausibly lyrical poem which sounds like a traditional biography immensely abbreviated and accelerated, such as Auden's sonnet "A. E. Housman" (1938):

> *No one, not even Cambridge, was to blame*
> *(Blame if you like the human situation):*
> *Heart-injured in North London, he became*
> *The Latin Scholar of his generation.*
>
> *Deliberately he chose the dry-as-dust,*
> *Kept tears like dirty postcards in a drawer;*
> *Food was his public love, his private lust*
> *Something to do with violence and the poor.*

Lyrical Antibiography

In savage foot-notes on unjust editions
He timidly attacked the life he led,
And put the money of his feelings on
The uncritical relations of the dead,
Where only geographical divisions
Parted the coarse hanged soldier from the don.

Here is pungency, sharpness of line, clear perspective; Auden has taken a few choice details of Housman's life and through a process of psychological triangulation inferred the whole. But why are such lyrics so rare? Why are our anthologies not crammed with such rapid and devastating character studies? The answer lies, I think, in the fact that few lives are suitable for treatment within the compass of a lyric poem. The usual subjects of panegyric—the king, the hero, the noble patron—do not much commend themselves to songlike brevity of expression. Flattery requires amplitude; and as the recitation of the list of accomplishments gets longer and more detailed, the poem is likely to sink out of the lyrical and into some lower, more earthy domain: not song, but representation. Poems like Tennyson's "Ode on the Death of the Duke of Wellington" strain at the boundaries of the lyric, tread out their grave measure, seem in danger of swelling into full-scale biography.

Housman fits inside a lyric because his life was uneventful, suppressed, involuted, tremulous, like the lyric mode itself. Indeed, the most salient features of Housman's biography exist, not in public life—to the world at large Housman was almost invisible—but in phantasmagoria, the imaginary classical antiquity where swordsmen and librarians embraced effortlessly and full of passion. Auden's skill at describing Housman's personality by lyrical means is noteworthy: much of Housman's reticence, his guilt, is suggested by the fact that his secret homosexuality is demoted to a simile, "tears like dirty postcards in a drawer." I think it is generally true that biographical lyrics work best when the subject is someone turned away from the world of deeds, of social accomplishment; one of Gerard Manley Hopkins's few successful character-pieces is a poem about St. Alphonsus Rodriguez, who spent forty sober and tranquil years as a janitor at a Jesuit college in Majorca. The lyric poet who wishes to write about an emperor or a swashbuckler is far from helpless— for one thing he has a body of mythological parallels to guide and focus his imagination—but the lyric poet who wishes to write about a saint, a scholar, another poet, anyone outside the world of the *Tatler* or *People* magazine, will find that his task is much simpler. What invites prosaic representation will not facilitate lyric poetry.

It seems, then, that lives unsuitable for the standard biographical approach—the endless accumulation of detail rendered significant by some psychological hypothesis—are precisely the lives most suitable for biographical lyrics. This suggests that there is some antithesis between the lyrical mode and the biographical mode, at least according to our usual conception of the biographical mode. This is what I mean by lyrical antibiography: we turn to the lyric in order to verbalize intuitions of identity that would not fit into regular biographical discourse, matters too extreme or fantastic or impudent to belong in a dignified narrative of someone's life. The gist of Housman or Alphonsus Rodriguez is interior, almost beyond the possibility of evidence; and where facts are lacking or irrelevant, the lyrical imagination is liberated, given permission to invent a nonworld, an antiworld, a plane of reality at right angles to our commonplace surfaces, a locus where fleeting ideas and feelings can embody themselves without the normal constraints of science.

I believe that poetry, if it constructs a secure and well-defined region of operation, will seem nonlyrical, even if that region is obviously unreal; we do not credit the Eden of *Paradise Lost* as an actual place, but it is a zone of being that has a proper weight, ecology, physics—it does not seem especially lyrical. A lyric poem usually posits some poorly constituted space full of metaphors and other sorts of shifty half-objects; when Coleridge and other romantics speak of the dissolving and deconstructive powers of the imagination, they are moving toward a theory of the lyric. People who have the odd fortune to reside inside lyric poems, like Housman and Rodriguez, normally are indeterminant and evasive folk who resist neat formulae of identity. Indeed they are often outside of history entirely, for many lyric poems are inhabited by the unborn and the dead; a lyric like Ben Jonson's double ode on Cary and Morison moves from a child who refuses to be born to a noble soul siderealized beyond the human. If there are any two classes of men about whom it would be difficult to write a two-volume biography, one might suggest a fetus and a specter oblivious of its past life; and they are precisely the species that appear comfortably in lyric poems.

There are many long poems not in themselves especially lyrical but containing passages of a lyrical nature; and a study of one or two such passages might prove helpful in determining the relation of lyric to biography. John Donne's "The Progress of the Soul" (1601) is a "biography" of the soul that dwelt in the fruit of the Tree of the Knowledge of Good and Evil; and if ever there was a proper theme for lyrical biography, this is it, for Donne conceives this soul as completely characterless, a neutral spark that flits from fruit to bird to fish to she-ape without contamination or conclusion, an endless metamorphosis of identity, an animate hovering. The poem is full of remarkable passages:

> Out crept a sparrow, this soul's moving inn,
> On whose raw arms stiff feathers now begin,
> As children's teeth through gums, to break with pain;
> His flesh is jelly yet, and his bones threads,
> All a new downy mantle overspreads. *(ll. 181–85)*

Donne is fascinated by these half articulations of a blank creative germ, these potentialities that precede any gross definition of form. Indeed, it is hard to imagine any biography more lyrical than that of an unhatched bird.

But perhaps I am being unfair in choosing a biographical poem that does not concern a human being. Let us turn instead to Tennyson's "Enoch Arden" (1862), a fictitious story, but, as scholars have pointed out, a narrative of a situation that was near the center of Tennyson's emotional life: the feeling that he was a kind of ghost returned to trouble the lives of those whom he loved. To this extent it may be called an autobiographical poem. The poem tells, in simple blank verse, the story of a goodhearted sailor, long shipwrecked on a deserted island and at last found, restored to England to become a furtive witness of his loving wife, now married to his best friend, and of her children by two husbands. Much of the poem is workmanlike narrative, as rich in circumstantial detail as a story in prose:

> Enoch Arden, a rough sailor's lad,
> Made orphan by a winter shipwreck, played
> Among the waste and lumber of the shore,
> Hard coils of cordage, swarthy fishing-nets,
> Anchors of rusty fluke, and boats updrawn. *(ll. 14–18)*

But sometimes the verse calls attention to itself, grows incantatory and gaudy, full of anaphora, lyrical:

> *No sail from day to day, but every day*
> *The sunrise broken into scarlet shafts*
> *Among the palms and ferns and precipices;*
> *The blaze upon the waters to the east;*
> *The blaze upon his island overhead;*
> *The blaze upon the waters to the west;*
> *Then the great stars that globed themselves in Heaven,*
> *The hollower-bellowing ocean, and again*
> *The scarlet shafts of sunrise—but no sail.*   (ll. 587–95)

At last Enoch is discovered by a crew strayed off course, and he approaches them

> *Brown, looking hardly human, strangely clad,*
> *Muttering and mumbling, idiotlike it seemed,*
> *With inarticulate rage, and making signs*   (ll. 634–36)

All that blazing has, it seems, burnt away his brain until he has lost every human faculty, undergone what Samuel Beckett calls loss of species. The sailors take him home, and Enoch Arden slowly is assimilated back into European society; and this assimilation is accompanied by a shift from the lyrical to the narrative mode. As a creature of pure sensation, uninflected by civilization, amorphous and gibbering, Enoch is a lyrical figment; as a man with complicated social relations, restrained and carefully qualified, he must fall out of the lyrical.

There is a sense in which every poet, as he starts to write a lyric, must undergo this same transformation. Insofar as he is a lyric poet he must extricate himself from the prose of things, abandon his usual identity, become a denizen of a high-pitched sensational feeling-world. Tennyson is a case in point. In "The Holy Grail" (1869) the pure Sir Galahad cries out "If I lose myself, I save myself!" (l. 178); and this cry resonates throughout Tennyson's later poetry. In "The Ancient Sage" (1885), another quasi-autobiographical poem, Tennyson versified a peculiar experience, what he called a "waking trance. . . . This has generally come upon me through repeating my own name two or three times to myself silently" (*Mem.* 1:320):

Lyrical Antibiography

for more than once when I
Sat all alone, revolving in myself
The word that is the symbol of myself,
The mortal limit of the Self was loosed,
And past into the Nameless, as a cloud
Melts into Heaven. I touched my limbs, the limbs
Were strange not mine—and yet no shade of doubt,
But utter clearness, and through loss of Self
The gain of such large life as matched with ours
Were Sun to spark.   *(ll. 229–38)*

I propose that every poet, when he composes a lyric, must for the moment enter into a domain of intense nonidentity; and therefore when we as literary critics try to construct the subject behind the poem, the persona used by the poet, we are puzzled, for we discover a nonperson, an un-Tennyson or anti-Shelley difficult to reconcile with such biographical information as we may possess. As we have seen, lyric poems with a biographical intent tend to present, not a clear portrait, but a shrunken oblique thing, or a corpse, or a cloud; and when we study what appear to be autobiographical lyrics, we will find the same sort of entity. The image of the author, if reconstructed from the evidence of a lyric poem, does not yield a distinct character full of telling quirks and anecdotes but instead an unearthly and disconnected sensibility, full of an inhuman largeness of passion, or tumult, or lethargy, or apathy, a field of feeling that refuses to coagulate into a particular man. The lyric poem seems to offer us insight into the depths of the poet, into his most precious and revealing experiences, into the *real* self compared to which the social person is only a hollow mask; but I think that this insight is generally illusory, that no critical labor will succeed in reconciling the poet as inferred from his lyric poems with the poet who likes to smell rotten apples, or flirts with his half sister, or loses all his money in a mechanical wood-carving scheme.

Certainly a biographer of Tennyson who neglected to record the poet's swervings into sublime anonymity would be remiss in his duties; but whatever ingenuity he might expend to relate such mystical states to Tennyson's matter-of-fact public life will, I think, be superfluous. Indeed, the author of every lyric poem is Anonymous. Certain modern theorists have said that this is true of every text, lyrical or otherwise; but most texts offer an impression, a shadow, of a subject and an object, in a fashion almost impossible in a lyric poem. W. H. Auden has noticed that in love poems the object of admiration is essentially arbitrary: "It is quite in order that a poet should write a sonnet expressing his devotion to Miss Smith because the poet, Miss Smith, and all his readers know perfectly well that, had he chanced to fall in love with Miss Jones instead, his feeling would be exactly the same" (*The Dyer's Hand,* p. 458). One might go one step farther than Auden and suggest that, in a lyric poem, the emotion expressed is as independent of the lover as of the beloved, a free-floating affection or loathing that affiliates itself with no one in particular. It seems that a measure of the lyrical quality of any poem is the degree to which it fails to terminate either in a man who feels or in an object felt; a lyric poem is that which hovers.

The easiest way to test the relation between biography and lyric poetry is to ask what sort of biography we would write of a poet if we knew nothing about him except his lyric poems. George Bernard Shaw, in *The Quintessence of Ibsenism,* quotes two opinions of Shelley, one from a contemporary reviewer who called him a devil, and another from Matthew Arnold—his famous reference to Shelley as a beautiful ineffectual angel beating his wings in a void. Shaw thought that the first opinion was more correct, and better tended to confirm his own high opinion of Shelley; but a biographer of Shelley could not go very far if he could describe his subject only as an angel or a devil. The implied author of many of Shelley's poems is indeed an angel, or a continent, or a heavenly body, or the universe's ground of being, a range of personae tending to interfere with proper biographical scrutiny. From the perspective of contemporary accounts Shelley was a moody promiscuous fellow expelled from Oxford; from the perspective of his lyrics he was an angel writing love poems to an ellipsis mark. These perspectives will not easily converge, though occasionally, as in the *Epipsychidion,* they do attain a partial focus.

There are a few poets who went to great lengths to make a genuine lyric autobiography, to embody themselves in a series of short poems. One of them was Yeats, who set out, as he said, "with the thought of putting my very self into poetry" (*Essays and Introductions,* p. 271); to some extent his whole career is a continual experiment on that theme, though the notion of self mutates strangely as

Yeats discovers which fractions of identity can be conveyed in a lyric poem. One difficulty with the concept of writing autobiography via lyric poetry is that the intensity and compression of a single poem tend to present a momentary feeling as something absolute, invariant; so that a poem about disappointment in love seems to suggest that this mood is incurable, that the poet's dreariness, which has already infected the cosmos, overclouded the sun, and made the trees weep, will prolong itself until Judgment Day. But other poems suggest that this is not the case. Autobiography ought to be able to transcend all such changes of emotion, to posit an overself that varies between sadness and joy; but the lyric mode seems incapable of offering a mediate self moving through various feeling-states. No amount of rapid transitions from one emotion to the next can remedy this essential defect.

> *IV.*
>
> *My fiftieth year had come and gone,*
> *I sat, a solitary man,*
> *In a crowded London shop,*
> *An open book and empty cup*
> *On the marble table-top.*
>
> *While on the shop and street I gazed*
> *My body of a sudden blazed;*
> *And twenty minutes more or less*
> *It seemed, so great my happiness,*
> *That I was blessèd and could bless.*
>
> *V.*
>
> *Although the summer sunlight gild*
> *Cloudy leafage of the sky,*
> *Or wintry moonlight sink the field*
> *In storm-scattered intricacy,*
> *I cannot look thereon,*
> *Responsibility so weighs me down.*
>
> *Things said or done long years ago,*
> *Or things I did not do or say*
> *But thought that I might say or do,*
> *Weigh me down, and not a day*
> *But something is recalled,*
> *My conscience or my vanity appalled.*

These are two sections of Yeats's poetic sequence "Vacillation" (1932). It is an autobiography in which all the prose of life is deleted, and what remain are a few flashes of ecstasy and despair; but these glimpses, these photographs shot with lightning, do not add up to an image of a man. The shock of juxtaposition of these contrary states of feeling makes a considerable aesthetic effect, but it inhibits us from imagining the full character who traveled between them. Yeats, one might say, dwells in the white space between the sections of the poem, hidden from our view. We try to draw lines to connect them, to form the picture of a sensibility; but there are insufficient data, and the face does not constitute itself among so much contradiction, so much vacillation. T. S. Eliot wrote a strange book called *After Strange Gods: A Primer of Modern Heresy* (1933), denouncing Yeats, Lawrence, and Pound—indeed, fearing for their souls; most of his argument would be hard to recommend, but in one passage, discussing Lawrence, he diagnoses accurately the aesthetic error of Yeats's "Vacillation": "It is in fact in moments of moral and spiritual struggle depending upon spiritual sanctions, rather than in those 'bewildering minutes' in which we are all very much alike, that men and women come nearest to being real" (p. 46). To write lyric autobiography, the poet must assume that he is most himself in moments of extreme feeling; but it seems more likely that his blaze of nerves and his season of melancholy will be, however precious or memorable, the occasions when he is least characteristic, self-possessed, determinate. Intense feeling is anyone's feeling; all men who have a toothache are the same man. This is one reason why lyric poems often closely imitate or translate previous lyric poems; if you have described your toothache well, you have also described mine.

A lyric poem tempts us to autobiographical interpretation because it is often so overtly intimate, suffused with personalness, that we imagine that this intimacy points in the direction of the poet, when in fact its true object is the poem. But anyone who tries to verbalize a moving experience and then rereads his account at a later date is likely to feel a certain estrangement from his earlier mood; and I suspect that this feeling of recoil is keener in great poets than in most of us. Every utterance, no matter how authentic, will eventually take on the aspect of a deliberate mask or prevarication; and Yeats developed the doctrine of the Mask or antiself precisely because his autobiographical urge was strong. To write an extensive canon of lyric poetry is to record the story of a soul; but it is easier to say that it is the story of a soul diametrically opposed to one's own, such is the intensity of self-alienation between the poet and his lyrics.

Once when Yeats was a young man he heard, when half asleep, a voice that was not his own voice speaking through his lips, saying "We make an image of him who sleeps, and it is not him who sleeps but it is like him who sleeps, and we call it Emmanuel." This self-oracle seemed so important to Yeats that he recorded it in his posthumously published autobiography (*Memoirs* p. 126), and in *A Vision* (p. 233), and in his novel *The Speckled Bird* (sec. 1, p. 9). He felt as if he had been snatched away by the Sidhe and a heap of shavings or a log shaped in his likeness had been left in his bed as a sign of abduction; and surely this declension from man into the dead image of a man represents the nightmare of a poet who feels that his emotional life is being stolen from him and replaced by a body of poems, as if his collected lyrics constituted a changeling or golem mocking the sensibility of the man behind them. Eliot says of the poet that "the man who suffers and the mind which creates" (*Selected Essays,* p. 10) have little to do with each other; but in the case of Yeats there is a certain anxiety that the man who suffers will be usurped, expunged, by the mind that creates. Our deepest feelings, the feelings recorded in lyric poems, seem not to pertain to ourselves at all, as if we were only the vicars of our own moods.

So the strategy of composing an autobiography by lyrical means seems to fail. But there is perhaps a subtler method for introducing an autobiographical aspect into lyric poems. A poet who acknowledges within his poems the fact that the feelings expressed are not his own but belong to some artifact, some conscious mask, seems to preclude every possibility of autobiography but in fact, strangely enough, enables it. I cannot display myself in a poem; but I can display a false self, emphasize its falsity, and then by the repudiation or destruction of that bad image give some sense of the shock of nakedness my face would give, were I able to present it. God cannot be directly manifest, but by the smashing of an idol something of his impossible presence can be suggested. Yeats was a master of such outrageous self-images: golden birds, mad old ladies, all manner of remote sham personae erected only to collapse; what gives "The Circus Animals' Desertion" (1938) its astonishing force is precisely this rejection of a series of incorrect Yeatses in favor of some genuine gross lapsed self hinted at but not quite displayed at the end of the poem. In a letter written near the end of his life, Yeats said, "When all the sensuous images are dissolved we meet death" (*Letters*, p. 917); and I think that he meant that, after a lifetime of creating images of himself, his final task was to undo those images. The lyric is not very useful for the usual kind of autobiography; but for the autobiography of self-dissolution it is a fine tool indeed. It is possible that every literary composition exists in a state of tension between a constructed identity and the deconstruction of that identity; and that much of the savor of poetry comes from the struggle between autobiography and the lyricalness that opposes it.

Bibliography of Works Cited in Text

Auden, W. H. *Collected Poems*, ed. Edward Mendelson (1976).
———. *The Dyer's Hand* (1962).
Donne, John. *Selected Poetry*, ed. Marius Bewley (1966).
Eliot, T. S. *After Strange Gods: A Primer of Modern Heresy* (1933).
———. *Selected Essays* (1969).
Tennyson, Alfred. *The Poems of Tennyson*, ed. Christopher Ricks. (1969).
Tennyson, Hallam. *Alfred Lord Tennyson: A Memoir* (1897).
Yeats, W. B. *Essays and Introductions* (1961).
———. *Literatim Transcription of the Manuscripts of William Butler Yeats's The Speckled Bird*, ed. William H. O'Donnell (1976).
———. *The Letters of W. B. Yeats*, ed. Allan Wade (1954).
———. *Memoirs*, ed. Dennis Donoghue (1972).
———. *Mythologies* (1959).
———. *The Variorum Edition of the Poems of W. B. Yeats*, ed. Peter Allt and Russell K. Alspach. Macmillan, 1957.
———. *A Vision*, second edition (1961).

§
Acknowledgments

W. H. Auden's "A. E. Housman" is reprinted with permission of Random House, Inc. / Alfred A Knopf, Inc., from *Collected Poems*, edited by Edward Mendelson. Copyright 1976.

Lines from "Vacillation" are reprinted with permission of Macmillan Publishing Company and A. P. Watts Ltd. on behalf of Michael B. Yeats and Macmillan London Ltd. from *The Poems of W. B. Yeats: A New Edition*, edited by Richard J. Finneran. Copyright 1933 by Macmillan Publishing Company renewed 1961 by Bertha Georgie Yeats.

Contributors Notes

Index

Contributors Notes

DANIEL ALBRIGHT had the pleasure, for seventeen years, of being a colleague of Cecil Lang's at the University of Virginia. He now teaches at the University of Rochester. He has written books on Yeats, Tennyson, Stravinsky, the theory of the lyric, and concepts of representation and personality in modern fiction.

KAREN CHASE is the author of *Eros and Psyche*, a study of the fiction of Charlotte Brontë, Charles Dickens, and George Eliot. She is currently completing a book on *Middlemarch*.

WILLIAM E. FREDEMAN is Professor of English at the University of British Columbia. The author of *Pre-Raphaelitism: A Bibliocritical Study* and editor of *The P. R. B. Journal,* he has also written many monographs and articles on Victorian poetry and bibliography, including the Rossettis, Tennyson, William Bell Scott, Arthur Hughes, Thomas J. Wise, and Thomas Bird Mosher. A Fellow of the Royal Society of Canada and of the Royal Society of Literature, Professor Fredeman is coeditor of *The Journal of Pre-Raphaelite Studies* and is now completing a multivolume edition of the letters of Dante Gabriel Rossetti.

JEROME McGANN is Commonwealth Professor of English, University of Virginia. His most recent book is *Towards a Literature of Knowledge,* a study originally delivered in 1987 as the Clark Lectures at Trinity College, Cambridge, and the Carpenter Lectures at the University of Chicago.

J. HILLIS MILLER is a Distinguished Professor at the University of California at Irvine. His most recent books are *The Linguistic Moment* and *The Ethics of Reading*.

Contributors Notes

ROSS C MURFIN received his master's degree and doctorate at the University of Virginia, where he wrote his dissertation under the supervision of Professor Cecil Lang. He has since taught at Yale University and the University of Miami, where he is Professor of English and Associate Dean of the College. The author of *Swinburne, Hardy, Lawrence, and the Burden of Belief* and *The Poetry of D. H. Lawrence: Texts and Contexts,* he is currently working on a book tentatively entitled *Novel Representations: Victorian Fiction in Its Own Mirror.*

DAVID G. RIEDE received his Ph.D. at Virginia in 1976 under the direction of Professor Cecil Lang. He is the author of numerous articles on Romantic and Victorian literature, and of books on Swinburne, D. G. Rossetti, and Arnold. He is a professor of English at Ohio State University.

HERBERT F. TUCKER, a professor of English at the University of Virginia, has published numerous articles on nineteenth-century British poetry and two books: *Browning's Beginnings* and *Tennyson and the Doom of Romanticism.*

CAROLYN WILLIAMS is currently associate professor of English at Rutgers University (New Brunswick). In addition to articles on various nineteenth- and twentieth-century topics, she is the author of *Transfigured World: Walter Pater's Aesthetic Historicism,* whose dedication celebrates her permanent debt to Cecil Lang.

Index

§

Index

Index

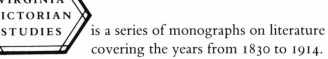 is a series of monographs on literature covering the years from 1830 to 1914. Contributions may be editorial, critical (historical or theoretical), biographical, bibliographic, comparative, or interdisciplinary.